Where's Your Mama Gone?

Where's Your Mama Gone?

Kay O'Gorman

Gill & Macmillan

Gill & Macmillan Ltd
Hume Avenue, Park West, Dublin 12
with associated companies throughout the world
www.gillmacmillan.ie

© Kay O'Gorman 2008
978 07171 4099 2

Typography design by Make Communication
Print origination by TypeIT, Dublin
Printed and bound in Great Britain by MPG Books Ltd, Bodwin,
Cornwall

This book is typeset in 11.5 Minion on 14.5.

The paper used in this book comes from the wood pulp of
managed forests. For every tree felled, at least one tree is
planted, thereby renewing natural resources.

A CIP catalogue record for this book is available from the
British Library.

5 4 3 2 1

Dedicated to my grandchildren, especially to Nell,
whom I've never met

and

For the ones who inhabit lives
where belonging is torn and
longing is numbed.
— JOHN O'DONOHUE

Neither in environment nor in heredity can I find the
exact instrument that fashioned me, the anonymous
roller that pressed upon my life a certain intricate
watermark whose unique design becomes visible when
the lamp of art is made to shine through life's foolscap.
— VLADIMIR NABOKOV

Last night I dreamed
blessed illusion ~
that I had a beehive here
in my heart
and that
the golden bees were making
white combs and sweet honey
from my old failures.
— ANTONIO MACHADO (TRANSLATION BY ROBERT BLY)

Contents

Acknowledgments

I want to thank my agent Jonathan Williams for his encouragement and belief in the book, for his painstaking reading of the manuscript, and for his meticulous, creative and literary critique. My thanks also to Gill & Macmillan, especially Fergal Tobin, who took on this book enthusiastically.

I want particularly to thank Robin Blake who first read the manuscript in a very rough draft; his suggestions were invaluable. My friend and editor Katy Brittain, for our never-to-be-forgotten days when we laughed and cried together over the manuscript. I'm also grateful for Alison Walsh, Matthew Blake and Mark O'Neill's contributions.

Finally, Joe, this would not have been possible without you. You helped me realise my dream of writing this book, and for that I thank you from the bottom of my heart. I know this isn't the first or the last of many dreams we will share together.

Author's Note

This is a true story. Much of it was painful and difficult to write, but I felt compelled to do so. I continue to have deep feelings for my family, and harbour no wish to hurt anyone unnecessarily.

Chapter One

I wonder what my father would have felt, as he cradled me in his arms the night I was born, if he had known the hurt I was going to cause. In later life, after he had a few drinks taken, Daddy would tell how he had been afraid I was cold and, holding me too close to the fire, had burned my feet.

My parents' marriage was an on-off relationship that must have caused quite a scandal in the Ireland of the 1940s. They had been married for three years, but were living apart when they found out I was on the way. This was a fact my father never missed an opportunity to mention. The story goes that it was my father's drinking and womanising that drove my mother away, but there was another reason. As a child, my mother had developed rheumatic fever, leaving her with a damaged heart. She spent a lot of time in bed and was continually seeing the doctor. Daddy would get angry about this, shouting and roaring that all his hard-earned money was being wasted on doctors and that there was nothing wrong with my mother. I believed him. In general, I felt responsible for my parents' situation. I was convinced that they would not have had to stay together but for me.

When Mammy left my father, which she did often, she would go to the farm in Ballintee where she had grown up. She seldom took me with her, which I didn't mind much. I have few happy memories connected with my mother's mother. For the least thing, she would lock me in the bedroom, in the dark. She was tall, thin and very stern, and I was terrified of her. She was a farmer's daughter herself, with a back bent from hard work, and a red mark around the calves of her legs, left by her wellington boots. My maternal grandfather was a different matter: small and quiet, he let his wife be the boss. I loved how he would scratch my back as we sat by the fire.

I spent much of my early childhood being looked after by different people. My father was a superstitious man who would not stay in a house with only a child for company, so when my mother was not with us, and as the evenings drew in, he and I would take off in his old Ford Anglia, from wherever we were living at the time, to find someone to look after me.

First, my father would send me to his sister, my Aunt Bid, but she already had three young children herself. Next, we would try Ballintee, the farm where my mother was staying. My mother's family had little time for Daddy, as they always blamed him for my parents' separations. I would be sent to the door, which involved a fearful long walk up the front path; the path had high hedges on either side, which I couldn't see over, and which seemed to tower up to the sky. When I got to the door and knocked, the answer was always a firm 'no', before the door was shut in my face. Despite my rejection, on my nervous walk back, I used to put on a big smile to let my father see that he shouldn't be upset. My real worry was that he would be angry.

Finally, after Daddy stopped off for a few pints here and there, we would reach the cottage where his own parents lived. By now, evening would be well set in and my grandmother always made the same remark, 'What are you doing out with that poor child at this time of night?'

He would say nothing, while I jumped to his defence.

'It's not his fault. Mammy is gone again.'

My grandmother would turn back inside, grumbling to herself, and I would look up at my father reassuringly. All was well and we could stay. After all, he was the apple of his mother's eye: her only living son out of seven children.

This grandmother, whom I called Ma because my father did, was a tiny round woman. I never saw her legs. She was always dressed in a long skirt to the ground and a black shawl that served many purposes. She tied it around her waist when she was cooking and cleaning, pulled it tight about her shoulders to sit by the fire, and covered her head with it when she went out.

Perhaps because we shared the same birthday, my grandfather and I had a special relationship. Old Daddy, as I called him, was a big, gentle man with a full head of silver-grey hair. He never, to my knowledge, raised his voice to anyone, especially not to his wife. I remember my times with my father's parents as golden days. I played out in the orchard, which was full of all kinds of wonder: huge trees weighed down with beautiful juicy apples; blackberry and gooseberry bushes straining under the weight of their fruit. I would have a bottle of water given to me in the morning, and some bread and jam, and off I'd go. I had a house made in every corner of the orchard and there was an arch with red roses where I used to play at weddings.

Most of the back yard was covered by a beech tree which, when I climbed it, was like a village to me. On one branch, I had the post office; on the next a garage, or a pub, and so on. Philomena, my doll and only other companion at this time, was greatly loved by me but was not allowed into the house. I had left her up in the tree one day and she'd got wet through. No matter how dry Philomena was, my grandmother always said there was a smell of damp from her and that I could catch my death by holding her close to my chest. Once Ma got a notion in her head, nothing would shift it. I explained this to Philomena. I told her everything because she was my best friend.

Every now and then, my grandmother would shout out of her bedroom window, 'Where are ye?' and I'd slide out of the tree and come running to the window to have one of the special sweets she doled out. Lozenges, she called them. They tasted terrible but I would always take one, not wanting to offend.

Ma would pour tea for Old Daddy and me. This was served up several times a day with a slice of bread and jam and, like everything she gave us to eat or drink, it tasted of smoke. A pot was kept brewing constantly on the hob by the fire so she could pour and sip tea all day to her heart's content.

One of Ma's great interests in life was her front garden. Here there was no such thing as a neat bed of flowers. There was just a confusion of plants and herbs, deliberately wild and wonderful and giving off intoxicating aromas and all the colours that were ever seen.

Few sounds reached my grandparents' home, though one you were sure to hear twice a day was the Angelus. It would ring out from the chapel bell at twelve noon, and again at six in the evening. The men of the area would doff their caps and hold them against their chests whilst thumbing a quick sign of the cross on their foreheads. The women would bless themselves more extravagantly: up with the right hand to the forehead, down to the stomach, then with a diagonal sweep to the left shoulder, and across to the right. They finished with a loud 'Amen' and raised their eyes towards heaven. Whichever of my grandparents I was near when the Angelus rang, I would imitate.

Sometimes Old Daddy used to take me by the hand for a stroll down the lane beside the orchard. With Philomena tucked under my arm, we'd go through the fields, picking flowers and gabbing away to each other, or would stand looking into the stream that ran along the back of the house.

'Old Daddy, where does it end?' I would ask. 'Where does it come from?'

'It comes from the mountain and ends in the sea,' he would answer simply.

He would tell me about fairies and leprechauns.

'Look,' he would say in a loud whisper, pointing to the undergrowth on the opposite bank. 'There's one. Ah, you missed it. Never mind, you'll catch sight of it next time.'

Old Daddy had been a postman and my father followed in his footsteps. This meant that he had to be up at four every morning, which caused me great anxiety when we stayed with my grandparents because of the peculiar arrangement of rooms in the house. The front door opened into the kitchen. There were two bedrooms on the left. Ma slept in the one at the back, and Old Daddy in the front one. There was also a big bedroom to the right of the kitchen, which is where we would sleep; my parents had had this room for a while after they married. They had separated this room from the rest of the house, making an entrance into it from the back yard, so it was self-contained. This meant that when my father left in the morning, I felt a terribly long way from my grandparents.

My dread was made worse by my father. He had the habit of giving me a nudge just as I dropped off to sleep at night. 'What's that strange light shining on the wall?' he would say in a muffled whisper, or, 'What's that noise outside?' Such things bothered him greatly. He'd start on about ghosts, telling stories of banshees and how people would wash themselves in urine to keep away the fairies. If you found a comb in the road, it was sure to be the banshee who had dropped it. Banshees had long hair to the ground, and woe betide you if you ever saw one's face. I lay awake in terror and fought against sleep, not wanting to have to wake up alone in the haunted room after my father had gone to work. I would beg him to put me into Ma's bed in the morning. He would promise to, but he never did.

We could expect my father home from work around three in the afternoon, after he had had a few pints. He always started the day with a drop of whiskey, a Baby Powers, which he kept under his pillow, and I could be sure that he would definitely be going to the pub later that night, and me with him. 'I can't expect my poor mother to look after her day and night,' he would tell the lads with great pride. When I heard this, I felt that I was a nuisance to everyone. In the pub, I was put lying on a long wooden seat, my father's heavy postman's coat over me. I would listen to the talk and laughter, always punctuated by shouts of 'Up Dev!' as they hoisted glasses of stout in the air. I'd hold on to the brass buttons on my father's coat for safety, as the men gave me sips of Guinness until I eventually fell asleep.

We would stay there until he felt like going home, or some trouble started. One particular night, the guards raided the place after closing time and there was great panic. They were rapping on the door and I was being lifted over a big yard gate at the back, my father vaulting over behind me, as we made our getaway. Ma was often up when we got home, not at all pleased with her son. On one of those occasions, when they were having harsh words over the lateness of the hour, she shouted at him that she wouldn't have us in her house if he was going to keep the hours of a heathen. Then she picked up a cup and smashed it against his forehead, which left blood running down his face. I was hysterical as he angrily bundled me outside and into the car. We drove around, searching for someone to take us in, or at least take me. Maybe he was hoping for sympathy, going to his sister and my other grandmother; if so, he didn't get any and we slept in the car. In the morning, he took me home to his mother and nothing more was said until the next time.

My father was a well-educated man. Taught by the Christian Brothers, he could speak the Irish language fluently — had a gift for it, or so he told me. Had he not taken the notion to be a postman, he said, he could have been a schoolteacher. He would always impress on me that he was no ordinary postman, doing the rounds on some old push-bike. A bright green Morris with 'P agus T' printed in yellow on the side of it — Posts and Telegraphs — that's what he drove, collecting and delivering the mail to estates like Mount Juliet in Thomastown, and to big farms and pubs where he was sure to be given a good drink.

He took infinite pride in his appearance: never a hair out of place and his uniform pressed to perfection; the badge on his peaked cap dazzling; his brass buttons gleaming; the shirt an immaculate white; and you could see your face in his black shoes. He walked straight, head up and, although slight of build, when describing another man, he would often say, 'He was a big fellah, like meself.' 'Call me Mister,' he would instruct the lads in the pub, and most of them did. To him, all this was a sign of good character, but he had no patience and a tongue that would lacerate you. He could not be told anything, for he knew everything. He always had an eye and a soft word or two for a good-looking girl.

My mother was gentle and refined by nature and always ready for a laugh, if there was occasion for it. She was not well educated but she was certainly pretty and had style. Before her marriage, she had worked for a couple of years in London as housekeeper to a wealthy family. Mammy told us that that was where she had discovered her love of good china and fine linen. She was tall and slim with beautiful curly, dark brown hair that she wore down her back. People were always telling her how lovely she looked. I remember a flowery dress she had, tight at the waist with a wide skirt. She wore it for a children's tea party we once had in the garden, and sat on the ground with the skirt spread out all around her and her legs tucked underneath. Her hair was dressed high on her head and she looked like my idea of a princess.

My father and mother tried living in various small houses, but when my little sister, Mary, arrived, they returned to my father's parents and the big room with the separate entrance. As a baby, Mary was very troublesome, crying a lot and frequently holding her breath until she turned blue.

In 1949, when I was just five, I started my education. The National School was beautifully perched upon a prominent hill, surrounded by woods and with a view of the village. There were just two classrooms; in one, the mistress taught the younger children while, in the other, the master took the older ones. I always got a little smile or a wink when I saw the master, who knew me from the pub. He was usually there with my father; they were good friends. One of the things they had in common was the delicate health of their wives, and it was for this reason that Mammy developed her own fascination with the master's wife.

'Did you see the master's wife today?' she would ask when I got in from school. 'How did she look, poor woman? Sure, if she can get over the autumn of the year, she'll be all right for another twelve months, please God.'

I liked school. There were about forty children there, and we were not under any great pressure to learn. Most of the mistress's efforts went into the pupils who were going into the master's classroom the next year, so the rest of us had plenty of time to play and to get to know each other. At lunchtime, we would eat our bread and butter as quickly as possible so we could play hide and seek in the woods. The school had outdoor lavatories and there was a heap of big leaves put in there for wiping your bum.

After school, I would run down the hill as fast as I could, and always at the back of my mind was the worry: would Mammy be there or would she be gone again? My way home took me past two churches: the Catholic church, which was familiar and did not particularly worry me, and, almost opposite it, the dreaded Protestant one, which did. We were taught to think of it as a blighted plot of land; if we went inside the gates, we would never see the face of God. Only rich people went in there, their ill-gotten gains won off the backs of the poor Irish Catholics.

'It is easier for a camel to go through the eye of a needle than for a rich man to enter the kingdom of God,' our own priest told us with a great thump of his fist on the pulpit. We all knew whom he was talking about.

Much fear had been instilled in me from an early age, but most of all I was afraid of God. He knew everything I was thinking and everything I had done; and I often had bad thoughts about my sister, because she would be crying for something, and my mother would give her everything and tell her she was a good girl when she obviously was not. It made me angry that she received so much notice, but I knew that God did not like me thinking that way, and would surely punish me.

My bad thoughts about Mary gripped me particularly on Saturday nights when Mammy, to be ready for Mass the next morning, devoted herself to teasing the tangles out of my sister's unruly hair. During this arduous process, they went through all the people in the village who would be there, naming them one by one, until the comb ran smoothly through her curls. Mary moaned and wriggled but, when it was over, Mammy would clasp her hands, look into her eyes and tell her she was so beautiful and good. I didn't agree at all, and hungered for the undivided love and attention I felt Mary was getting from my mother. Now and then, I would sidle up to my mother and try to sneak on to her lap, but she would tell me firmly that I was too big.

The four of us would go to Mass in the morning, entering as a family before my father left us to join the men on the right of the church, while we took our places on the left with the women, their heads covered with a shawl or a scarf. We were not allowed to look around us or speak, which was very hard to remember since I always thought of something important that I wanted to say to my parents during Mass. Outside, when it was over, people wished each other good morning. Then the women made their way home to cook the Sunday dinner, while the men either slipped into the pub or went home to read the papers. If my father came home with us, it would be a family day. If he went to the pub, my mother would tell us, 'It would be better to wait for your father to come home before we eat.'

Most of the time, the dinner was burnt to a cinder before he got home, but he didn't care. He was full of the drink and chat of the pub.

Chapter Two

When I was six, my parents had a chance of a fresh start, which they decided was needed. We piled our belongings into a trailer and set off into what was, for me, the unknown. I had always lived in this County Kilkenny village and now, with a sense of dread and excitement, I was heading twenty miles away to Thomastown, in another part of the county.

The house turned out to be small but, unlike my grandparents', it had an upstairs. The front door opened straight out on to the road, but we had a nice back garden with a brook running through it. I loved the place from the start, though my mother was not at all impressed. Having been used to a fine farmhouse before she married, she now worried about where in this poky place she was going to store her beloved bone china.

Looking back, I realise that our sleeping arrangements in the upstairs room were odd. My father and I occupied one bed, while my mother and Mary took the other. I see it now as my parents' method of birth control, the only kind available in Ireland in 1950.

However, the new home failed to ease the tension between

my parents. This was most obvious at mealtimes. My mother insisted that the table be set perfectly, with a spotless cloth and cutlery in the precise position. No elbows on the table, no slurping or eating with your mouth open, and no talking as far as Mary and I were concerned. Because my parents hardly spoke themselves, the silence lay like an undigested lump in my stomach and I could hardly swallow my food.

After some of their rows, they refused to speak directly to each other.

'Ask your father has he enough,' my mother would say to me.

'Have you enough, Daddy?'

'Tell your mother I have.'

'Mammy, he has.'

This could continue for weeks and it usually had something to do with my father going back on the drink. After months without a drop, he would suddenly be missing in the evening. At last, after midnight, in he would come from the pub, with a bunch of his 'cronies', as my mother called them. The three of us would be upstairs in bed, listening as he fried whatever food was in the house. My mother would be raging when he eventually came up to us to make his peace, the smell of sausages climbing up the stairs behind him. His attempts only made matters worse and he would go back down, leaving Mary and me mad with hunger. The food was usually burnt and inedible because my father would forget about it while he belted out rebel songs such as 'The Wild Colonial Boy' and 'Kevin Barry'.

After what seemed like hours, the cronies would leave and there would be quiet. Soon enough, we'd again hear my father's footsteps on the stairs. He would be at the bedroom door, full of self-pity, announcing that he was going to drown himself in the Nore. Mammy's reply was contemptuous: 'Go ahead. Who cares?' But I would run and hold on to him, shouting, 'I care, Daddy. Please don't.'

'He has no intention of killing himself at all,' Mammy would say. 'He's only trying to make us feel sorry for him.'

In previous days, Mammy and my sister would have gone back to the farm after such a row. But now I was going to convent school and the nuns would not be pleased if I were missing because my father was driving me around the country looking for a relation to take me in.

I found it hard to settle in my new school. The other children called me a 'country bumpkin', and I trailed far behind them in my work. Though I struggled hard to fit in, I was betrayed every day by my style of dress, especially by the cardigans my mother had knitted. She also wouldn't allow us to use certain words, a legacy perhaps of her days in London, but it caused me to be mocked.

'I dropped my handkerchief in the lavatory,' I might say, and be answered with roars of laughter.

'You mean your *hankie* in the *toilet*,' I would be told.

I had never as much as seen a nun before. Encased in starched white wimples, their faces never held a smile. They wore black leather belts around their waists — most convenient for our punishment. The sound of their great beads rattling, and the swish of their heavy skirts as they swept along the corridor, overwhelmed me.

'Good morning, Sister,' we would chant every morning, full of apprehension as the lesson began.

The nun would take her position in front of the fire, the back of her skirts hitched up to let the heat get at her legs and rear, while we sat shivering in our desks.

Once, I was called up to the top of the schoolroom to face the class. Pointing dramatically at my eyebrows, Sister Francis Xavier boomed, 'This girl has a weak character. See how her eyebrows meet in the centre of her forehead? It's a sure sign.'

She pushed me back to my desk. I was scarlet with shame. The minute I arrived home that afternoon, I got my father's razor and shaved off my eyebrows. They never grew properly again, so perhaps my character improved.

My sister and I were not allowed outside to play with the other children. 'They're townies; they know too much,' my father told us mysteriously.

But listening to them laughing and having fun, I longed to be amongst them. I wanted to know all the things they knew. Perhaps I could even make a friend; we could share our secrets and walk to school together. I desperately wanted real life to be the way I'd heard it was in *Little Women* and *What Katy Did*.

An opportunity for my father to make some extra money arose. The telephone exchange in the post office was going to operate twenty-four hours a day. He got the job of manning the exchange at weekends but it meant staying on duty all night. Not wanting to be alone, he took me with him. It felt like a great adventure. The phone seldom rang, but the excitement of waiting was intense.

The exchange was above the post office in a huge dark room with a high ceiling. It had a few dull books on the shelves and leaflets about pensions and postage rates scattered about. It smelt like my father's uniform: a mixture of ink, rubber bands and lead pencils. I liked it.

Daddy's overcoat came into play once again because, when it got late, I was put on a table to sleep. I felt more and more that I was his child and quite distant from my mother. Her family always said, 'You're your father's daughter all right.' I wasn't sure what was meant by this, but began to suspect that maybe it was not a good thing for me to be.

In spite of the separate sleeping arrangements, my mother was soon pregnant again. She was confined to bed most of the time, which made the pregnancy seem very long, but when at last my second sister was born, I instantly loved her. I couldn't wait to take her for a walk in her new pram. She was christened Alison.

The birth meant that we moved house again. To my delight, it was to the terrace where I had envied all the children playing together. Now I was going to be one of them!

My mother was delighted with our new home. It had an indoor lavatory — or 'toilet' as I now called it. There were two bedrooms; Mary and I had one, leaving the other to my parents (still keeping to their separate beds) and the baby. Downstairs, we had a front room, a kitchen and scullery. There was a tap in the house, which meant running water. There would be no more taking a bucket to the well or pump several times a day. And we also had electricity for the first time. Everything was perfect.

One day, our father brought home a wireless. He spent hours experimenting to find the best position for good reception until it was put on a high shelf where only the adults could reach it. I remember my mother standing on a chair with her ear pressed close against the radio, trying to hear through the static. She never missed the news and was full of talk about Princess Margaret and Squadron Leader Peter Townsend.

I had made my First Communion at this stage. I was seven, a big girl who was supposed to know right from wrong. In my father's mind, for instance, it was right to give a wide berth to those 'townies' living on either side of us, and wrong to talk to them. But in this, I was wilfully defiant.

Now I had my first best friend. She lived next door and her name was Breda. We used to take a short cut to school together over some railings. My father, who saw danger in anything and everything, said that a big man would jump out and do terrible things to children who went that way. It didn't stop us. As we walked along, we used to discuss what this man would do. We thought he would kidnap us first, then cut off our arms and legs, and maybe even our heads. Breda and I had so much to say to each other, and in such a short time, that we were always late for school.

'Here's me and my shadow,' the nun would say when we arrived in class breathless. We were not allowed to sit beside one another.

My father disliked Breda's family, as he did all our

neighbours. He would not give them the time of day, but would incessantly criticise the way they spoke and looked. I knew Mammy agreed with him only to shut him up. Sometimes when he was at work, she and Breda's mother would have great chats at their back doors, but they were never mentioned in front of my father. I lived in fear of him finding out that my mother and I had secret friends.

The ban on playing outside remained in force. When Mary and I came home from school, we were not allowed out again until morning unless it was to hang out the washing. I used to get a terrible teasing at school about this. The children would surround me, chanting, 'Granny granny grey, she can't come out to play.'

Polishing and buffing the varnished floorboards upstairs until they shone was one of my jobs. I hated doing this, but would not dare complain. We also had to do all the shopping. Real men, like my father, didn't shop, even if they had a car.

By now, we no longer had the Ford Anglia. There had been a fire in the garage where it was kept, and my father had no proper insurance, so we suffered a total loss. He ranted about this for ages, blaming everyone but himself.

Without his car, my father took to the push-bike and, once a month in the summer, he pedalled to his parents' house — the house he was going to inherit, he told me proudly, he being the only son. I would go with him in a seat on the bar of the bike, to trim the laurel hedges that Old Daddy could no longer manage. As he cycled along, I became obsessed with the thought that he would die on me while pedalling up a hill. I would chatter non-stop, as if to keep him alive. 'Look, Daddy, look! Did you see the magpie? One for sorrow, two for joy, three for a wedding and four for a boy'. All I could hear was his panting breath.

When Alison was about a year old, my mother got pregnant again. She was very upset, crying day and night, and just lying in her bed. I knew from overhearing things that it was not good for my mother to have more children. After about three months, the doctor sent her to hospital because of her weak heart. She had to stay there until the baby was born. This was dreadful for her, and just as bad for us children.

A cousin from my father's side, Una, came to look after us. At sixteen, she was not much more than a child herself and, though she did her best for us, the job was a heavy weight on her shoulders, a weight my father did nothing to alleviate. Each day, he cycled straight from work to the hospital to see my mother. He spent hours there, doing what an attentive husband should do, but my hunch is that he enjoyed the hospital for its own sake. It had scores of young nurses and he got a boost from the attention they paid him. After his visit, he went to the pub for the rest of the evening. We hardly saw him during that time.

Alison did not take to Una: it was me she wanted and she would become hysterical when I was out of her sight. I was nine and missed months of school because of this, but nothing was done about it. Alison was suffering terribly, bawling day and night. For a long time, we had no idea that this was caused by a chronic ear infection. I waltzed her around the house to stop her from crying until I thought my arms would fall off.

As Christmas drew near, Una's family wanted her with them and we went to stay with another of my father's sisters, my Aunt Ellie, and her family in Kilkenny. I loved everything there. It was a home with two parents in it all the time and, lying in my bed upstairs at night, I felt cosy and cared for. You could hear the big town clock ringing out every hour, which filled me with a sad longing — for what, I didn't know. Today, if I hear a clock chiming, in any town, it touches me inside as I remember a lost time.

My father continued his hospital-and-pub routine. I often wondered why we could not be brought in to see our mother, especially since it was Christmas, but we never were. I didn't understand. She was having a baby, not suffering from a contagious disease. I wanted to say this to my father, but I was too frightened.

On New Year's morning, my father told us we had a new sister. When the initial excitement and relief had worn off, people would say to my father, 'Sorry it wasn't a boy.' It made me feel furious on my sister Geraldine's behalf, though I knew that my father had desperately wanted a son.

Soon we went back to our own house and Una returned. My mother had to stay in hospital for another six weeks, but they couldn't keep the baby there that long, so Aunt Ellie took her. Geraldine was a quiet, dimpled little soul and was no trouble.

For about a year, coming up to the age of eleven, I had been suffering from pains in my joints. Sometimes they swelled up, though no one took much notice. Mammy was at last allowed home from the hospital and was so shocked to see my swollen fingers and knees that she insisted that my father take me to the doctor. The diagnosis was rheumatic pains, a serious matter because of my mother's medical history. The doctor sent me home with a prescription for prolonged bed rest. I was not to walk but had to keep my feet off the floor, as he put it sternly. I was in bed for eleven months.

The district nurse called every day to wash me, give me breakfast, and lend Mammy a hand with a few things in the house. She had become very weak after Geraldine's birth and could no longer climb the stairs. Once she was down in the morning, she was unable to come back up to me until my father came home and carried her upstairs. So there she would be downstairs, from time to time calling, 'Are you okay?' and me shouting back, 'I'm grand.' They gave me the wireless for company. I would listen to Radio Luxembourg at night and sing along with all the hits. I once overheard my mother saying that she had sat in the kitchen and cried to hear me singing and she unable to come up to me.

I was still in bed when my new sister came home from Aunt Ellie's. The cot which my uncle had made was beside my bed and my treat every morning was to have Geraldine put in with me, just for a few minutes. She would gurgle and smile. My aunt and uncle were heartbroken at having to give her back. They were worried that, as my mother was sick, Daddy could not be relied on to look after the new baby properly. Something of the kind must have been said, because relations between my father and his sister were rocky for some time afterwards.

I spent my time listening to the radio and reading comics. No one mentioned school and neither did I. A few friends came to see me at first, but the visits quickly tailed off. Strangely, my isolation didn't worry me.

The only regular visit I had was from the priest, once a month, to hear my confession and to give my mother and me Holy Communion. We had to fast from midnight to receive the Sacrament and the house would be spotless upstairs and down to make the place fit for the Holy Eucharist. Complete silence was expected during the visit; no one was allowed to chat to the priest, who was in a special state of grace since he was carrying the Body of Christ.

The whole event took only a few minutes. Heralded by an altar boy, who wore a white surplice and rang a hand bell as if his life depended on it, Father Drea would arrive in his Mass vestments, covered by a heavy black overcoat in winter. He had the consecrated Host in a lidded chalice, which was hidden under a beautifully embroidered silk veil. He would breeze in, making the sign of the cross, and would hear Mammy's confession in the kitchen. He would give her penance and Holy Communion and then come up the stairs to me. My heart raced as I sat bolt upright trying to think of something to tell him that would not sound stupid, something different from the last time. My opening words came out in a sing-song: 'Bless me, father, for I have sinned; it's a month since my last confession.' Then I took a deep breath, and gabbled.

'I told lies. I took the Lord's name in vain.'

This was all I could think of.

'Bless you, my child' was Father Drea's response. He never

showed any reaction to my confession. 'Say three Hail Marys and three Our Fathers for your sins.'

In a rapid whisper, he ran through the incomprehensible Latin words of absolution and made the sign of the cross on my forehead. Then I closed my eyes and opened my mouth for the consecrated wafer to be placed on my tongue. Before I reopened my eyes, he was gone. I lay back and breathed a sigh of relief as I tried to poke the Body of Christ off the roof of my mouth with my tongue, where it always got stuck. You couldn't use your fingers for that job; it would be a mortal sin.

Mortal sin loomed large in the minds of all Catholic children. Venal sins, like the two I had confessed to, were like pencil marks that could be easily rubbed out. But a mortal sin was like a deep blot of ink on your immortal soul. If you died before you confessed it, you would be lowered into the fires of Hell for all eternity.

One day, to my utter horror, I realised that I was bleeding between my legs. I was eleven years old and knew nothing about the facts of life, so naturally I thought I was going to die from the loss of blood. When my father came home, I called him upstairs, shaking with fear. I told him I was bleeding 'down there'. He looked stricken and spun round and ran downstairs. Now I was sure I was going to die. But he carried my mother up to me and left us alone while she explained that this was just me growing up. It was normal and nothing to be afraid of.

I had gone to bed a child and, when I was allowed out of bed, I was a young woman. My muscles were very weak and the soles of my feet were so soft that to take more than a few paces was excruciating. So here I was, learning to walk again, and becoming a grown-up.

When I went out, everything was changed, and I was made to feel different. Boys were looking at me strangely. I had breasts now. I didn't like them because they distinguished me from the other girls of my age, none of whom was as developed as I was.

I longed to fit in: to be like them. Catching a glimpse of myself in a shop window, I thought I was fairly pretty.

My father did not encourage mirrors in our house. 'The sin of pride,' he would bellow if he caught us looking at our reflections. At the same time, he would make me walk around the kitchen with the sweeping brush under my armpits so that I would not slouch my shoulders, but stick my hated chest out for all the world to see.

There was one boy, Paddy, about fifteen, whom I saw on the way home from school. He seemed to like me. I thought he was wonderful. We used to snatch a few words when we could, but it wasn't often. In the mornings, when I went to eight o'clock Mass, Paddy would be waiting for me and we would exchange furtive glances. I knew I was in love with him. But one night, as I was going around the house singing, 'Once I had a secret love', my father took me aside and said menacingly, 'It's a secret no more, me girl!'

From then on, he kept a close eye on me.

When I was thirteen, and Mary eleven, we made our Confirmation together. It was customary for children to be taken to visit both sets of grandparents on this day, but we did not go to Mammy's parents, because my father was unwelcome; they disapproved of his drinking ways. We did, however, make the pilgrimage to the little cottage with the orchard and the beech tree, and were treated like royalty by Old Daddy and Ma. This was to be the last time I would see Ma, who died a few months later. Her death was to bring about a new upheaval in our lives.

Chapter Three

My paternal grandparents' cottage seemed to have been in Ma's name and, as expected, my father inherited the property. It was on the understanding that Old Daddy, who spent most of his days laid up in bed, could stay there as long as he wanted. So, before we knew what was happening, Mary and I were out of our schools, packing our bags and returning to the village.

Back there, even though we had been no farther away than the next town, and had regularly visited our grandparents, we were treated as strangers. People were not too friendly and I found I missed my friends Breda and Paddy.

The village was a small place, with three grocery shops and three pubs, a post office, a surgery, a presbytery where the parish priest lived, the Catholic and Protestant churches and the national school. I was now fourteen and should have been at secondary school. But with three young sisters and three adults in the house, two of them bedridden, someone had to do the looking-after and it was taken for granted that this was to be my job. Education was never mentioned again: my working life had begun. I don't remember having any particular feelings about my new situation. I took it all in my stride.

Having got used to all the modern conveniences of our terraced house, we now had to adapt to life without them. There was a great deal of coming and going with chamber pots since there was only a chemical toilet in the backyard. There was one great consolation, though: this house had no stairs. Our water was drawn from the well in Noonan's yard, a five-minute walk away, and carried home in a bucket for the cleaning, laundry and cooking.

My grandfather was in the little front bedroom where he had always been. Mother and father slept in the big bedroom, in their separate beds as usual.

In the morning, after my sisters had gone to school, I would first give my grandfather his breakfast: a boiled egg and brown bread. Then I would put food on a tray for my mother, Geraldine and myself. Geraldine was three now and would spend most of the day sitting beside Mammy in the bed. Breakfast was a time for chat, laughter and song. Mammy would sing in her wheezy, weak voice 'Put another nickel in in the nickelodeon'. Her friend Eileen sometimes came in to see her, and I would be sent about my business so they could chat in private. My mother was not always happy. She would scream at me at times because I could not do something right, and would cry as she tried to explain from her bed how to make custard or gravy. How I wished I had a mother who would take the top off my egg in the morning and ask if I had slept well. Instead, I felt this tremendous responsibility for her wellbeing and happiness.

Old Daddy was easier to please. Give him the newspaper and he would read it from cover to cover. The only paper that was allowed into the house was the *Irish Press*, which my father bought. My grandfather would cut out the Dagwood cartoon every day, and anything else of interest to him. He liked me to sit on the side of his bed so he could show me his clippings.

We could expect my father home any time after three in the afternoon. He had a Volkswagen now, which I dreaded to hear coming, because it meant that peace was at an end.

'The devil makes work for idle hands,' he told us. Mary and I had to polish the brass buttons on his jacket, cap and overcoat, our shoes, and his, until our arms ached.

If he didn't go to the pub, he would be in bed by seven, since he had to be up so early. Because he slept in the room with my mother, this meant that we couldn't go in to talk to Mammy and that she couldn't read in the evenings. Of course, on the nights when my father went to the pub, there was nothing about him needing his sleep.

My mother had her good and bad days. If it was a bad one, I would have to steel myself to tell my father when he came in, 'Mammy is not well today, Daddy.'

'I suppose that's because I went for a couple of drinks the other night. Am I not entitled to after a hard day's work?'

In the middle of all this, I would take a peep at Old Daddy through the open door of his room and he would give me a wink. This was a comfort. When we were all exhausted and my father had gone off to bed, the relief felt wonderful. As soon as we heard him snoring, we would creep up and kiss Geraldine and my mother, asking if she was okay. I knew in my heart that she was not. When I was in bed myself in my grandmother's old room, which I shared with Mary and Alison, I would hear my mother trying to catch her breath.

My fifteenth birthday arrived and matters improved when I got a bicycle. It quickly became my most treasured possession. With its carrier basket on the front, it made shopping suddenly almost easy and, better still, during the long summer evenings, I could go for a spin and enjoy a bit of freedom. Time to dream of all I was going to do with my life!

My father and grandfather were not getting on well at all. My father would go for days without going in to see him, though he had to pass by his open bedroom door to come into the kitchen. And Daddy was always lecturing us about honouring our father and mother.

My mother no longer had good days. She was worn out. One

morning in early December 1959, I went up with her breakfast and she patted the bed beside her. I knew something was very wrong. When I looked at her, a shiver went through me. The skin on her face and neck seemed almost transparent.

'Will you get Joe for me like a good girl?' she whispered. 'Ask him will he come over and take me home?'

Joe, her younger brother, a kind and caring man, was the only one of my five uncles still living at the farm. I was about to go and do what she'd asked when she put her hand on mine.

'Before you go, I want you and me to do something.'

She was making a huge effort to get out the words. 'I have a bit of money put away for you girls and when each of you is twenty-one, you will get it.'

She handed me a piece of paper on which the details were written. She wanted me to sign it, so only we four sisters could touch it. I was very upset, but I had to listen carefully because her voice was so faint. I nodded, not caring about the money, not wanting to think what this conversation might mean. My mother seemed to drag the breath into her lungs as I got a pen and signed. Then she took hold of my two hands and with a heave, lifted her head off the pillow.

'This is between you and me,' she gasped. 'You mustn't tell anyone, do you hear me?' She fell back exhausted.

'I promise you,' I said. Inside I was praying, *Please, God, don't let her die.*

I got on my bike, and pedalled for all I was worth. It took me nearly half an hour to get to Ballintee. When I breathlessly gave my uncle the message, he ran to the car without a word. I cycled as fast as I could after him and was pushing the bike through our gate when I saw him carrying my mother out in his arms, wrapped in a blanket. She had her head buried in his shoulder. Neither of them looked at me, nor said a word. Delicately he put her on the back seat of the car and then ran round to the driver's side. I stood there watching as they drove away. I don't believe I even waved goodbye.

Old Daddy called me up to his room. He kept saying, 'You poor child. You poor, poor child.'

Suddenly I was crying as if my heart were breaking.

My father was very quiet when I told him that Mammy had gone to her mother's. The news seemed to make everything worse. He went and stood in the room they shared, the room he still believed to be haunted.

Geraldine could not stop crying. I wanted to cry again but not in front of my father, there was a part of me that didn't want him to think that I was against him, by crying over Mammy.

Emptying the chest of drawers of his clothes, he announced that he would not be sleeping in their room until she got back. 'I'll sleep in yours, and you four can sleep in here.'

It made me feel close to my mother, sharing her room with my sisters. We were glad to be together, so we could talk. My father did not offer to take us to see her, and we were too afraid to ask. His silence was deafening.

Christmas was near. Alison and Geraldine firmly believed in Santa Claus, but Mary and I had no money to buy them presents.

'I'm going to go and see Mammy, and get her to ask my father for some money,' I told my grandfather.

'Whatever you say,' he replied.

I cycled over and saw my mother for the first time in a fortnight. She looked no better, but her face shone when she saw me. She said I mustn't be worrying about not coming over to see her, because she understood how things were. I gave her all our news and finally said, 'Would you ask Daddy for some money so that I can get Christmas presents for Alison and Geraldine?'

'I haven't seen him since the day I left the house,' she said.

Her eyes were brimming over with tears. I couldn't believe it! I had thought he was keeping us away because my mother was not well, just like in the hospital when she had her babies.

When I told Mary what my mother had said, she was raging.

'We should have known,' she said bitterly. 'Sure, he wouldn't be welcome the way he goes on.'

Mary was far stronger than I was, and not afraid of upsetting anyone, not even my father. She said she would ask him straight out for the money. Our younger sisters were asleep by the time he came in from the pub. As he sat at the kitchen table ravenously eating his heated-up supper, I knew by his manner that he had a good few pints in him. My stomach felt knotted with fear. Thirteen-year-old Mary stood defiantly in front of him, hands on hips.

'We want some money for Christmas presents for Alison and Geraldine,' she said, looking him straight in the eye.

'I have them got,' he said, his voice cold and his hard blue eyes flashing with anger. My sister held her nerve.

'What did you get them?'

'Slippers.'

The word sounded like the lash of a whip. I looked at Mary in despair as he stood up from the table, his supper still uneaten, and pushed away the chair. He put his face right up against hers.

'Why don't you mind your own bloody business?'

Then he turned and strode into his room. My body shook at the slam of the door.

Mary's face was scarlet. I saw her hands down by her sides, fists clenched, knuckles white. But it was no good: we had made him angry and now we were worse off than ever. How were we going to give our sisters slippers on Christmas morning, when they were expecting dolls and prams?

One evening, soon after this, we recognised the sound of my father's car, much earlier than usual. He was in a terrible state when he came into the house.

'Have ye seen my wallet?' he asked, looking around wildly.

We hadn't. He dashed up to his bedroom, searching like a madman.

Please, God, let him find it, I prayed. I wanted him to go out to the pub and leave us in peace. But there was no sign of the wallet.

The next morning, he went to work as usual. I said to Mary, 'What are we going to do if he can't find his wallet? He'll be in the house all over Christmas if he has no money.'

'I'll have a look,' she said. She raced up to his room. The next thing, she was back with his wallet in her hand.

'It was down between the bed and the wall,' she told me triumphantly.

The wallet was bulging. She put it on the table and we stood and looked at it as if it were going to bite us. Then we were laughing hysterically.

Eventually, we opened the wallet and were amazed at all the banknotes. We started counting, but when we reached £300, we got frightened.

I wonder if he knows exactly how much he has?' I said.

Mary ran and put the wallet back, but we couldn't stop thinking that we would never get an opportunity like this again. When Alison and Geraldine had gone to school, we brought the wallet down for another look. This went on for ages, putting it back, and bringing it down. At last, we counted the money properly. It came to more than £300.

'I bet he has this amount of money every Christmas, while we're always scrimping and saving. It's money he gets from people for Christmas boxes and he keeps it for himself to drink.' Mary was carried away by her anger. I was too anxious to be angry. In the end, we took a bundle of notes out of the wallet.

My father arrived home early. Coming in the door, he said, 'Well, any sign of my wallet?'

'We found it between the bed and the wall,' Mary said, handing it to him. He seemed puzzled.

'I'm sure I looked there.'

He opened it and started to flick through the money as Mary and I held our breath. Then he put his hand into his inside pocket, took out more notes and crammed them in the wallet. Putting it in his inside pocket with a pat, he went to his room without a word. I thought Mary was going to explode with rage.

We got Alison and Geraldine what they wanted and even bought one or two things for ourselves. My father did not seem to notice any of this or, if he did, he never said. He may have thought we had got the presents from our maternal grandmother and, if we had, he would not want to know about it.

He did not take us to see our mother at Christmas and, as far as I know, he went nowhere near her himself. He spent most of the time in the pub, which suited us fine. I'm sure my grandfather had a good quiet laugh over the wallet episode, but he never said a word.

Even though we had taken money, Mary still decided to teach my father a lesson. She was so angry with Daddy that she told him she would go and live at my grandmother's with Mammy, which she knew he would hate.

'Has she gone?' he asked, coming in from work on the day she'd told him she was packing her bags.

'She has.'

He sat down to his dinner without another word. I missed Mary terribly, as did my sisters, but he didn't seem to care.

Chapter Four

Coming up to my sixteenth birthday, I was full of anticipation. I was sure I would be allowed to go places now, to dances and to the pictures. Nearly every day, I cycled over to see my mother. I couldn't talk to her the way I used to and all the time I was there I felt my grandmother could not wait for me to leave. My father was not too pleased about my visits either.

'Do you know they don't want you over there? They never did.'

It didn't matter. I was going and that was that.

When I brought Old Daddy's breakfast up to him, he said, 'I don't usually interfere, child, but this time I feel I have to. Don't let your father stop you seeing your mother, d'you hear me?'

'Yes.'

'You want to please your father at all costs, but you must promise me you won't let him stop you going to visit her.'

I promised and I meant it.

Just before my mother left home, a local boy came into my life. Michael Kelly had come back after two years in England. From the first, I took his fancy. He would come down to our house, circling around the road on his bicycle, looking for a glimpse of me through the window.

This was very exciting, but my mother could see him from her bedroom waiting for me to take a step outside, and she began to worry.

'Be careful,' she told me. 'I know he is a few years older than you. He knows more about the world, and anyway, you're too young to be thinking about boys.' Michael was twenty to my almost sixteen.

I would venture out cautiously, thinking I was terrible-looking: too plump, blushing, and with long brown curls down to my waist like a child's.

'Stay where I can see you,' my mother would say.

Dutifully sticking to the bit of road in front of the house, Michael and I exchanged a few embarrassed words.

'Do ye go out at all?' he asked, letting the wheel of his bike tick as he freewheeled in a circle.

'I do the shopping,' I said, sounding like an old woman.

'Where do you go to school?'

'I've left school. I look after my mother and grandfather.'

I thought that sounded more grown-up, and people said I looked eighteen.

Michael was slim, of medium height, with fair hair and very pale skin. He wore drainpipe trousers, winkle-picker shoes and his hair was long and slicked back with Brylcreem.

'A Teddy Boy,' my mother said. I had seen such boys in magazines, of course, but not in real life. But here was one right in front of my eyes and, on top of that, he was interested in me.

'I'll see you then,' he said, standing on the pedals and shooting away down the road with a ring of his bell.

God, how stupid I had sounded! I'd made a total eejit of myself. But the strange thing was, Michael kept coming back, and I looked forward to his visits.

I begged Mammy not to tell my father. We both knew that if

he heard that I was talking to a boy, he'd be like a devil. She warned me, 'Stay away from that boy.'

I let none of this put me off and, once Mammy had gone to Ballintee to her mother's, it was easier to see Michael. One day, he asked me to go to the pictures with him. I blinked in disbelief.

'What did you say?'

'There's a good film on in Callan. My father will lend me the car.'

His father was the village hackney man.

'I'll have to ask,' I said.

How was I going to get my father's permission?

'Michael Kelly has asked me to go to the pictures,' I announced that night, in a shaky voice.

He looked up from his dinner sharply, then turned back to his plate. Deliberately, he cut a sausage in half but made no comment.

'Can I go?'

'No.'

I knew that was it. So I retreated at once but, when I talked it over with Michael the next day, he had a good argument.

'They expect you to be a grown-up about everything they want you to do, and they treat you like a child when you want to do something yourself.'

I must remember that in a couple of months when I reach sixteen, I thought.

All the time, I continued to cycle over to see my mother and, of course, this gave me a precious chance to see Michael. On my way back, he would meet me halfway and we'd laugh and chat as we cycled along. Sometimes, if the road was clear, we would stop to kiss, the bicycles between us.

I was besotted, feeling loved and wanted. Nothing else mattered as long as I had Michael.

I never mentioned to my mother that I was in love. In truth, she did not seem like my mother any more. She was frail and helpless, more like a child who had to be protected than an adult to confide in. We no longer chatted and laughed. She sang no more happy songs.

My sixteenth birthday arrived. The first thing I did was wish Old Daddy happy birthday with a kiss on the cheek and a bunch of flowers in his room. I loved sharing this day with him because it made us feel more closely connected. He thought I was special and I knew he was.

It was a beautiful, sunny day as I cycled over the Kyle Road to see my mother. The farmers were coming from the creamery with their horses and carts. They waved and raised their caps as they passed, knowing where I was going having seen me so many times on the road. The empty milk churns clanked and bobbed behind them. I went on a few miles and turned into the narrow winding lane that led up to my grandmother's. It was the kind of boreen you would read about in a fairytale. At the bottom of it was a well, fed by a spring, and it had the most wonderful-tasting water. Then there was a division in the road, with clusters of trees in the fork, so tall that they seemed to brush the sky. Opposite the trees was a lodge called the 'Grand Gates', one of three entrances to the 'Big House' where the gentry lived. Old Daddy knew many ghost stories about the Big House. He told one about a horse-drawn carriage which, on certain nights of the year, drove straight through the closed gates at midnight.

My grandparents' house was the second along this road. Opposite was a space where wood was chopped for the big open fire in my grandmother's kitchen. The fireplace had wooden benches at each side and from here you could look up and see the clear blue sky or the stars at night. My grandmother baked her own bread in big black pots on this fire and it would make you weak at the knees to smell it. When she put a big pan of onions on, you could pick up the delicious whiff from way down the road. There was no electricity, so oil lamps lit the house at night, throwing strange moody shadows. It was a place

to frighten little children, something from which my grandmother appeared to get great satisfaction.

I don't remember having presents on my sixteenth birthday.
It was the same as any other day really.

Eventually, I started for home. I was hoping to meet Michael
and suddenly there he was, cycling powerfully towards me. He
braked violently and I could see that he was anxious.

'Quick,' he said. 'My mother's heard about us meeting. Hide
the bikes!'

He threw his bike into the hedge, then grabbed mine and did
likewise. He forced himself through a gap and into a field.

'Come on,' he said, catching me by the hand.

I gathered my dress around my legs and struggled through
the hedge.

'Keep down. Someone might see us,' he said.

He pulled me on to the long grass. It was the first time I had
ever lain down with a boy. I knew nothing at all about sex. It felt
exciting to be so close. We started to kiss. Our kisses were
usually very hurried, in case we'd be seen, but this was different.
Michael rolled on top of me. There were things going on down
there that I did not understand. Then I felt a stab of pain and
shouted, 'You're hurting me.'

I was all sticky inside my underwear and down my legs. I was
embarrassed and ashamed. What would he think of me? Within
minutes, I was on my bicycle. I flew home as quickly as I could.

When I got back, I was sure Old Daddy would know by
looking at me that something was wrong. I could not face him.

'Are you all right?' I called.

'I am, child.'

I went into the bedroom to think. My head was full of
questions. As I was taking off my wet underclothes, quiet tears
ran down my cheeks. Why had Michael reacted in this way to
his mother knowing about us meeting? In one of our hurried
conversations, he had told me that she considered me a townie,
leading her son, the innocent country boy, astray. Mrs Kelly

knew all belonging to me, didn't she? My father delivered the post to her post office every day. And could I be pregnant? How did you get pregnant? I still had no knowledge of the facts of life. At first, I thought it might happen if we kissed. I didn't remember much about my mother being pregnant — only that she had been in hospital for most of the time. I'd never asked questions about any of it. My feeling towards Michael had, until now, been innocent and romantic, but what had happened felt dirty and sinful.

I had not seen Michael for days. By cycling over a back road to my grandmother's, I didn't have to pass through the village and he didn't come down to the house. I was sure he didn't want to see me after what had happened between us. But sooner or later I had to go to the village for messages and, as I cycled up, there he was standing at the door of his mother's shop.

'Where have you been?' he asked me.

So we were speaking again.

'Home.'

'I looked for you. I had this for your birthday, but you took off before I could give it to you.'

He pulled a small jewellery box from his pocket. I opened it. Inside was a beautiful gold locket. I felt a mixture of relief and joy. Michael still liked me after all, I thought.

Three weeks after I'd turned sixteen, my Uncle Joe pulled up outside the house and blew the horn. I ran out.

'Go and ring your father and tell him your mother is not well at all.'

I cycled up to the post office as fast as I could.

'Will you ring my father, please?' I asked the postmistress, Michael's mother. 'Tell him to come quick. Mammy's very bad.'

Within an hour, my father arrived; he wanted me to go with him. My mother's friend Eileen looked after my sisters. When we arrived at the farm, my great-aunt Lizzie was there. She had been a matron in a hospital in London; now she was taking care of my mother.

My father and I stood one on each side of Mammy's bed. My poor mother was just lying there with her eyes closed. I could not be certain that she knew we were there. Then Aunt Lizzie said, to no one in particular, 'Her pulse is very weak.'

'Why is she saying things like that in front of your mother?' my father asked me. 'How does she know if she can hear her or not?'

I shrugged, not knowing what to say. I looked across the bed at him as he struggled to gain control of the situation. But my great-aunt paid him no heed. I wished he would be quiet. Then my Aunt Lizzie looked at me and said, 'I'll leave ye to have a few words together.'

'Thanks,' I said.

I knew my father took this as his right and felt no need for thanks. He was bristling as he stood there as straight and stiff as a rod.

'Can you forgive me?' he said to my mother. All that moved was his mouth, not another muscle.

She opened her eyes and, without hesitation, answered clearly and firmly, 'No.'

The silence between the three of us was stifling. It was the last word I ever heard her speak. I did not want to lift my gaze from my mother's face and look at my father, afraid of the anger and indignation I would see. Oh, why did I have to witness this?

When I went home to be with my sisters, I told them how ill Mammy was. My father did not come back until the next morning; he told us all that our mother was dead.

We were not expecting to hear such news and were not prepared for it. How could she not be there any more? There were so many things I wanted to tell her, of what had been going on in my life and my thoughts and plans for the future. Now it was too late. My little sisters were crying; they were frightened and lost, having been kept in the dark about it all. My father made no attempt to comfort them. He wanted me to go back to the wake with him. Alison and Geraldine were hysterical at the idea of being left alone again, but he needed me. He was afraid no one would speak to him, and with good reason. I knew that Mary, who still lived in Ballintee, would not.

There was not one word spoken as we drove along the familiar road. I started to cry, knowing I would never cycle over there again to see my mother. Then there was the thought of looking at her dead body.

Before we got out of the car, my father turned to me and said, 'Are you all right?'

I blew my nose and wiped away my tears. I told him I was, so we went in. I wanted to look anywhere rather than at the bed, so I tried to study the people coming in and out. Chairs were set around the room. Some of the neighbours had come to say the rosary, their beads dangling from their fingers, and entwined in their hands. The older women wore shawls pulled up over their heads. The men swiped their caps off as they walked through the door and held them in their hands like steering wheels.

'Isn't it terrible sad?'

'So it is. And herself only thirty-nine.'

I forced myself to look at the bed, and was surprised. Mammy was lying there exactly the same as she had many times before, when I had crept in to her, thinking she was asleep. She looked ready to open her eyes with a laugh.

'Ah, I caught you,' she'd say. 'You thought I was asleep!'

But those eyelids were never going to open again. Mammy was not going to smile, or sing, or give her big hearty laugh. I wanted to run over and wrap my arms around her.

It seemed as if the whole world were trooping in to pay their respects. I left the room and went outside. I could not listen any more to people talking about my mother in the past tense. That evening, her coffin was taken to the church.

It was a huge funeral that left the next morning for the

cemetery, after the Requiem Mass in the same church where she had been married nineteen years before. The priest, in his black vestments, accompanied by an altar boy swinging the incense burner on its rattly chain, walked ahead of the coffin. We, her family, all wore black diamonds on our sleeves. The coffin bearers were my mother's five brothers. Just as they came out of the church door, a shower of light rain fell through the rays of the sun, lasting about three minutes. During this time, everyone stood still.

'Happy is the corpse that the rain rains on,' the mourners said to one another.

It is customary in Ireland for a married woman to be buried in her husband's family plot, but Mammy had left instructions that she wanted to be buried with her own people. This made the split in our family all too obvious. Old Daddy and my two young sisters were not there; my father thought it would be too much for them. His five sisters were there to support him. I stayed by his side throughout the service, while Mary was with my mother's family. I remember thinking we should all be together on this dreadful day.

After the coffin had been lowered, I watched the handfuls of earth my father showered on to its lid. I imagined my mother's frail body shaking inside from the impact and suddenly put my hands to my face and began to sob. My father clutched my arm.

'Pull yourself together, for God's sake!' he said.

But I couldn't.

There was such an air of loss; people didn't seem to want to leave the graveside. I hated the thought of my mother being left in that lonely place. At last, our two families went their separate ways with hardly a word spoken between them. I was trembling so much, my father took me to the pub, into the snug, where the women went for a bottle of stout. He sat me down and bought me a large whiskey: his answer to every crisis. I felt calmer after my first whiskey, being used to only sups of Guinness. We went back home, which didn't feel like a home any more. My father's sisters were waiting for us, worried about how my father would cope now.

In the days that followed, with my sisters gone to school and my father at work, Old Daddy and I would try to talk. But, for the first time ever, we had no idea what to say to each other. I wanted to ask him so much about my father and mother, their life together and what he thought had gone wrong — why, for instance, she wouldn't forgive him. One burning question I wanted to ask, but couldn't, was if my father would be different now. But being unsure of how Old Daddy felt about his only son and not wanting to have to take sides between them, I thought that perhaps I was better off not knowing.

Each day, at the time I would have been setting off to see my mother, I would go out the back yard and look over towards Ballintee, and scream aloud from the crater of loneliness at my centre, 'Mammy!'

Then I would listen. There were times when I was sure she called back to me. I would curl up and lie on the end of Old Daddy's bed. I knew she would have come back if she could have. I don't know how my sisters felt. We never spoke about my mother.

My father carried on as before: going to work, then to the pub. He did not comfort us or ask for our comfort. After a few days, Mary wrote to know would I ask him if it was all right for her to come home. He said it was.

Getting his second daughter back was a feather in his cap and something he could tell his cronies about in the pub. He would not say much about her leaving home but that she wanted to come back to him was a different story. So, without delay, he and I went once more up the quiet boreen. Outside the house, he told me to go and get my sister.

'What kind of humour is he in?' Mary asked me at the door.

'He's delighted you're coming home.'

'Sure he is,' she said sarcastically.

We walked back between the tall hedges and reached the road. My father had the engine running, as he always did.

'Are ye all right?' he asked as we climbed in.

'We are,' we said, in one voice. But it did not sound very convincing.

Chapter Five

My mother's death and my encounter with Michael had all taken place within weeks of my sixteenth birthday. Afterwards, I began to lose weight and people were remarking on it. Many agreed with Old Daddy's notion: that I was pining for my mother. It seemed the obvious explanation. Eventually, my father had to take notice of my pale, pinched face.

'I suppose I'd better make an appointment with the doctor,' he said, turning his eyes up to heaven at the thought of the expense.

An appointment was made for me to see the doctor in Callan, about seven miles away. There was one in our village, but our family doctor, who had attended my mother, was the one I was to see.

'I can't take you,' my father said. 'Get the hackney car in the village.'

It was run by Mr Kelly, Michael's father. I'd had only a few words with Michael since my mother's funeral but, when I went up to book the hackney car, I met Michael coming towards me on the road.

'Where are you off to?'

'To book the car. I'm not well, so I've to go to the doctor's tomorrow.'

'I'll drive you myself.'

I thanked him, but I didn't mention this offer to my father, and, the next morning, Michael called for me. Since there was no school that day, we took Alison and Geraldine with us; they were delighted to be going for the drive. The three of them waited in the car while I went in to the surgery.

There was no one in the waiting room, so I saw the doctor straight away. He was a distant man who, to my knowledge, never addressed anyone by their Christian name.

'How are you?' he asked.

'I'm not too well really. I'm feeling sick all the time.'

He asked me when I had had my last period. I blushed and told him that I had no idea, because I never took any notice of it. He stared at me hard and clicked his tongue.

'I'll examine you and see what's the matter.'

There was a couch on one side of the room. I got up and lay on it, shaking all over.

'Just relax.'

He came over and started to lift my skirt.

'Relax,' he said again. 'The sooner we get this over, the better.'

I was trying, but the more I tried, the more tense I became. I could feel him probing around and I started to cry.

When he had finished, he turned his back to me and washed his hands. I got down off the couch.

'Do you have a boyfriend?'

'No,' I answered in sudden panic.

'Well, that's strange,' he said, spinning on his heel to face me. 'Because you're pregnant.'

I couldn't believe what he had just said. I stared down at the lino, wanting only to get out of the place, and did so as soon as I decently could.

'You look like you've seen a ghost,' Michael said when I reached the car.

'I can't tell you now,' I whispered frantically.

I fumbled for my purse, shook out some coppers and gave them to my sisters, saying, 'Go over to the shop and get some sweets for yourselves.'

When they had got out of the car and run off skipping and laughing, I turned to Michael and blurted it out.

'I'm pregnant.'

He bit his lip. That was his only reaction.

'Don't worry,' he told me after a few minutes. 'It'll be all right. I'll come down to your gate tonight and we'll think of something.'

I was so frightened, and he was so cool.

My younger sisters were in bed and Mary was at the table doing her homework when he arrived around 9 o'clock. My father was not home, thank God. I heard the bicycle bell and ducked out of the house, in a state of anguish.

'What am I going to do? My father will kill me.' I was crying. 'How could you do this to me?'

'Jesus, will you calm down?'

'Don't tell me to calm down! What have I got to be calm about? What'll I do?'

'I'll get some money,' he said soothingly. 'We'll go to England.'

'England? How can I leave my sisters, and our mother only after dying?'

He gave me a sheepish look.

'Come here and give me a kiss.'

'No! This is no time for kissing. I'm going inside. Come down tomorrow night and tell me what you've planned.'

It went on like this for weeks. Michael came down almost every night with nothing but empty promises. He had no work and no savings — nothing that was going to help us start a life together.

Meanwhile, I guessed I was about fourteen weeks' pregnant and I was finding it hard to hide my growing stomach.

One day, I was up the village doing the shopping when I met Michael's married sister Iris, over from England to show off her new baby son.

'I see you're putting on weight,' she said to me.

She was not normally a friendly person, so she must have suspected something to have spoken to me at all. She looked me up and down enquiringly, which made me very uneasy. To think that Iris had noticed my size made me feel even bigger. If Iris had twigged, so might others. This started me thinking about going to England, in spite of having to care for my sisters.

To be pregnant at that time was the ultimate shame, and sometimes it led to people doing desperate things. I once overheard Mammy and Eileen whispering about a young girl who had gone off and had her baby in a field, all on her own, like an animal. When they found her, she and the baby were rushed into hospital, nearly dead. It was a terrible scandal and the thought of it terrified me. I would go mad if Michael did not think of a plan soon.

When Michael came down that night, I told him about his sister's remark.

'Don't take any notice of her,' was all he said.

What's the use of telling him anything? I thought to myself. Nothing bothers him. I thought of the girls in the convent laundry in Thomastown. It was said that some of them had babies and that was why they had been sent there. They were allowed out for a walk on a Sunday, like sheep, one behind the other and staring straight ahead. Would I end up there and not be allowed to keep my baby? Tears stung the back of my eyes.

'I'm going in,' I said irritably.

As I passed Old Daddy's room, he called me. 'Come here, child, and tell me what's bothering you.'

I sat on the bed beside him, looking at his gentle face and thoughtful eyes. Without warning, I burst into tears. He said nothing, just patted my hand. 'It can't be that bad,' he said at last, softly.

'Yes it is,' I sobbed. 'I'm pregnant. That's how bad it is.'

'How long have you kept this to yourself?'

'Since I went to the doctor that time.'

I looked at his sad face and felt so guilty for letting him down.

'What will my father say? Please don't tell him!'

'You'll have to tell him sometime.'

'Yes, I know.'

He simply put his finger to his lips to show that they were sealed.

My father came home about midnight and was eating his supper. We were all in bed, but I was not asleep. Suddenly there was an unmerciful pounding on the front door.

'Hold your patience, whoever you are,' he called out through a mouthful of food.

The pounding continued, and then a woman's voice shouted, 'Open the door this minute.'

The whole house was awake now. We girls sat up in our beds, wondering what was going on. We heard my father go to the door and open it.

'What's so important — '

'What age is that eldest one of yours?'

It was Mrs Kelly. My father did not appear to hear her at all, but went on with his question: '— that you have to disturb a man at this hour of night?'

My sisters were looking across the room at me.

'What's Mrs Kelly doing down here?' Mary asked. 'Why does she want to know your age?'

I shook my head. Mrs Kelly was determined to get my father's attention.

'That young one of yours is pregnant,' she shouted.

There was a deathly silence. I held my breath. Mary gasped in horror. We waited for my father to explode, but he didn't. He only said, in an almost light voice, 'What can we do about it at this time of the night?'

My sisters looked at me, their eyes and mouths wide open. There was a pause.

'What age is she?' Mrs Kelly repeated.

'She's just gone sixteen.'

Another pause.

'Right,' she said. 'We'll talk tomorrow.'

We heard her steps going back down the path. I made out voices other than Mrs Kelly's, saying 'Goodnight' to my father, and realised that Michael and his sister had been with her.

As the door shut, I thought: now I'm going to get it. At first, there was no sound, only my father tidying away his plate. Then he called from the kitchen. 'Come down here, Kay.'

Unbelievably, he still sounded calm. It seemed impossible that he could be taking this in his stride. He tipped his head at me to come into his bedroom. He was sitting on the side of his bed, looking lost.

'Have you any idea what you are going to do?' he asked.

'No.'

'Do you want to get the baby adopted?'

'I want to keep my baby no matter what.'

Not for one minute, in the midst of all my fears and confusion, had I considered giving my baby away. It was mine.

'Then he will have to marry you. Do you understand that?'

'I do.'

'Go to bed then.'

As I turned and twisted in my bed, I could hear my restless father in the other room. Eventually I heard him get up and go to work as usual at four in the morning. I lay there, full of guilt, wanting to comfort him and tell him that everything would be okay, like it used to be when I was young, when we two were on our own.

I talked to Old Daddy, who told me not to worry. I did my best not to, but he looked so sad. When my father came home from work that evening, he wouldn't touch his dinner. He said to me in a voice that, for him, was gentleness itself, 'Well, we'd better go and meet these people.'

The Kellys lived at the back of the shop and post office. By village standards, they were rich. This was almost entirely because of the single-minded efforts of Mrs Kelly. The story goes that she had started working in the post office for a penny a week in the 1930s, and had never missed a day's work or an opportunity to better herself. Now, in 1960, she seemed to own half the village. She had three houses: the shop-house itself, another just beside it, and a third outside the village. She also owned the garage and petrol pumps.

Her living-room, behind the shop, was cosy, with a big couch in front of an open fire roaring up the chimney. Having presented ourselves at the door, my father and I were grudgingly invited in. I noticed a wall cabinet crammed full of china and thought of my mother and how she would have loved that. For a while, I was not listening to the discussion in the room, but was far away, wondering what Mammy would say if she knew the condition I was in. I was snapped back to reality by Mrs Kelly's voice.

'I suppose you two have had a chat.'

'We have,' my father said. 'Kay wants to keep the baby, so the only right thing for them to do is to get married as soon as possible.'

Mrs Kelly spoke through tight lips. 'I see. Well, Michael is fine with that. It seems he wants to marry her.'

'That's that then. The sooner, the better.'

I half-expected this to be the end of the matter, but my father had more to say.

'I don't have any money myself, after burying her mother,' he said firmly. 'So I won't be able to help in that way at all.'

I wanted the ground to open and swallow me. How could he say that? Had he no shame?

'Their mother left them a few pounds each, when she died,'

he said. 'Unfortunately, I had to draw it out last week, to put tyres on the car.'

I looked at him wildly. I had forgotten about the money. How had he known about it? And how had he got his hands on it? Carrying on like that, no wonder he was always dwelling on my mother coming back to haunt him. When he came home drunk, he would say that he felt her presence in the car at the Merry Dance, a part of the road where he said he had experienced many strange happenings. He would tell us that Mammy was not happy and had something to say. I used to feel sorry for him when he went on like that, especially since I had heard from my mother's own lips that she would never forgive him. Now I was wondering what kind of man my father really was.

Chapter Six

Within a fortnight, Mrs Kelly had set up the wedding. In that time, she could not bring herself to look at me. As far as she was concerned, this was none of her precious son's doing.

'The only reason I am agreeing to this,' she said, 'is that I don't want to spend the rest of my life looking at my son's illegitimate child running around the streets of this village.'

She had total control of the wedding arrangements because she paid for everything, including my wedding ring and pink dress. I was not allowed to wear white — obviously not being a virgin, as Mrs Kelly took it upon herself to inform me. I didn't know what this word meant because the only one I had ever heard of was the Virgin Mary.

In the weeks before the wedding, Michael and I had the freedom to see each other whenever we wanted. Michael said we should have sex, because it was a way of feeding the baby. I believed him, of course, and I certainly was not going to deprive my child of anything. But I didn't like it and felt ashamed afterwards, imagining that people were thinking about us doing it all the time. I was so young and I believed he loved me as much as I felt I loved him. Michael seemed happy enough to be getting married and, in my naiveté, I thought that we would live happily together forever.

We married in August 1960. Michael's brother was best man and Mary, dressed in blue, was my bridesmaid. The benches on the bride's side were not crowded. Those who did turn up came entirely from my father's side of the family. Two of his sisters were there, with looks that would wither you. One of them had given me a slap on the face before we left for the church, saying that I had brought shame on the family name. None of my mother's family was at my wedding. I was told they had not been invited.

If I had died in the church, it would have been a relief. My stomach was so sick, I couldn't concentrate on the ceremony and now can remember it only vaguely. Afterwards no one came to congratulate me or to wish us well; in the photographs, taken outside the church, we all look grim. But for the clothes we were wearing, you would think we were at a funeral.

The next ordeal was the reception. It was held in an old farmhouse belonging to a distant relation of ours. The meal was set out in the parlour just off the kitchen. The spread was plentiful: chickens, hams and cuts of beef. There was a two-tier wedding cake and plenty of drink: bottles of porter, gin, whiskey and even a drop of poteen.

I can't say that I enjoyed any of it. I was like a stranger at my own wedding, not knowing where half the food and drink had come from and unable to name most of the guests. As the alcohol took effect, the dancing started. Michael's cousin, a great accordion player, got couples up to dance.

I didn't dance. Why should I, when I had never danced before? And besides, Geraldine was sitting on my lap, clinging to me and crying because I was about to go to London for a week. That was an eternity to a five-year-old and she just after losing her mother. But go I must, for what was a wedding without a honeymoon?

When the time came for us to leave, Mary dragged Geraldine

from me and, with tears running down my face, I was bundled next to my husband into the back of Mr Kelly's car. Michael hadn't spoken more than a half-dozen words to me all day and yet here we were at the start of our married life together.

The plan was that we were to be put up for a week by Michael's sister, Iris. She had extended her holiday to be at her brother's wedding and would now be travelling back with us. We went by car to Rosslare, then ferry to Fishguard and train to London.

A cabin was booked on the boat, for the happy couple. I had never been on a boat, but I could not really appreciate it. I couldn't even stop crying. It seemed so overwhelming. Suddenly, I was a married woman and would be spending the rest of my life with a man whom I hardly knew. And yet, as soon as we closed the door of the cabin, before the ship had even sailed, Michael was all over me. Though how he could, with me looking like a blob, with a red nose and eyes and my big stomach, was beyond me.

The next day, after a seven-hour train journey, we were met at Paddington station by Iris's husband, Greg. As we drove through the streets, Greg started pointing out famous landmarks. This was for the benefit of his new sister-in-law, but my attention was elsewhere. As Greg spun the car round a traffic island, saying, 'This is London Bridge', I had my head out of the back window, vomiting.

The house seemed gigantic to me, with room after room on floor after floor. It was full of lodgers — all men, except for one girl, Jan. Most of them knew Michael, because they were from around the village at home. They didn't know me, but they knew my father, so I was Mr O's daughter. I didn't know how I was going to cope in the house with all those people. They were well aware that we had just got married, and me only sixteen, and they could see the size of me. I thanked God we were staying only a week.

I envied Iris. She seemed to have everything: pretty looks

and a handsome husband, two lovely children and beautiful, fashionable clothes. On top of all that, she moved through life full of confidence. I felt timid and dowdy in comparison.

During the week, we didn't go anywhere or do anything special. London to me was huge and frightening. Michael just went to the pub at night with the lads from the house, coming back late and stumbling up the stairs.

Once I went out shopping with Iris to get some presents for my sisters. I was so looking forward to going home and telling them all about the house, the clothes, and what I thought London was like. Apart from that, just to say I had been was enough for me.

I had no idea where we were going to live when we got home. It didn't matter as long as we were back. Then the bombshell dropped. Mrs Kelly phoned to tell Michael that she didn't want me around the village in the state I was in. We were to stay in England until the baby was born. I couldn't believe it! My father would go mad. Who was going to look after my little sisters? I was lost without them, Old Daddy and even my father.

Going out into this huge city terrified me. I felt I didn't have a person in the world to talk to. Having come from a place where I knew everyone I met, and could expect a smile, a wave or a couple of words, however trivial, I found London so unfriendly. When I asked Iris if I could do anything for her, she would say, 'everything's under control'. So, I spent most days in our room feeling sorry for myself, thinking of all the things I should be doing at home. Michael got a job as a carpenter. I hadn't even known he was one. After work, he would go to the pub to meet the lads, as he called them.

Mary wrote. Since I was no longer at home, she had been made to leave the technical school. She was furious with my father, with Mrs Kelly and with me. She had wanted to finish her schooling and do something with her life but because of me, she had been denied this chance. Looking back in later years, I wonder if this might have been a source of resentment.

One day, as I was lying on the bed, I felt a tiny kick in my stomach, and then another, as if the baby were fighting to arrive through my skin. I lifted my jumper and looked at my navel. It was bulging like a little pod, and I was sure that was where the baby was going to come out. In a panic, I ran downstairs to Iris.

'It's started!' I screamed. 'It's coming.'

'Can't be,' she said coolly. 'It's not due for another three months.'

'Are you sure?'

'Quite sure.'

I hauled myself back upstairs and said nothing to anyone about the worrying state of my belly button, but one good thing had happened: I now realised there was a real baby in there. I started to visualise it, even talked to it and suddenly could not wait for the day to come when I would hold my very own child. It took away some of the lonely feelings. I started to knit baby clothes and, as I listened to the click of my knitting needles, I dreamed contentedly of all the things I would soon be doing with my child.

Just a few weeks before the baby was born, I woke up in the middle of the night and saw that Michael was not in the bed beside me. I lay still and listened. We were sleeping in the back half of a big ground-floor room which was divided in two by large wooden doors. In the front room, Jan the lodger slept on a couch, and it was from that direction that I could make out faint whisperings. The dividing doors were slightly open and I crept out of bed to peep through. I could see my husband and Jan together. I didn't say or do anything, but simply tiptoed back to bed. The noise they were making carried on, but I had only one thought. When my baby was born, I could go home to my family, and not feel guilty. I put my hands on my tummy. I would love this baby as no baby had ever been loved before and we would have a great life together. My sisters would cherish it as much as I did, and Old Daddy would take it for walks and tell it the stories that he had once told me. We didn't need Michael.

He hadn't known it, but in his thoughtless way he had given me what I wanted. I had it all planned in my mind by the time he got back into bed beside me. I lay still, breathing evenly, waiting for him to fall asleep.

Chapter Seven

I was in no way prepared for the birth of my child. Not being able to find my way beyond the corner shop, I had not been near a doctor since my first brief consultation. But as I entered my last month, Iris suddenly said, 'You'd better go and see someone.'

She made an appointment.

The doctor was not pleased to find me so far gone and not even booked into a hospital. As far as I knew, in Ireland, when the baby was coming, you just turned up and had it. He told me not to mind Ireland. I was only sixteen and hadn't attended any antenatal classes, whatever they were.

He fixed me up at a maternity unit. I inspected my belly button every morning and found it getting bigger and bigger. There could not be much longer to wait.

When the contractions started, I was two weeks overdue, by the doctor's reckoning. I was huge and helpless and beginning to think that the baby was never going to arrive. It was late afternoon and, as soon as the pains began to feel stronger, Iris took me into hospital.

From the start, the nurses treated me with disdain for being so young and ignorant. I was plunged into a hot bath, which made me writhe in agony. I lay in the water, gasping; I couldn't get out and I couldn't be still. They pulled me out in between pains, and whisked me into an empty two-bedded room where one of the nurses wanted to examine me internally. She ordered me to open my legs. I asked her why and she told me. In one short sentence, all my theories about giving birth through my belly button were shattered!

The examination took some time. I annoyed the nurse further because I couldn't relax or even understand how, in that position, they could expect anyone to. Then my waters broke and my agony intensified, giving me barely enough time to draw breath. The nurses left, handing me a little black switch attached to a flex; they told me to press it if I wanted someone. Closing the door, they left me alone.

I did not believe the labour could get any worse, but it did. I was up on my knees, thrashing around the bed, frantically pushing the button in my hand for someone to help me. No one came. I was screaming from the very pit of me.

At last a nurse came.

'Lie down in that bed and behave yourself!' she said. She caught me by the arms and shoved me back, with a hard slap on the backside. But I could not stay down. I was up again as if on a spring. I put my face close to hers in the hope of getting heard, and roared with all my strength, 'Please help me, please, please!'

She lifted her hand and gave me another slap, this time on the face. Then she marched out again.

This lonely ordeal went on from nine in the evening until six the next morning, during which time I prayed to God to let me die. Every so often, a nurse would come in and tell me to be quiet, which I was not able to be, so I would get another couple of slaps. Eventually I began to lapse in and out of consciousness. I remember two nurses coming in and trying to sit me up. But I was falling all over the place like a rag doll. Then they tried getting me out of the bed.

'Put your feet on the floor. It's time to go.'

Their voices sounded far away. I tried to stand but I was too weak. They ended up dragging me along the corridor. I looked down and saw that my legs were covered in blood. I felt near death.

Then we were in a white room with huge lights blazing down on a high narrow bed. There were more people around me now. I was not sure if any of this was real or not but I heard a man's voice telling me, 'Don't worry. It'll be all over soon.'

I tried to smile at him but no longer had the use of my face. They laid me on a table, put my legs in white stockings and hauled them up in the air. I could see the man they called 'Doctor' standing at the end of the bed with what looked like a knife in his hand. He bent down and suddenly I felt a warm gushing sensation around my thighs and a feeling of relief spread through me.

'It's a boy,' someone said, in a matter-of-fact tone. The next moment, I was aware of a hoarse cry and then a small, wet body lying across my left leg. At six o'clock in the morning, my son had been born.

I thought my heart was going to explode with love as they placed him in my arms. He was big, over 9 pounds in weight. He was perfect and he was mine. I don't know how long the doctor took to stitch me. They let me hold my baby all the time he was doing it, so I didn't care.

That night, when Iris and Michael came in, I carefully watched my husband's face to see what he made of his son. He was obviously embarrassed to see me breast-feeding and was itching to leave. Strangely, at that particular moment, I didn't mind. All my worries about our relationship had been pushed aside. I may not have felt like a wife, but I definitely felt like a mother. This was what I had been born for.

Ten days later, Michael and Iris came to take me home. I felt weak, but I insisted on carrying my baby. Everyone was very quiet in the car on the way. It puzzled me, but I decided not to break the silence by saying something and getting the deaf ear. Or maybe they were afraid of waking the baby, I thought. Then, as we walked up to the house, Michael grabbed my arm and stopped me. His face was even whiter than usual as he said, in a low voice, 'We have something to tell you before you go in.'

'What? Tell me quick.'

Everything tore through my mind: my sisters, my father, an accident.

'Your grandfather is dead.'

I stared at him. 'Old Daddy?'

He nodded. 'Yes. And buried.'

I stood still on the pavement. Vaguely I felt Iris take the child out of my arms and did not resist. How could this be? How could he leave me? And just when I had my baby, and needed him. Tears spilled down my face. I would never see Old Daddy again. I stood there and wept. Then my baby started crying and Iris said, 'He's upset because you are.' I smothered my sobs, took him from her arms and went into the house. There I sat feeding him and watching big salty tears fall on to my little boy's head.

We christened the baby John James, after his two grandfathers. I watched my son in an obsessive way. As he slept, I sat beside him, knitting with a passion to keep from thinking about my mother and Old Daddy. Every week, I had something new finished for him. My only solace was the thought of going back to Ireland and being with my family.

Michael came home late every night. I'd be awake in bed, mad to talk to him about the things I was thinking of.

'When are we going home to show them the baby?'

'Soon,' he would say. 'Soon.' He'd speak in a coaxing voice, ready to promise me anything. I quickly got to know what he was after.

Once it was over, and he turned away to go to sleep, there was no more talk about going home. I did kick up a row for a new pram and got my way. I would take J.J., as we called him, for a walk every day, venturing farther from the house each time. I would talk to him as we walked, telling him my plans, how much my sisters would love him, and all the people he would meet. When the ice-cream van passed us, its chimes playing jangly tunes, I would say, 'When you are big enough, I'll buy you all the ice cream you can eat, so I will.'

Now that my son was born, I desperately wanted to turn us into a family. I besieged Michael with ideas and questions. Could we go for a walk together some Sunday? Would he come home straight from work just once? I wanted him to get to know his child by helping me bathe him or by putting him to bed. But it was no use. He told me I was a nag. Then I'd stop asking him to do anything, hoping that J.J. would somehow get through to him without my urging. It never happened. The only time Michael paid attention to me was for those few minutes at night.

I could never get it across to him how sore and frightened I was of having another baby. 'You'll be all right,' was all I got from him. The nurse had given me a packet of condoms when I was leaving hospital and explained how to use them. I asked Michael and his answer came back with a smirk and a swagger: 'You won't get me to use one of them yokes.'

I had made one good friend in the house — Jan. I never mentioned the night I had seen her and Michael together, and she had no idea that I knew what had happened. I was surprised to find that I bore her no grudge. My feelings were entirely taken up with J.J.

I knew that Jan felt sorry for me because she had witnessed my difficulties with Michael. I had become deeply self-conscious, awkward and anxious. But I was glad to have someone to talk to, someone who listened and even answered me when I spoke.

One night, Jan suggested that I get a job. She knew there was one for a couple of hours in the evening, in a factory, packing brassieres. I was all excited. If Michael would come home from work and mind the baby, I would be able to do it. Iris and

Michael were in the kitchen one day, arguing about money, as they often did: how much he owed her, and how much he could give her. So I threw in the question about me getting a job. They just looked at me blankly and went straight back to their argument. I kept on at Michael until he was tired listening.

'All right! Go ahead, and don't be annoying me.'

So I got my first paying job. I liked meeting the other workers and, even more, enjoyed planning things to buy for J.J. out of my wages. But I was in a fool's paradise. I had to give it up after a week because Michael never came home to look after the baby — not once. Iris herself had too much to do, looking after the house and cooking for the lodgers. After a while, I earned a little bit of pin money, though, when I started looking after her little boy.

A few months later, when J.J. was six months old, out of the blue Michael announced that we were going home for a couple of weeks. I couldn't believe it was going to happen at last. I wrote and told my sisters.

I thought the journey would never end. J.J. and I were both seasick from the minute we set out on the boat. At Rosslare, we caught a train to Waterford, where Mr Kelly met us at the station. The first thing he did was reach out to J.J., who went straight into his arms with a big smile.

Mr Kelly was a powerfully built man, over six feet in height, and normally very quiet. I felt proud that J.J. had gone so happily to his grandfather, and was delighted at the look of pleasure on Mr Kelly's face.

Chapter Eight

Coming near the village, we swept past the Grand Gates, the entrance to the big estate, and I automatically made the sign of the cross in my mother's memory. Then we drove straight to Mrs Kelly's shop. This was one part of the visit I had not been looking forward to. I hoped for, but greatly doubted the prospect of, a warm welcome from my mother-in-law.

'Well,' was all she said when we arrived, but she was delighted to see her son and new grandson. In a minute, J.J. was high up in his grandfather's arms again, looking down like a lord on the rest of us. Mrs Kelly tickled him under the chin and gave me a stiff handshake, without looking me in the face. Even J.J.'s presence could not work miracles. I would go on calling her Mrs Kelly forever, while she avoided giving me any name at all.

Then she turned to Michael. 'Are ye coming in or do ye want to go down the road first?' She meant to my father's.

'We'll go down first,' he said.

'You take the car, so,' his father said. With that, he tried to give the baby to Michael, but there was no way J.J. was having any of that. Mr Kelly and he seemed to have bonded firmly. I was thrilled.

'You have to come with me,' I said to J.J. 'Your aunts will want to see you.'

I took him screaming from his grandfather's arms. Mr Kelly chuckled with delight as we drove off.

During the short drive, I said nothing. I had a sickness in my stomach at the thought of seeing my father. Over the last fifteen months, so much had happened to our family: two deaths, a marriage and a birth. After London and motherhood, I did not know if my father would still have the power and presence that had loomed so large over my life.

He was there as I got out of the car and fixed me with a long look. And then I saw the tears.

'Look at you. You left a tubby teenager and now you look like an old woman!'

My eyes were full also — partly for him seeing me like that, and partly for myself. I wiped away my tears, and then I looked at my sisters standing apart from me as if I were a stranger. When I got inside the house, I stared into Old Daddy's room, still able to picture him with his scissors, carefully cutting something out of the newspaper. Nothing was said and the moment passed.

My father was talking to Michael. 'How long are ye staying?'

Michael shrugged. 'Don't know.'

'In the shop you're staying?'

'That's right.'

My sisters were arguing over whose turn it was to hold J.J. He was having the time of his life with all the love and attention. Yet my father had taken hardly any notice of him. He and babies had never mixed comfortably.

I took a moment to study my sisters: Mary was fifteen now, Alison nine, and Geraldine nearly seven. My younger sisters seemed very thin and had a tense look about them; they hung back from me. I went over to Geraldine, put my arms round her and told her I had missed her. Her scrawny little arms tightened on me and she said she'd missed me too. Letting her go, I thought I felt her relax but when I tried to do the same with Alison, she shrank away.

'I missed you,' I said, watching her face.

'Did you?' was all she said, before running off outside, as if she'd thought of something else to do. The loss of our mother and the strain of living with Daddy and his unpredictable moods had told on them all. How I wished I had been there for them: if only she knew that none of this had been my choice. I felt so guilty.

It was lunchtime; we had tea and sandwiches. I noticed Mary and my father bickering away. Mary caught me smiling at the two of them. 'It's no laughing matter,' she said fiercely.

We were staying in the house Mrs Kelly owned beside the shop. It had two rooms and we slept in the back one. The front one was full of car tyres, gas cylinders, and other stuff from the garage. The smell of rubber and oil made me feel sick, but I didn't dare complain.

We ate our meals at Mrs Kelly's. She would close the shop for an hour at lunchtime and the men would eat first. Only when they had finished would she and I eat, usually in silence. Then she would open the shop and post office while I washed up and prepared J.J. for our ramble down the road to my father's. My son was getting very big and spoiled. Apart from being up in his Grandfather Kelly's arms, he liked nothing better than my sisters carrying him around and fussing over him. He was a charmer all right.

Alison and Geraldine were unhappy; I could see it. I was burning to talk to them about our mother, and how they were feeling, but it was like an unwritten law: don't mention her. I was afraid that if I spoke about her, I might make things worse for them.

When I mentioned it, Mary said she did not want to talk about it. 'She's gone. Talking won't bring her back, so what's the use?' She felt the same on the subject of Old Daddy. 'Why do you have to keep on about it?'

We had been home for two weeks now and there was not a word about us going back. I was superstitiously afraid to mention it, thinking that if I did, it would hurry on the day. When people asked, I felt stupid saying that I didn't know, but this was how it was between Michael and me.

Then, once again, Michael and his mother made the decision. Out of the blue, Michael said, 'We're not going back. I'll go over myself and get the pram and the other things.'

I was so pleased that it never entered my mind to question the way this had been decided, with not a word to me. Michael went to London and got our stuff, including the pram that J.J. now refused to sit in, and, when he returned, he got a job locally. Mrs Kelly bought him a Morris Minor to go to work, but she told me, in no uncertain terms, 'I don't ever want to see you in that car; do you hear me? It's for Michael.'

I never told anyone what she'd said. It was too humiliating.

Michael was having a great time; it was as if he had never got married. One day, he was going to the races in Tramore, and he came to the garage to get petrol at his mother's pump. He had his first cousin, Rita, in the car, all dressed up in her finest, and a girlfriend of hers in the back. Michael and Rita were around the same age, twenty-one. She was glamorous, with beautiful clothes and long brown hair to her waist. Looking at her, I felt dowdy and insignificant.

Mr Kelly was standing there with J.J. in his arms, and I was beside them, watching him fill up the tank. Michael never looked at us. It was as if we were invisible. Maybe the same thought came to Mr Kelly for he said to me, 'Go on, get into the car and go with him.'

I looked at him to see if he was serious. He was.

'Don't worry about the child. I'll look after him.'

With that, the shop door nearly came off its hinges, and Mrs Kelly marched out, her face purple with rage. She had heard it all.

'Are you mad?' she blazed at her husband. 'Michael, off you go now. Go on this minute, I tell you!'

She was flapping her hands at him to get away. Michael grunted, and hung up the pump nozzle. He slipped into the driver's seat, started the engine and was away without a backward glance.

I turned to Mrs Kelly, almost crying out in exasperation, but the look on her face stopped me. It would seem that she saw me as the girl who had stolen her son's life away, and she would do her best to give it back to him.

Some days after this, I noticed that my ankles were swollen and I couldn't pass water. I was wondering to whom I should talk about it when Mr Kelly remarked, 'You look all puffed out; you'd better get yourself over to the doctor.' He nodded in the direction of the surgery. 'He's just gone over there now.'

So I went to this doctor for the first time and, after a brief examination, he told me I was four months' pregnant.

'How old are you?' he asked me.

'Seventeen,' I told him. 'This is my second baby.'

'I want you to go to bed and I'll be down after you.'

When I got to the shop, I told Mr Kelly that I was pregnant and that the doctor was coming later. He asked me, 'Was that the first you knew of it?'

I said, 'Yes.'

For some reason, I was not looking forward to telling Mrs Kelly that I was pregnant, but I thought it would be bad manners not to tell her. I waited until the shop was empty of customers and gave her my news. She was not pleased.

The doctor arrived shortly afterwards, and said, 'Hospital for you. Your kidneys have packed up. Another couple of hours, and God knows what would have happened.'

'Will you let my father know, please?'

'I will, to be sure,' he said as he left.

My father was with me in a matter of minutes. He had not been into the house before and I saw the disapproving looks he threw at the front room. We took J.J. down to Mary and drove on to the hospital.

'This brings back memories,' my father said.

Then I told him of my fear of dying young, like my mother. If I did, who would look after J.J.? I didn't mention Michael, but it was understood between us that he would not be up to the job. I think my father was sorry that he had mentioned Mammy.

'You'll be okay,' he said, but I was not reassured.

At the hospital, the first thing they did was drain off the urine and, after that, I felt much better. But with my kidneys continuing to malfunction, I had to remain in hospital for several more days. Michael came to see me one evening. I wished he hadn't bothered, he was so drunk. It was just as supper was being brought in and he immediately tucked in and ate mine.

People in the hospital would say, 'You're so young to be having a baby.' When I told them it was my second, they would be speechless.

I still didn't feel right when they discharged me two weeks later. I had been home a couple of hours when I started to bleed and I had to be rushed back in again.

My father came to see me every day, saying, 'It's hard to break the habit of a lifetime.'

I was put in the ward in which my mother had waited for Geraldine to be born. Several of the nurses remembered my father. How could they forget his charm? He would talk to me about how things had been between him and my mother. He was, according to his stories, the one who had tried everything to make their marriage work. I didn't want to talk about it and would get upset, cry and bleed more. God help him, I thought.

J.J. was still at Daddy's house. Mary adored him. He slept with her and she would not let him out of her sight.

I thought of Mammy a lot, especially when I saw mothers coming in to visit their daughters or to see their newborn grandchildren. I wished she was there, sitting on the bed, telling me stories about when my sisters and I were born. I developed a powerful yearning for this and began to hope that the baby I was trying to hold on to would be a girl.

Michael made the odd appearance, asking me when I was coming home and saying he missed me. Then I began to think that maybe this crisis was a good thing. My husband might appreciate me a little more in future.

I was let home after six weeks and went to stay at my father's, so I would not be on my own if I started to miscarry again. Michael was far from happy about this — he couldn't stay with me because there was not enough room in the house.

It was midnight that first night when he came down roaring drunk: 'I want my wife back, d'ye hear me? I want her back now!'

He had the whole house awake, including J.J., who began to cry. My father got out of bed and went out to try to reason with Michael, but he was beyond reason. He took a swing at my father. 'Blackguard!' my father said and threw himself at Michael. The two of them wrestled. We were watching at the windows. None of us knew what to do. Then I started bleeding again.

That put an end to the tussle. Mary ran out screaming to my father to come quick. In he came, holding his jaw. Michael was forgotten as we got into the car and drove back to the hospital.

I was six months gone by now, a very dangerous time to lose the baby, so it was decided that I should remain in hospital until it was born. I couldn't help thinking how ironic it was to find myself in the same position as my mother. I could not settle and was very discontented, worrying that J.J. would forget me or feel abandoned. I knew he was loved and looked after but still I kept fretting, which did not help my condition at all.

I was allowed home for J.J.'s first birthday; the baby was due soon and it would be safe enough. My son was not walking yet, probably because he was carried everywhere. The minute he saw me, he put out his arms for me to take him. I was ecstatically happy to be able to hold him, be it for only a couple of minutes. My sisters, my father and I had a great party for him as he crawled excitedly around the place, but Michael did not appear.

Four days later, I went into labour. I was very frail, having been laid up for so long, but this birth was not as gruelling as the first.

Although she was nearly full-term, our baby daughter was tiny, weighing only three pounds, and was rushed off to the premature ward to be put in an incubator. But I got to hold her for those all-important seconds just after the birth. I was full of tenderness and love for her and called her Katie.

When it was time for us to go home from hospital, Mrs Kelly said we could live in the house that she had on the outskirts of the village. My father scouted out the place and told her, 'Kay is not moving in there until the floors are covered and there's a cooker in it.'

The work was all done in a matter of days.

Chapter Nine

This house seemed to hold all my dreams. When we moved in, I thought we would be bound to live happily ever after. I was seventeen with a year-old son and a new baby girl. There was no mother telling Michael to go to the pub for a couple of pints, and no lads, as in London, to tempt him. Now I was sure my husband would come straight home after work.

Our new home was a council cottage that Mrs Kelly had bought years before and was the very house in which Michael had been born. It was one of six, on an uphill stretch of road, less than a five-minute walk from the village. All were similar in style, with three bedrooms and a kitchen. There were five steps down from the front door to a cement path that crossed the lawn, flanked by low evergreen hedges and ending in a wrought-iron gate. A fine copper beech stood at the entrance.

At the back of each house, there was a half-acre of land. Mr Kelly had all kinds of vegetables growing in ours, and a small plot of potatoes. There were apple trees and, on a stretch of grass, a clothesline. Beyond that was a lush green wooded hill from which the schoolhouse looked down on us.

Like most people in rural Ireland, we had no running water

in the house. There were two barrels out in the back yard, collecting rain for washing. Water for drinking and cooking was brought up the hill, in buckets, from the village pump. Once more, we had a chemical toilet out the back, for which I would cut neat squares of newspaper, and thread them on a loop of twine. Although toilet paper could be had, old newspapers were free.

The kitchen had a small open fire over which we sometimes made toast. It had a gas cooker — the gas came in cylinders — and there was a lovely dresser, full of plain, hard-wearing crockery.

The bedrooms were colourful and bright: flowery wallpaper, floral curtains and vividly patterned rugs. I wanted to put my touch on it, to paint the walls, varnish the floorboards, and lay only the best rugs on them.

With two babies in towelling nappies, there was a lot of washing. Most of the time I had a line strung across the kitchen; this made the house very damp which, I thought, was why the children always had colds. When we had firewood, I would light up a big blaze, take out the tin bath and wash my babies in front of the fire. This was great fun. I was completely wrapped up in my children. The one thing I craved was for Michael to pick them up and play with them, but he showed little interest. My children were such an enormous part of me that by ignoring them, he made me feel worthless.

Michael was never short of work. He seemed to have the contract to refurbish every pub in County Kilkenny. They paid him his wages on Fridays and got the whole lot back across the bar over the next seven days. I seldom got a penny from my husband and had to go to my mother-in-law for almost everything. She kept a tight rein on me, making a record of every item I bought, be it a loaf of bread or a pint of milk. Apart from their bottle, my children's diet was simple enough: guddy — sugar and bread softened in milk. If I went to Mrs Kelly for anything extra, questions were asked. I was treated almost as a child, kept dependent on the charity of my mother-in-law. Mrs Kelly saw nothing wrong with keeping an eye on my expenditure.

At two months, Katie was still very frail. She was a big worry and I never felt that she was thriving. She got every bug going, and you could see the threads of her veins through her milky white skin. Sometimes I stood over the cot, listening to her congested rasping, and found myself drawing my own breath in time with hers, willing her not to stop. It was a responsibility I carried alone.

Michael got up every morning with a hangover, grabbed the baby's gripe water, and made for the door. That was the last we saw of him for the day.

'I wish you wouldn't drink that,' I once called down the steps after him. 'Your mother won't let me have any more of it.'

He always swore that gripe water was the best cure ever invented for a hangover — not surprising for, as I found out years later, the stuff contained alcohol.

From the top step of the house, I could look down over most of the village, including my father's house in the distance. Mary was good to me; she came up to me now instead of me going down to her. This meant that I could sit with Katie on my lap and take note of her tiny breaths.

Mary told me that my father didn't give her any pocket money, and she wanted to get a job and some independence.

'You do it,' I told her. 'I'll look after Alison and Geraldine; sure they're up here every day after school anyway.'

Mary got a job as a residential nanny, looking after a little boy in Waterford city, during the week. She also had a boyfriend, Tom. He had a car, and used to pick her up on Fridays and drive her home. She would stay with me because my father would not let her in the house after she had left him 'in the lurch', as he saw it. Every weekend, Mary brought some small gift for me or for one of the babies.

Katie was growing stronger and I was becoming less

frightened. My health was improving, too, but I was still only seven stone and could never put on weight. I wanted to so much. Michael's glamorous cousin Rita was lovely and rounded and if I could be less bony and more like her, so I thought, Michael would love me.

I was finding time to be busy around the house, forever rearranging the furniture. From somewhere we got an old and comfortable couch. I had varnished the floors the way I wanted them, and put down only the best rugs. I was delighted with the result, but Michael's only comment was 'Will you stop moving the bed around? Every night it's in a different place in the room.'

After dark, while the children were asleep, I sat up sewing and knitting until Michael came in. Mrs Cuddihy, who was in her fifties and lived next door, would come up nearly every night to keep me company for a couple of hours. She would look at me at times and say, 'You're ashen, child. Why don't you go to your bed?

'I'll wait up for him.'

'I'll stay with you so.'

We would both be too tired to talk. All there was to break the silence was the clicking of my knitting needles. More often than not, I would drop off to sleep on the couch, to be woken by Mrs Cuddihy when she heard Michael's car.

After his night at the pub, I would have a job to haul him up to bed. But the shame I carried around with me was even heavier. The burden was all mine. *I* was the disgrace. When I went down to the village, I finished my shopping as fast as I could, unable to face people. I was the one who had got pregnant at sixteen, and had had to get married. I was a bad person — that was what everyone was thinking and what I believed. If I could just make Michael happy, people might think differently. These were my core feelings at age seventeen.

In his mother's eyes, Michael could do no wrong. If he had no money, she gave it to him. I was in the shop one evening when he staggered in. He leaned over the counter, breathing beer, until he caught her eye. He didn't have to say a word. She left the customer she was serving, shot open the till and came over to him with money in one hand, and a packet of cigarettes in the other. He took them without a word of thanks and went off again, making no sign that he had seen me.

Even if he didn't love me, my husband still wanted sex and I worried about getting pregnant again. The only birth control in Ireland was the so-called safe period. I assumed that not getting my period for three months after Katie was born was just my body slowly returning to normal.

One day I was out at the clothesline, bringing in bed sheets that had frozen into stiff boards, when I doubled over in pain. For a minute, I couldn't move. Mrs Cuddihy, who had come up to watch the children, thought I had been in the garden a long time. She came out to see if I was all right and found me on my knees, blood running out of me.

She got me in and ran for the doctor but he was away, so she went to the shop. Mr Kelly drove his wife up. In she came like a tornado. It was the first time she had been in the house since we'd moved in.

'My God', was the first thing she said. 'Look at the state of my house!'

She had a bundle of old linen under her arm for mopping me up.

'Let me see. What's the matter with you?'

She had been holding the sheets tightly to her chest, as if to stop herself from rushing around putting everything back the way she'd had it, but she eventually threw them on the bed in a gesture of despair.

I told her I was in terrible pain and bleeding.

'You'll be all right,' she said.

In the end, they got me into the car and took me to hospital.

'You're having a miscarriage,' the nurse told me in a businesslike manner. 'You must stay very still because we have none of your blood type.' She gave me an injection and I don't remember any more. In the morning, they did a D and C, and confirmed that I had been three months' pregnant, but now my baby was gone.

I went home the next day. Mrs Cuddihy and Mary, between them, had been looking after the babies, and they tried to make my homecoming a happy occasion. But I was far from well, and could not stop the tears from flowing every few minutes. A couple of neighbours came in to say how sorry they were, and tried to console me. 'It's a blessing in disguise,' they said. 'You've enough to look after.'

I couldn't see it that way. I felt empty. I had another shock in store when Mrs Kelly appeared again. She went through the house like a blast of wind, replacing the rugs that I had removed. 'My god, where do you get your ideas from? It's like a tinkers' camp. She came close to me and wagged her finger under my nose. 'This is not your house; always remember that!'

For several days after my return from hospital, I lay around the house, not able to do much. I had lost a lot of blood and had not been given a transfusion. There was no compassion from my husband, no conversation, nothing about what had happened.

Mary was worried about me. I couldn't take an interest in anything.

'Go and see that new doctor. Tell him how you're feeling,' she said.

Dr Hoyne had recently come to the village. He was younger than the other doctor and listened as I told him about my miscarriage. Then, for some reason, I started to talk about Michael's drinking, though I had never mentioned it to anyone before, not even to my own family.

'Well, look after yourself,' he said, reaching for his prescription pad. 'For a start, take one of these, three times a day

— it's Valium, a new drug; it does wonders. If you need more, come back to me.'

Home I went with my packet of tablets, but it wasn't until a couple of days later, when J.J. was out with Grandad Kelly and I was sitting in front of the fire with Katie on my lap, that I took one. It seemed only ten minutes before I started to feel strange. As we fell to the floor, I managed to turn my body and cushion my baby's fall. I don't know how long we were there. When we got up, I felt shaken and frightened and threw the tablets into the fire.

Michael found it extremely difficult to speak to me with any degree of civility, but I'm sure if you had asked him then about our marriage, he'd have said there was nothing wrong. His attitude had changed from indifference to hostility; he seemed to be fed up with the whole marriage. My father must have known the truth, or a bit of it, but he was angry with me because, for once, I was defying him.

Daddy was coming up at twelve and one o'clock in the night, drunk, to pick up Alison and Geraldine. They would be fast asleep and I'd have to wake them up, to go home with him to that cold house. I would stand on the top step and watch him drive down the road, weaving from one side to the other.

One night, he and Michael had one of their rare drinking sessions together. They came up from the pub and my father began insisting that I sit on Michael's lap and be nice to him. I wished he would tell Michael to be nice to me for a change, but I did as he said. Michael stood up abruptly, saying he was going to bed, and I fell to the floor with a bump.

I was humiliated and angry but it gave me the courage to say to my father, 'Go home on your own. I'm not going to wake those children at this time of night.' He straightened and steadied himself, like he always did in drink, and walked stiffly out of the house. From my usual perch, I watched him. The lights from a couple of the houses around were still flickering.

All nice and safe, I thought; no drunken men and fatherless children. There was no sight or sound of my father's car going through the village. He would know that I would be watching to see him get home safe, so he went into the pub.

For two days, there was no sign of him. When he did come up to the house, it was early in the evening and he was neither sober nor drunk, but in that place between. He seemed a little shame-faced.

'Can we talk?' he said.

I drew out a chair for him.

'It's very lonely down in that house on my own.'

'I thought it might be.'

'I will be home early from now on. So I'll bring the girls home with me now.'

It was half a question. He searched my face to see if I was agreeing with him. He hurried on. 'I was thinking maybe I could get you one of those twin-tub washing machines, and give you ten bob a week to wash our clothes for us.'

A washing machine! That was what I had dreamed of. A big, stupid grin spread across my face.

'I'd love that, Daddy.'

I got my twin-tub, and my ten bob a week. It took eight buckets of water to fill the tub for the washing and eight more to rinse. Our barrels did not hold enough for such a thirsty machine, but I was so proud to have it, I thought nothing of carrying the water up the hill from the pump.

J.J. was not walking yet. He was two years old and very spoiled, driving around in the car with Mr Kelly. Katie was way ahead of him; she was walking at nine months and, although small and thin, was full of life and good humour. I was nineteen now and pregnant again. I dreaded the actual birth.

Mary and Tom were getting married. I reminded her how, at bedtime, our mother used to shout up the stairs to us, 'Say three Hail Marys for a good husband.' I felt my sister must have said more prayers than I had. They spent hours planning the wedding and their future together. He was a good man. I was happy for them.

I went into hospital to have my third baby, and Mary took time off work to look after Katie and J.J. She disliked being in the house with Michael: she hated his drinking and coming in at all hours.

When my baby arrived, she was just what I'd wanted, a beautiful baby girl weighing nine pounds. It was 1963 and I called her Jackie after Jackie Kennedy, the American First Lady. This was two months before the President was assassinated.

J.J. was walking at last. He was like a little old man from being with his Grandad Kelly. He made me laugh: 'Grandad has a big job on in the morning,' he would say as I tucked him into bed. 'Get me up early, will ye, Mammy?'

Mr Kelly would take him for a couple of hours and I was delighted that he was giving J.J. the attention he needed from a man.

In the long summer evenings, Mrs Cuddihy and I would stand at the window and see the girls and boys of my age pushing their bikes up the hill past the house. She would say to me, 'They're off to the Carnival in Piltown. Wouldn't you like to be with them, child?'

'No,' I would say, allowing myself to think about it for a minute. 'I'm happy with my babies.'

Still, I would go out to the gate and look wistfully up the road after them. They would be carefree, laughing and chatting. Of course, I didn't belong with them. Nor did I belong with the married couples of the village. There was one old woman who was always up and down the road. Whenever she saw me, she would say, 'You made your bed. Now you'll have to lie on it.' I hated those words.

Michael went to everything that was on, but then, he was a man and it was his right.

'Why do you bother to come home at all?' I heard myself ask him one morning. I hadn't meant to say it out loud. I had been lying awake beside him for an hour, thinking. And out it came.

'What did you say?' he mumbled.

'You heard me.'

'Don't be stupid. I come home because this is my house.'

'Everything I say is stupid as far as you're concerned.' I began to cry.

'Oh, for God's sake, don't start. I can't stand it!'

But once the tears arrived, I could not stop. He sprang out of bed, banging his toe against the new baby's cot and waking her.

'Let me out of this madhouse!' he shouted.

A feeling of hysteria swept through me.

'Stay and talk to me for a minute.'

I knew I was degrading myself and making him angrier, but I wanted something from him, a declaration of love, something, anything to hold on to. He darted out of the room to look for the gripe water for himself. The three children were crying, but I put up with it until he left. They sounded distant as I covered my head with the threadbare blanket. At times, I felt terrified at the reality of my life.

Putting my overcoat on over the jumper and slip I wore in bed, I rolled out, shivering, on to the cold floor. There was white frost as thick as paint on the inside of the windows. I went down to fill the children's bottles with hot milk. I should have brought in the firewood the night before, I thought to myself, but it had been too cold to go to the shed.

J.J., at the age of three, and Katie still liked their bottles. I filled three and went up to them, all crying in their cots, their faces and hands purple and covered with snot. They jumped for joy when they saw their milk and sucked contentedly as I changed their sodden nappies.

Sometimes in the morning, the four of us would get back into bed for the warmth, and snuggle up together. With their bellies full, the baby and Katie might drop off to sleep again.

Then J.J. and I would slip out of bed, packing the pillows around his little sisters to keep them from slipping over the edge. He was my little helper. I would get him dressed and ready for his grandfather and one of their mystery trips. Then I would go out to the shed to bring in some coal and wood, depending on what was there. Our fuel had to be carefully rationed. Often it was Mr Kelly I had to thank for both. He'd throw some in the boot of his car when he got the chance. 'Don't mention that,' he would say.

I would light the fire and turn the clothes that were hanging in front of it. By then, the little ones would be awake and I would dress them as warmly as possible, heat some guddy for Katie and watch her feeding herself, while I sat with Jackie on my knee. They were beautiful children. My heart throbbed with pride and love for them.

Chapter Ten

'Have you a sore foot or what?'

'No, I haven't. Why?'

My father had come early to pick up my sisters. He had a few drinks taken, but was in a reasonable state.

It was winter and he had brought a rare treat — some meat — and I had cooked it while he played with Katie. She was his favourite; she loved to sit on his knee, even while he ate, babbling away to him as he fed her bits from his plate.

'You're limping. Come here and let me look at that shoe.'

I lifted my foot. There was a hole the size of a half-crown in the sole and I had hardly noticed it.

'My God!' he roared, jabbing his finger into the hole. 'Why are you wearing those old things?'

'Because they're all I have, Daddy.'

'To think of it,' he said. 'That blackguard sitting in the pub, morning, noon and night, and not a shoe on his wife's foot.'

He looked around angrily. 'I'm taking you out of here, the whole lot of ye. It's a disgrace! Gather your things.' He began yanking nappies and clothes off the line, making a bundle, which he pushed into my arms. Then he opened the front door.

'Come on.'

We set off in the Volkswagen, much faster than his usual stately speed, but when we reached Mrs Kelly's, my father stopped with a jerk. Out he got, walked round and pulled my door open. Bending down, he slipped the shoe off my foot.

'Come on.' He caught me by the hand which forced me to hobble behind him into the shop, with the baby on my hip. The place was full of customers having a gossip while waiting their turn.

'Do you see what this child has to wear?' he shouted furiously to the shop at large, waving the worn-out shoe in the air. The power of his voice made the place go silent. 'And that young pup is out drinking every day and night of the week.'

Finally his eyes rested on my mother-in-law behind the counter. Carrying on as if she had heard nothing, she seemed unable to speak. My father was at no such loss.

'That bloody house is freezing and they have no food most of the time.'

He jerked his thumb at me. 'She was trying to make custard with water the other day because she had no milk!'

The people in the shop stared. Some of them had their mouths open, but not Mrs Kelly. Hers just twitched into a weak smile. She continued to ignore us. He looked around, challenging anyone to answer him.

'I can't keep out of it any longer,' he declared. 'I'm taking them home with me, for their own good.'

With that, he turned, pulling me after him. Within minutes, my three children and I were installed in my father's house.

Much later, I was lying awake, waiting for something to happen. I was certain Michael would come spoiling for a fight with my father and, sure enough, at one in the morning, he arrived, rapping on the windows and shouting my name. Soon everyone was awake. With babies crying and Michael's hammering, it was like a madhouse. This time, to everyone's relief, my father decided against a confrontation.

'Ignore him,' he said softly at my bedroom door. 'He'll go away.'

Eventually all did go quiet and I stole to the window to look out. In the moonlight, I could see Michael clearly. He was lying curled up on my grandmother's flowerbed. After a couple of hours, the cold woke him and he started making more racket, but we ignored him as before and, in the end, he went away.

The next day was painful. My father left for work and my sisters for school. J.J. was asking for his Granddad Kelly, crying as if his heart were broken. The real problem was that we were all hungry. There was no more food in this house than in the other one. All I knew was that I couldn't go to Mrs Kelly for anything. So we sat it out for the day, eating only bread. I thought my father would be in around three, and I'd ask him to get some shopping, but when he finally came home, it was past eleven and he was the worse for drink. Never even noticing our hunger and giving out all the time about Michael, he stomped off to bed and was snoring within a couple of minutes. Some time after midnight, Michael was hammering on the door again, but we were all too hungry to care.

The minute I heard my father stirring, at four in the morning, I got up and went down to him. I was about to ask where I was supposed to get some food, but this time he was ahead of me.

'Go to Norris's,' he said. 'I went in there for a few drinks last night on the way home. They'll give you what you want.'

Then he seemed to remember the thing that had brought us to the house.

'There's a pair of shoes belonging to Mary. See if they'll do.'

They fitted.

Norris's was a bar and general store which had been in the village for generations. I couldn't show my face in that shop; the Kellys would be furious. So, keeping my sisters from school, I sent them for what we needed. Meanwhile, I gave each of the babies a hot bottle of nearly black tea, with plenty of sugar, something they were used to whenever Mrs Kelly was on the warpath. All in all, being at my father's was not much better than being at home.

In one way, it was worse. My father could not bear the children crying or making a noise. He expected complete silence for himself, just as he had when I was little.

After we had been four days at my father's, Michael came back a third time. It was eight in the evening. My father was there and went out to the door.

'Well, boy, what do you want?'

'I want to know will they come back,' Michael mumbled.

My father shook his head. 'Things will have to change,' he said quietly.

'I know.'

My father said nothing for a minute or two, then, 'All right, maybe ye should give it another chance so.'

'I have the car on the road,' Michael said.

Within half an hour, we were back in our own house. I was not consulted about the matter. J.J. wanted to know if he could see his Granddad Kelly the next day. I told him he could and he danced for joy.

The house was as cold as ice and there was no firewood as usual. Michael went out again, promising to get some. Two hours later, he had not returned. So we went to bed to keep warm. Then, in the middle of the night, I heard noises in the kitchen and knew he was back. He didn't come to bed and, after half an hour, I went to see what he was at. I found him lying stretched out on the kitchen floor, unconscious and stark naked. His skin was as white as a plucked chicken and his clothes were nowhere to be seen. Half-coaxing, half-dragging, I got him into bed.

In the morning, the children woke up at seven, hungry and wet. I struggled out of bed to start the morning routine. Going into the kitchen, I pulled back the curtains and saw Michael's clothes, hanging in all their glory from the tree in the front garden: pants, vest, shirt, trousers. My first thought was to run out and bring them in. I thought again. I would leave them there for the world to see and for him to discover.

'Where are my clothes?' he shouted hoarsely to me from the bed a couple of hours later.

'How would I know?' I replied innocently.

He wrapped himself in a blanket and came into the kitchen, shivering. 'God, it's cold,' he grumbled.

'It's the same every morning. Something to light the fire with — that's what you went out for last night, remember?'

'So how the hell did I come home with no clothes on?'

I just shrugged and went back to the bedroom to settle the children.

Eventually he spotted the decorated tree. Still wearing the blanket, he went and retrieved his clothes, and was dressed when I returned to the kitchen. I could tell he would be making for the door at any minute, to escape and spend the day forgetting us. I suddenly felt the anger rise up in me.

'Talk to me', I said, in a shrill voice. 'Don't you even want to know why we left you?'

He stood there, with a half-smile on his face, making no attempt to answer. I lost control.

'Don't you care about us?' I screeched. 'Is that it? Please say something.'

J.J. was tugging at my skirt. 'Don't shout, Mammy.' I picked him up and held him close.

'You're upsetting the young lad,' Michael said.

'Don't talk like it's nothing to do with you. His name's J.J. and, for God's sake, he's your son.'

I had never in my life been so savage towards my husband. He stood there, no focus in his eyes, while J.J. whinged. At that moment, Mr Kelly walked in.

'What's going on here?' he asked, frowning. He looked around. 'And why is the fire not lit for the youngster?'

He searched Michael's face and then mine.

I shrugged. 'There's nothing to light it with.'

J.J. was wriggling in my arms and craning towards Mr Kelly, so I put him down. The three-year-old ran and wrapped his arms around his grandfather's leg.

'Come on, little fella. We'll get something for the fire.'

When they had gone, I felt ashamed that Mr Kelly had heard me arguing. Michael stood there. He was impenetrable.

'Have you anything to say to me?' I asked.

'Nothing. My father is getting you something for the fire. What more do you want?'

'Some day you'll be sorry for all this.'

It was not idle talk. It felt like a prophecy.

Michael hesitated and stood looking at me. I thought I saw fear in his eyes, but it was only for a minute. Then he let out a big laugh and walked past me and out the door, as easy as you please. That laugh made my stomach turn over.

All day I could not settle. Usually I talked myself around to being comforted in some way. I'd remind myself how lovely the children were, or that we had a roof over our heads. But this attempt at gratitude for what I had just didn't work for me this time. I kept panicking because there was no food in the house. How would I face Mrs Kelly after all that had happened?

When her husband came, I told him I wasn't feeling very well.

'Please, would you get me some shopping — just a few things?'

He considered. 'All right, but you'll have to go yourself sometime,' he said gently.

'I know,' I said, blessing him in my heart because it did not have to be that particular day.

The dread of going down the village did not leave me quickly. In our community, nothing went unnoticed, and everyone was consumed by everybody else's business.

On a Monday morning, there was a competition about who would be the first to have their washing hanging out. A count was kept of when a woman cleaned her window or swept her front steps. If you got a new coat or hat, its price would be carefully worked out by the neighbours, and a great debate would take place as to whether or not your family could really afford the extravagance. It was the same in church. Great importance was attached to who got to the altar first for Communion and, if some young girl was missing from Mass, the other women would not rest until they had found out the reason; dark secrets were always suspected of being at the bottom of it. And, given that the village cars were all known by their sound, if a strange one were heard, curtains would be twitching.

'I wonder who that was, at this time?'

'Maybe someone is home from England at Sheas'.'

'That'll be it. I'm sure we'll find out soon enough anyway.'

If someone made so bold as to go to Kilkenny in the middle of the week, this would create great interest and a hum of talk.

'I see the So and So family passing. It's unusual for them to go to town today. I wonder if anything is wrong.'

'It's not like him to waste petrol unless he has good reason.'

'Maybe it's old Mrs So and So; she's not been well.'

'You could be right there. Or maybe one of the young ones got hurt.'

This conversation would carry on until every angle was covered, as Mr and Mrs So and So well knew, as they argued in their car! 'What will people think? They know full well that we never go to town only at the weekend. How could you have forgotten my mother's pension the one time I asked you to get it for her?'

'Why don't you get it in the village like everyone else?'

'It was your idea in the first place, so that people wouldn't know our business.'

'It's as bad for me. I won't be able to go to the pub now, all the questions I'll be asked.'

No one was happy until they got to the root of even the

slightest departure from custom. So I knew people would have much to say about my having left Michael for four days, then crawled back. I was ashamed and for a while it was impossible to face the village.

When Michael announced that he was 'off to Mass', this meant going for a cure. I'd been on at him to take us to the seaside in Tramore. In the end, one summer Sunday morning, he gave in. Miraculously, after a couple of hours in the pub, he did as he had promised. I had nappies, bottles, sandwiches, blankets for the beach — everything we would need. I was full of excitement. This was what I had dreamed of: doing things together, going places.

'Wait until you see where Daddy is taking us,' I gushed to four-year-old J.J. 'A big sea you can paddle in, bigger than any river you have ever seen.'

He looked at me, having no idea what I was talking about.

An hour or so later, Michael was backing the Morris Minor into a parking space in Tramore. Behind us was a windswept, soggy strand. It had started bucketing down about halfway through the journey, during which Michael had not spoken a word. Now he switched off the engine and yanked up the handbrake. Then he buttoned his coat, turned up his collar and opened the door.

'Where are you going?' I asked.

'Where do you think? For a pint.'

The rain was lashing the car, the wind whistling through the telegraph wires. The windows had fogged up. We could see nothing. In any case, we were not facing the sea. The children were getting cross, wanting to sit on my lap all at the same time. I let J.J. into the front, so he could play at driving. Then Katie wanted the steering wheel. She was not used to being in a car. I coaxed her into exploring down on the floor. The baby wriggled on my lap as I struggled to change her nappy.

Then they were hungry, so I opened the jam sandwiches and

the thermos of tea. We felt better after that, but the children were soon bored. I debated whether or not to take them for a walk in the rain, but we would have to sit afterwards in soaking wet clothes.

Panic flowed through me as J.J. and Katie began to fight again. I wiped the mist from the window and searched for the pub Michael had gone to. I couldn't see one.

What if he were to forget that he had us with him and take a lift back the 30 miles? How I wished I could drive. What if he'd had an accident, a fight? Should I try to lock the children in the car and go and find him?

I was afraid to leave them alone. I sang some of my mother's old songs to distract them, but it didn't work. They repeated the same questions, like a litany. When is the rain going to stop? Why are you crying? When's Daddy coming back?

The rain did not stop. Mammy was going insane and, while we sat imprisoned in the car, Daddy did not come back for nearly five hours.

He was all over the road driving home. It was hard to see through the downpour. Much of the way, I had one hand on the steering wheel, trying to keep us out of a ditch, while I held on to the baby with the other. The only words spoken were by me, to keep Michael awake, warning him of corners and oncoming cars.

At last we were home. At the front gate, I was glad to get the children out of the car. Michael sat on in the driver's seat, his eyelids drooping. Then I remembered. We had no milk. I had meant to get some on the way home. I tapped on his window. 'I have no milk.'

He revved the engine.

'I'll get it.'

It was the answer I'd been afraid of.

'No,' I said quickly. 'Why don't you stay with the children, and I'll run down for it?' He clenched his teeth and banged the steering wheel.

'I said I'll get it.'

'We'll all go down together, so,' I said. I grabbed the door handle but the car was already moving. I stood back sharply as he accelerated away.

It was still pouring, but I stood at the gate watching to see if he would pass the pub. He did. Then he disappeared around the bend to his mother's — for the milk, I hoped.

I put a match to the fire. The children were exhausted, crying and starving. I searched the cupboards. There was nothing

An hour passed. Getting the milk should be a three-minute job, so I decided on a desperate measure. I put the children into the bedroom, laying the baby in the cot and locking the door on them. I could hear their cries as I went out and jumped on Geraldine's bike, which was leaning against the house. It was too small for me but I flew down the hill on it, right to Mrs Kelly's shop.

There he was, leaning on the counter, trying to focus on the Sunday paper. Just him and his mother. I could barely breathe or speak, I was in such a state.

'Where is it?' I managed to hiss through my teeth. 'You came down for milk for your children, remember?'

I was shaking. He turned and looked at me as if in surprise, then pointed nonchalantly at a crate. I looked from him to his mother.

'Do you know what I'm going to do?' I was spitting the words, flaming with anger. 'I'm going to go up and drown the three children and myself in the barrels out the back. Do you hear me?'

They just looked at me blankly, then Mrs Kelly gave a high-pitched hoot of laughter and started busying herself with something behind the counter. A ball of rage swelled in my throat. I looked at Michael, who was back studying the paper. I stooped, picked up two bottles of milk and walked out.

Geraldine's bike had a little basket on its handlebars. I rammed the bottles into it and started walking up the hill. I was stumbling and making noises like a wounded animal. As I struggled to put one leg in front of the other, a middle-aged woman from the village, Mrs Noonan, was walking towards me.

'What's the matter with you, for God's sake?' she asked.

I laid the bike down on the road. With my face puffed and soaking from rain and tears, and my hair bedraggled, I almost fell into her arms. I clung to her, whimpering.

'I'm going to drown the children and myself.'

'Come on now, come on,' she said, patting my back.

She picked up the bike, placed it carefully against the wall and began leading me towards the nearby chapel.

'We'll go in here and ask God to give you the strength to carry on.'

'But I don't want to!'

'You have to, craythur.'

'Why? Answer me that. Why?'

She caught me by the hand and pulled me into the chapel like a reluctant child. I automatically made the sign of the cross and got into a pew. 'God help me. Please, please, help me!'

I knelt there and prayed from the deepest part of my being. In the peace and warmth, I felt some life coming into me. What I had said in the shop had just poured out of me. I had not thought or planned those words, but at that moment I had truly wanted to die.

Now I felt more composed and got up and thanked Mrs Noonan as best I could. I took hold of the bike and walked up to the house, the bottles rattling in the basket. The children were in hysterics. I hugged them and warmed the milk. After I had changed their nappies, I brought the three of them into bed with me and they soon fell asleep. I lay there and thought of the water barrels at the back of the house, and then of my father, all those years before, threatening to drown himself in the Nore.

When Jackie was a year old, I was pregnant again, this time with bad morning sickness. Some days, all I could do was lie in bed.

Mrs Cuddihy was up with me most of the time, helping with the children.

Before the new baby arrived, I thought I would put the three children into their own bedroom. Most of the time, they loved being together, talking, laughing and arguing. As I listened at the door, I thought they were priceless. One night, because I'd had a backache all day, I put them to bed early. Then I went to lie down but I soon heard a racket. It ended with Katie crying. Sitting up in the bed, I yelled at them to be good. Suddenly I felt a warm gush between my legs. I put my hand under the blanket and, when I looked, there was bright red on my fingers.

Stay quiet and it will stop, I told myself. Then I thought: I'm going to bleed to death and what will happen to the children?

'God bless all here.'

It was Mrs Cuddihy coming in the front door. Katie was calling her and so she went in to see the children. I knew that if I shouted out, I would haemorrhage more. After an agony of waiting, Mrs Cuddihy came in to me. The bedclothes were soaked. When she saw this, she put her hands to her face.

'Oh no,' she said. 'Not again.'

She ran out to get the doctor and Mrs Kelly. The doctor arrived first.

'You'll have to go to hospital,' he told me calmly.

'What will I do with the children?'

'Don't you worry about them. They'll be looked after.'

At this point, Mrs Kelly arrived.

'Well, Doctor, what's wrong with her?'

'She's having a miscarriage. We'll have to get her into hospital. I'll put her in my car and take her, if one of you women will come to sit with her in the back.'

'I'll go,' Mrs Cuddihy said.

'And I'll stay with the little ones,' said another voice from the doorway. It was my father-in-law.

The doctor gave me an injection, then carried me to the car, wrapped in a blanket. The children were crying, and everything was a mess. I knew I was losing the baby and, sure enough, it was gone before we got to the hospital.

This time, I didn't want to come home, not for anyone. I had been in hospital for two days. This loss felt different from the other one. The time before, I had not known I was pregnant. This time I had. So what was I to think now? Did the baby feel the need to leave? Did it know the chaos around us — that we were not happy, that its father and mother did not love one another? These unanswerable questions tumbled around in my mind, tormenting me. I realised that physical pain is nothing compared to what goes on in one's head.

But soon I had other things to worry about. The Electricity Supply Board came to cut us off, which happened more or less every time we got our bill. It was like a ritual we had to go through. The bill arrived, and I gave it to Michael. He stuck it in his pocket and forgot about it. Then, after a couple of weeks, the man came apologetically to disconnect us.

So, once more, Mrs Cuddihy and I got out the candles. 'Don't be worrying; sure Mrs Kelly will pay it,' she assured me.

'She has to know about it first,' I said wearily.

When Michael came home, he made no comment.

'How long will we have to wait to get the power back?' I asked him. It usually took him a couple of days to tell his mother. Mary's wedding was only a week away and she would be leaving for the church from our house. We *had* to have electricity.

'Don't ask stupid questions,' he slurred. 'I might as well get up. There's no peace in this place.'

He rolled out of the bed. Both of us were moody — he because of his hangover, and I had been cross in myself since losing the baby, a subject he and I had never discussed. I hated Michael for saying nothing to me about our lost child.

It was the usual morning carry-on. The children were hungry, wet and crying, and Michael could not wait to get out the door. I mentioned the electricity again.

'I'll do what I can.'

'Do what you can!' I screamed. 'Where are you going now? You'll have money for beer no doubt. I'm the one who as to go down to the village to shop. I have to face your mother and everyone else. You can be sure they all saw the ESB van yesterday.'

He went out the door, giving it a good bang. Mrs Cuddihy came up mid-morning to allow me to go to the shop. The instant I got to the front gate, I could see Michael's car parked outside the pub. It was a crisp fresh day as I walked down the road. The village was hushed. There was only the sound of a tractor in the distance. But as I drew near the pub, there were different sounds. I heard chatting and laughing, bottles and glasses clinking, bits of a song starting up. I went to the door and opened it enough to see in. The smell of beer and smoke hit me in the face. There he was, centre stage, a pint of stout in one hand, a John Player in the other, and a shot of whiskey at his elbow. A huge smile played on his face as he joked with some holiday-makers.

Something snapped inside me, like a frayed length of twine giving way. I suddenly lost all fear: of him, of Mrs Kelly, of what the village would say. I walked straight in and stood boldly in front of him.

'What the fuck are you doing here?' I shrieked. 'You bastard!'

I normally never swore but now everything was different. The whole place went still.

I looked around at the other drinkers and then back at Michael.

'We have no electricity! No money! How am I supposed to manage? What about our children? They don't know what it's like to have a father. They never see you. I hate you, do you hear me?' I was thumping him on the chest, using all my strength. Michael's pal, Packie, was trying to calm me down.

'He'll go home with you now,' he said, turning to Michael. 'Michael, this woman is upset. I think you should listen to her.'

I laughed bitterly. 'Listen? He never listens. He's a bloody pig.'

I swung round. I was going to tell the whole pub about my husband, about his drunkenness and filthiness. Michael pushed his face close to mine. 'Go home,' he said. He caught me by the arm to steer me towards the door.

'No,' I yelled. 'I'm staying here until you come with me.'

To my surprise, everyone in the place was agreeing with me.

'Go on, Michael,' someone said. 'Get it sorted out and then you can come back and enjoy your drink.'

But I had a better idea.

'No, he's not coming back. He's going to take the pledge. We're on our way to the priest this minute.'

To my astonishment, the publican himself, who knew even more about Michael's drinking than I did, was all in favour of the idea.

'Come here a minute,' he said to Michael. 'Now you have a young family, my boyo. Give it a try, won't ye? What have you got to lose?'

Michael hesitated. He looked defensively around the room. Then he put the pint to his lips, emptying it in one long swallow, his Adam's apple going up and down like a piston. He banged the glass on to the counter and snatched up the whiskey, which he drained in one gulp. Then he spun around and went out the door, with me after him.

To my amazement, he was walking up the road, swaying slightly, towards the presbytery. I followed him in disbelief and joined him as he stood, breathing heavily, at the front door. I rang the bell.

It was the same priest who had married us nearly five years earlier.

'What can I do for ye?' he asked.

I pointed at Michael. 'He wants to take the pledge, Father.'

'Come in, come in!' He was beaming.

He sat us down in his sitting room and asked Michael what

reason he had for wanting to do this and if he intended keeping it.

Michael sat looking at the floor. He mumbled that he had to and would do his best to keep it.

'All right so', said the priest, reaching for the Bible.

As we walked back through the tall trees lining the avenue, it seemed quite dark, even though it was the middle of the day. I felt a warm feeling towards Michael. I reached out my hand to put it into his, but he pulled his away.

'Get lost,' he said.

I withdrew my hand as if I'd been burnt.

Chapter Eleven

Michael had decided to take the pledge for three months. I could see from the beginning that he meant to keep it. He started renovating cars like a madman. This occupied the time he used to spend drinking.

When Mary's wedding day came, Michael would not go.

'What's the point,' he said, 'when I can't have a drink like everyone else?'

I could hear the bitterness in his voice: this was all my fault. He was cold and more distant than ever with me.

'How are things at home now?' my father asked me outside the church.

'Great,' I lied.

But in spite of everything, I enjoyed the day. I had a couple of Babychams and danced with Daddy, who tried to teach me to waltz. The drinks made me feel carefree and magnificent.

'For God's sake, don't get pregnant again,' he said, as we stepped around the dance floor. 'It will kill you. You look like nothing on earth.'

I hadn't realised I looked that bad; if I did, it was no wonder Michael didn't have a word to say to me.

'You should have a small Guinness every night,' my father said. 'It would build you up and put a bit of weight on you.'

'I'll see,' I said, but with Michael off the drink, I thought it might not be such a good idea.

In a fit of generosity, my father rented us a black-and-white television. I became an instant addict. We had only the one station: RTÉ. I wanted to watch it from the minute it came on, at five in the evening, until it closed down at midnight. The children were the same. We would sit and wait on the old couch for it to start. I'm sure Daddy's plan was that it would interest Michael, but he had no time for it. He was not drinking, so he was sulky. I tried to pretend that we were happy, but the house had no life in it.

'Look how well J.J. gets on with your father,' I said. 'He spends more time with him than he does with us.' J.J. had started sleeping at Kellys' the odd night now.

Michael went back on the drink a week before the three months were up. In one way, it was a relief because he had been so hard to live with. But from the day he drank again, he was as bad as ever, so it had all been for nothing.

I started to enjoy a couple of small stouts myself every night now, as my father had suggested. I found it gave me a feeling of wellbeing, and I even started having one or two during the day.

Michael was renovating a pub on the Kilkenny/Tipperary border. It had music at the weekend. This was a new thing in the 1960s, the singing pub. My father used to go himself and, one Saturday night, he called in on his way there.

'Why don't you come?' he said. 'Michael will be there. We could have a few dances.'

I was excited but nervous. Mrs Cuddihy said she would baby-sit, so, having had a drink first to give me Dutch courage, off I went with my father.

It was a small pub with a big room for dancing. The waltzes and quicksteps rang out into the night air and, as the evening went on and the drink flowed, we got into the set dancing.

Michael, who didn't have a step, left for some other pub when we arrived. My father was a natural; he brought me on to the floor to show me how it was done. No one was going to chastise Mr O' for taking out a novice. I seemed to pick it up quickly.

Other men asked me on to the floor and, to tell the truth, I liked the attention.

The next day, Michael said to me, 'You're making a holy show of me by going to the pub with your father.'

'Why don't you bring me?'

'That's a good idea,' he said, to my surprise. 'Tell your father I'll do that next week.' The next Saturday morning, as he was going out, I reminded Michael of his promise. He grunted and went off.

That night, I sat waiting patiently for him, dolled up in Mary's best dress, which she'd lent me. Of course, I should have known beforehand, but I spent a couple of hours waiting before I admitted the truth: he wasn't coming.

In the small hours, Michael returned home, all innocence. He said he'd forgotten about me.

It was 1965 and coming up to my twenty-first. Mary (who was now pregnant with her first baby) said I should go to Dublin for my birthday, because I had never been. She and my father both gave me money as a present. I had £40; I hadn't seen so much money since the time we had raided my father's wallet.

Michael and I arrived on a Saturday morning in the Morris Minor and went straight to the city centre. The department stores were full of wonderful things for the children, my sisters and my father. I could not believe the bargains. I was in a dither choosing — picking up one thing only to leave it when I saw something better. Michael was taking a great interest in what I was buying. He tried to persuade me — it was too small, too big; the children wouldn't like that rubbish. I was delighted until the penny dropped.

'You're not getting any of this money to buy drink,' I told

him. 'If I don't spend it here, I'll spend it at home.'

After my raid on the shops, we had to get somewhere to stay. Michael drove around until we saw a Bed & Breakfast sign.

'Could we have a room for the night, please?' I asked the woman in the apron who came to the door.

'No, I'm full up,' she said, giving us an old-fashioned look.

I noticed that almost all the houses on the street had B&B signs. We'd be bound to get a room in one of them. But the landlady of the next one made the situation much clearer.

'You're too young,' she said flatly.

I looked at her in disbelief.

'But we're married,' I protested, showing her my wedding ring.

'Pull the other one,' she said, shutting the door in my face.

The answer was the same all the way down the street, and I was close to tears.

'We'll have to go home,' Michael said.

'No,' I said. 'I'm going to keep trying.'

Knocking on the next door and getting the same response, I pointed to the phone I could see in the hallway behind her.

'Look,' I said. 'Could we use your phone? I'll pay for the call. It's to my mother-in-law and she'll tell you we are married.'

She looked at us dubiously, and then agreed.

I called Michael who was hovering at the gate; he rang his mother and, after she had spoken to the landlady, we got the room. The next morning, the landlady stood over us as we ate her big cooked breakfast.

'Are ye married long?' she asked.

'Nearly five years,' I told her with pride.

'My God, you only look about thirteen, the two of ye!'

'Well, we've three children,' I boasted. Michael was glaring at me as he stood up and left the table. I thanked the woman for the breakfast.

'The chapel's just across the road,' she remarked. 'Ye'll be in nice time for Mass.'

When I joined Michael in the room, he was fuming.

'For God's sake, did you have to tell her everything? I was never so embarrassed in all my life.'

After Mass, we packed. Michael was busy with the bags and checking his cash.

'We'd better sort ourselves out and pay the woman,' I said.

'You're the one with all the money.'

'Aren't you going to help? I might not have enough.'

'You should have thought of that yesterday,' he said, 'when you were spending all round you.'

I sat down to count what I had. It was 17s 6d, mostly in coppers. Downstairs, as Michael heaved the cases and shopping bags into the Morris Minor, I asked the woman what we owed her.

'That'll be thirteen and six,' she said.

So I had four shillings to take home with me. I was happy with that.

The village was coming into the twentieth century at last. Most families now owned a car and a television set. Then the people of the village got together to bring water into the houses, and everyone was delighted that the County Council was putting up streetlights.

One afternoon, I decided I would take us all for a walk to my father's: Alison, Geraldine, J.J., Katie, Jackie and myself. I had not been down there for about a year. Alison and Geraldine slept there, but they spent most of their time with me. I was glad that we had no key and could not go in — it all looked neglected and depressing. Instead, I decided I would show the children around the back garden where I used to play as a child. That was all changed too: running wild, not with flowers the way my dead grandmother had liked it, but with weeds. I just hoped she couldn't see the state of it.

I followed the children into the orchard. The apple trees had not been pruned for years and bore no fruit. The gooseberry and blackberry bushes were smothered with nettles and so was the arch of roses. I felt angry with my father for the shambles in this lovely place of my childhood.

Taking the children to stand under the big beech tree, I talked about the games I used to play in it. J.J. wanted to see for himself and, as I lifted him up, he put his hand into the branches and pulled out an old rag doll. She had no hair. Her painted eyes and features were faded, but I could still see them. He handed her down to me. It was Philomena! I held her close.

I had not seen her for almost fifteen years. I had played with her by the hour in that tree, but it seemed like a hundred years had passed since I was that child. A feeling of loneliness coursed through me. Once she had been so important to me. How could I have forgotten her? My four-year-old, Katie, was determined to have her.

'We'll have to put her at the fire to dry when we get home,' I said.

But before we even got there, Philomena's body had fallen away from her head. Katie insisted that I get out the needle and thread and mend her. They went everywhere together after that, Philomena tucked under Katie's arm during the day and beside her in bed at night.

J.J. and Katie were looking forward to Santa coming, and it was the first Christmas that Jackie knew what was going on. I wanted it to be special.

I began knitting Aran sweaters to make some money and managed to save enough to get really good presents: a bike for J.J. and a doll each, with eyes that opened and shut, for Katie and Jackie. Mrs Cuddihy hid the toys in her house until the big day.

On Christmas Eve, just before midnight, I was standing on the front step once more. The children were in bed and my sisters had gone home long before. I was enjoying the only bit of hush I'd had all day. It was a peaceful night, the quietest you could imagine: cold and with a bright moon. I could see clearly through the bare branches of the copper beech. It was a night when the sky and the ground mirrored one another, dreaming up another world.

I jumped when I heard Mrs Cuddihy approaching.

'Is it safe to bring the things up?' she called. Moments later, we'd got everything by the fire where Santa was supposed to leave it.

'Are your father and sisters coming up for their Christmas dinner tomorrow?' she asked as she sipped a cup of hot tea.

'Alison and Geraldine will be up here early. Mary, Tom and their baby will call in sometime during the day, but you know my father. He'll have to go for his drink.'

'Ah well, he was good to come and bring them home early tonight.'

Mrs Cuddihy was always inclined to see the good in everyone.

'I know he was,' I agreed with a sigh. 'But I know what it'll be like tomorrow too. He'll start on about my mother. He'll be crying, full of self-pity; it's all right for him to lament but we can't mention her. And we miss her too, Mrs Cuddihy. He should understand how we feel.'

She patted my hand, but I didn't want her to be nice to me. I was afraid that I would start crying. It was after one o'clock, so I stood up suddenly, as if to show her that it was bedtime. She got up to go.

'Are you all right, child? Do you want to talk?'

'I'd better not.'

'You'll have plenty to say, when the time is right,' she told me, a half-smile on her gentle face.

'Thank you for everything,' I said, suddenly bursting with gratitude and love for her.

We walked to the front door together. I stood on the top step and we waved to each other as she went out into the darkness of that Christmas morning.

Chapter Twelve

Getting to know people did not come easily to me. I felt stupid and worthless. I was sure people didn't want to know me but were too polite to say so. But by the age of twenty-three, I had finally made a couple of friends.

There was a teenage girl called Rose who lived nearby. She would come up to me for a chat some days and I enjoyed having someone to talk to about clothes, hairstyles and make-up — a subject on which she seemed to be an expert, in spite of being only sixteen. She let me try on some of her stuff and even gave me clothes to keep because we were the same size.

One day, she said, 'Why don't we ask Michael to take us down the village to the pub? They have dancing there at the weekends.'

It was the only way to do it in 1966; it would not have been right for any women to go without a man. I asked him would he take us and I couldn't believe it when he agreed. It was to be the next Saturday night.

Rose and I gave all day Saturday to getting ready. Of course, it had to be mini-skirts. Rose lent me a black one and a pink top, while she wore red with a black top. She had knee-length black boots and I wore a pair of black stilettos. We slapped on the black eyeliner and pale shiny lipstick.

I noticed that Michael made a great effort to look smart. He had shaved and put on his best clothes: a pair of black drainpipe trousers, a black shirt with a grey skinny tie and his winkle-picker shoes with orange socks. He wore his fair hair to his shoulders, swept back from his face, and when I looked at him, I had a flash of pride. He was handsome, young and modern, and he was my husband.

Michael decided not to take us to that particular pub, but to another that had dancing. As we climbed out of the Morris Minor, you could hear the band belting out the 'Tennessee Waltz'.

Rose and I went into the hall to find a table while Michael got the drinks at the bar. He came back with a bottle of stout for me, a bottle of Harp lager for Rose, and his own usual pint of Guinness. Without sitting down, he took a long drink and then asked Rose up to dance.

'Ask your wife first,' she said hurriedly.

'Will you dance with me then, Rose?' he asked.

She nodded.

'All right. Come on,' he said to me.

On to the floor we went. It was not like Michael to dance. He had always, to my knowledge, stayed propping up the counter. It was the first time I had ever danced with my husband after years of marriage.

'We could do this every weekend,' I said.

No reply.

It was not the twist, or anything like that, but the more old-fashioned kind of dancing where you held on to each other. Michael walked me carelessly around the floor, all the time looking at Rose, who was dancing with another fellow. Of course I knew what was going on in his mind.

'Stop flirting with Rose,' I said as the dance came to an end. 'She feels terrible and so do I.'

He looked at me in wide-eyed amazement. 'What in the name of God are you on about now?' he said as he steered me to my seat.

'Can I have that dance now, Rose?'

I took my stout with me to the toilet, not coming back until the dance was ended and I had drunk it and felt braver.

'Can we have another drink, Michael?' I asked.

'Sure, sure,' he said, going off to the bar to get them. Rose looked at me.

'Are you okay? I feel terrible, the way he's going on,' she said.

'Oh, I don't mind,' I lied. 'Will we go out to the bar to him?'

I thought if we were out there, he might not keep dancing with her.

We had five or six more drinks and I relaxed. By the time we decided to go home, my head was swimming pleasantly.

'That was great. Did you enjoy it?' I asked Rose.

'I did.' She was as drunk as I was.

Into the car we got, Rose in the back, and we began our perilous journey. We were weaving this way and that, hitting the ditches on both sides of the narrow road. I didn't think Michael was particularly drunk compared to his usual standards, so why was he hitting off everything? It took me a while to realise that he had one hand stretched behind him and was feeling Rose's leg. The back of the car was so small that she couldn't get away from him.

'Let me out,' I screamed. 'I'll walk home! Do you hear me? Let me out!'

He stopped with a jolt and out I got, slamming the door.

'You can't leave her there,' I heard Rose protesting.

'Why not?' Michael said. 'That's what she wants.'

'Well, I'm not staying without her.'

She was pushing the passenger seat forward and reaching for the handle. Impatiently, Michael pushed the seat back and opened the door.

'Get in,' he roared at me. For the sake of peace, I got in and then we set off again. When we got home and Mrs Cuddihy left, I wanted to talk to Michael about the way he had behaved, but all he wanted was sex. Full of resentment, I let him.

Michael and I never spoke about what had gone on that night, no more than we did about so many other things that happened in our marriage. But it was my first realisation that he would never change. When Rose came up after a couple of days, we did not discuss it either. At first, she seemed awkward, but when she knew I was not going to say anything, we just carried on like we used to.

Katie had started school and was making her own friends, and one in particular, Caroline Hickey. Caroline's mother, Maureen, was very attractive and had a smashing house. Her husband drank in moderation and never took a day off work. I held him up to Michael as an example.

'Why can't you be like Phil Hickey?' I asked. 'He has an interest in his children. He makes good money and he and Maureen go every place together.'

But Michael did not think much of them.

'When I'm about thirty-five, I'll settle down and be like him,' he told me sarcastically.

'That's nearly ten years away. We might be all dead by then,' I said. 'Think of all the time and money you'll have wasted.'

He didn't answer, but went off to waste some more of both.

Maureen Hickey was everything I felt I wanted to be and I was in hopeless competition with her. I made sure that when the children had their birthday parties, they had all the cake, sweets, lemonade and jelly that Caroline would have at hers. There would be about a dozen children in all and I would suffer agonies about the parents coming into the house to drop off their little ones. I cleaned and polished for days beforehand.

Once I invited Maureen to tea. It was to be in two weeks, so I went through fourteen days of worry. What would I talk to her about? What would I give her to eat? I would need a tablecloth to cover the marks on my old table. My chipped dishes and mugs were odd bits of this and that, nothing matching.

Saving my pennies, I bought a cup, saucer and plate and a jug and sugar bowl with a pattern of flowers around the gold-trimmed brim. I would love to have got the whole set. When I was buying them, I thought of my mother.

For sandwiches I got slices of ham and a fresh loaf from Norris's. I didn't want Mrs Kelly to know what I was doing. When Maureen came, I sat her down where I thought she could see the best of the kitchen. Then I left the children's bedroom door slightly ajar to give a view of what I thought was the best up there. I placed the sandwiches in front of her, carefully cut into triangles.

'Are you going to have anything yourself?' Maureen wanted to know.

'No, no. I'm fine,' I said quickly.

Actually I was starving, but I was not going to be seen using crockery that didn't match. So I looked at her as she ate and sipped her tea, trying not to drool.

'I see you don't have the water in yet,' she said, glancing around, 'I don't know how we ever managed without it.'

'Michael said he would have time next week to do it,' I lied.

Jackie wandered into the kitchen and shyly climbed on to my lap. After a few minutes, she looked over at the table and pointed. 'Mammy, where did you get all the new sugar and milk things? They're lovely.'

Turning bright red, I lied again. 'I had them all the time. Put away.'

Maureen and I talked a little stiffly about this and that, and, an hour later, she got up to leave.

'It's been lovely,' she said, smiling politely. 'Would you like to come over to me some day?'

'Yes, of course,' I gabbled. 'But I might have to bring the children.'

'That's all right.'

She gave a little wave as she got into her car.

I sat down and went over the afternoon. It had been an ordeal and I felt exhausted. Had Maureen been able to see how poor and shabby we were? Of course she had. Deep down, I knew it. It seemed that the more I tried, the more inadequate I felt. Short and shallow exchanges like this one only made me feel more hopeless.

To some extent, we behaved like any other married couple — by the time Jackie was three-and-a-half, I was pregnant again — but you'd have to be blind not to see that Michael and I were in desperate trouble. But in the spring of the year, I had my second son, Philip. He had blond hair and lovely blue eyes and I was thrilled.

'I need wool for my knitting,' I said to Michael, chancing my arm. 'Would you ever drive me to town to get some?' It was a Saturday afternoon. He had a good few drinks in him but, to my surprise, he agreed. J.J. was at his grandad's, as usual. Alison and Geraldine were there to mind Philip, so Katie, Jackie and I got into the car. We were only half an hour doing the shopping but, in that time, Michael was legless. We all got in the Morris Minor and he just sat there breathing heavily and staring at the dashboard. There was no way he could drive us home.

Katie looked at me and said with a frown, 'Mammy, why can't you drive?'

How hard can it be? I thought. 'Let me try, please,' I said to Michael.

He must have been in a bad state because he moved across to the passenger side without a word and fell asleep. I got behind the wheel. I knew the basics because my father used to show me when I was young. So I turned the key, put it into gear and slowly let out the clutch. With a jerk, we moved off.

In the back of the car, the girls were full of excitement at their mother's plucky move. We met only one car, at the sight of which I stamped on the brake and we screeched to a halt. The car went safely past and we set off again. By the time we stopped at our gate, I was feeling confident and proud. The girls ran in, shouting, 'Mammy drove the car home, and we never crashed!'

I waited behind the wheel for my sisters to see me, thinking I would keep at this, no matter what anyone said, including — in fact, especially — Mrs Kelly.

And so I did. The next Sunday morning, I drove the children proudly to Mass and, after that, I drove the car every chance I got. Mrs Kelly never said a word, though she must have seen me. I got braver as time went on and started to take the children for spins to all the places I used to walk to as a child. I would talk about my mother, and tell them the ghost stories Old Daddy had told me. They loved those stories.

I felt so grateful to Michael for letting me drive and this was a new feeling for me. He would not fill a bottle or change a nappy, but when he let me drive his car, I thought he was the best ever.

J.J. was seven now and it was time for him to make his First Communion. He was a strong handsome lad with a good heart and I felt an overwhelming surge of love for him on that day. Michael was not there, but everyone else of importance was: his sisters and baby brother, my own sisters, my father and Mr and Mrs Kelly. My son didn't mention his missing father, but I was painfully aware of his absence.

I was finding more and more relief in my Guinness. As long as I had that, I wouldn't feel as bad as I used to. It was like a bandage I could put over a wound. It seemed to soothe my troubled mind.

Nobody seemed to notice my drinking. By the time my husband and father came home, they were in no condition themselves, and my sisters were so used to the fumes of alcohol, they paid no heed. My only worry with my healing balm was how to keep the supply safe and plentiful.

Chapter Thirteen

My younger sisters had grown into very different personalities. Alison was self-contained, never discussing anything personal, while Geraldine would tell me everything. At sixteen, Alison was already two years out of school. She had got a job as a trainee in the post office in a nearby village where she lived during the week. She asked me if she could stay with us at weekends after she had an argument with Daddy when he caught her smoking in the bedroom. I told her she could, even though Mrs Kelly would be furious when she found out. Alison came to me on Friday nights; sometimes it was midnight. I would never ask her where she'd been. I worried that she'd go away to some big town and we'd lose touch with her.

Geraldine was still at school but now that Alison had gone, she didn't want to stay with my father any more. She also wanted to live with me.

'I suppose you can't wait to get away from me, just like your sisters,' my father would say to her. 'After bringing ye all up on me own, is this my thanks? I never brought another woman into the house after your poor mother passed away. God knows, it wasn't easy, and me still a young man, but I did it for ye. I know I'll end my days on my own, God help me.'

Geraldine would come up to me in the mornings, her eyes red-rimmed.

'I know I'm going to be the one who will have to stay with him for the rest of my life. If he would stop going on about ghosts, it wouldn't be so bad.' But no matter what anyone said, he would not leave the subject alone.

Normally Geraldine could talk for Ireland, but not with my father. She couldn't utter a word or he would belittle her, calling her 'the fool'.

One night, he came up from the pub around eleven, blowing the horn at the gate to call her out. As soon as she heard it, she started to cry.

I went to the door.

'Come in for a minute, Daddy,' I shouted. I watched him struggle out of the Volkswagen. His breathing was laboured as he came up the path, shaking his head and sighing at the effort. My father could be as old or as young as he wanted to be, depending on the situation.

'Well, girl?' he said at last.

I ushered him in and took a deep breath.

'Daddy, will you stop frightening Geraldine?'

Suddenly his face hardened and his eyes narrowed. 'What's that fool being telling you now?'

My anger surfaced. 'She doesn't have to tell me,' I shouted. 'I know what you're like. And don't call my sister a fool, because she's not one.'

I said all this in one breath. He looked from me to her and then he sharply turned on his heel, snapped his head back and walked out, with not a trace of the earlier old-man act. It was almost a repeat of his performance five years earlier, when we had been reconciled with the bribe of a washing machine.

As his car moved off, Geraldine and I went to the top step to watch him drive down home. By his car headlights we could see how he laboriously manoeuvred into the space beside the house. He always reversed in; this was so that the neighbours would think he had not been too drunk to park properly. 'That'll show them,' he would say, but nobody was fooled. The roar of the engine in the night, and the going backwards and forwards again and again to get the car straight would have told the world the state he was in.

Geraldine and I put our arms around each other and went inside, full of guilt. She stayed with me after that and, at the end of term, she left school for a job of her own. Like Alison's, it was also in a post office: Mrs Kelly's. We were all surprised, but delighted.

So, with my sisters both earning, they would each give me a pound note out of their wages, which seemed to me like a hundred. I would pile the children into the car at weekends and go shopping with my £2. We would all get a treat: a comic each for the girls, a Matchbox car for J.J., a lollipop for Philip, and six small Guinness and a bottle of port for myself. We would sing songs all the way home. 'Johnny was Shy' was J.J.'s. 'A Bunch of Violets Blue' was Katie's; 'Carolina Moon' was Jackie's; and we all sang 'My Bonnie Lies Over the Ocean' to Philip. The feeling in the car as we bounced along was like a bubble of security and love. I thought that if only Michael would allow himself to experience it once, it might transform our lives.

I used to drop him off at Paddy's pub on our way, and I was told to be there to pick him up at closing time. This was the same pub I'd sipped Guinness in at two years of age with my father, the one where they had lifted me over the gate when the guards raided it after hours.

Paddy and his sister Nellie lived over the pub. Both were in their forties and neither had married. They must have been wealthy because they had land and cattle all over the village, though to look at them you'd think they didn't have a penny. It was said that she hated the drink with a vengeance. But Paddy would walk up and down the street all day, an open bottle of stout standing in the pocket of his overalls, talking to the people of the village. He'd take a quiet nip from time to time but never spill a drop. Every couple of months, you'd be sure to see Nellie going around to their numerous fields, collecting the empties that he'd dumped. You would hear her before you'd see her as the bottles danced together inside her bag.

At closing time, Paddy would poke his head out quickly to make sure the coast was clear as he got ready to bolt the door for the hard drinkers. I would get out and run across to collect Michael. As quick as a fist to an eye, Paddy would put a small stout and a whiskey on the counter, free of charge, for me. 'Whiskey, *Uisce Beatha* — the water of life,' he would say as he downed a large one himself.

Like J.J. the year before, Katie made her First Holy Communion. All the mothers were very competitive. I wanted Katie to be the best-dressed child there and had been saving for ages for her clothes: a white frilly frock and veil. It cost 15 shillings, and white lacy knee stockings were included in the price. The night before, I put rags in Katie and Jackie's hair to make ringlets.

After the Communion, there was the usual special breakfast. Members of the family were there, just as they had been for J.J, but Mrs Cuddihy was ill for the first time since I'd known her and was not able to be there. The next day, I heard that she was in hospital, and I went in to Kilkenny to visit her. She looked just the same as always and was delighted to see me.

'I'll be home in a couple of days, please God.'

'We missed you at the First Communion,' I told her. 'I'll show you the photos when we get them back. But sure you'll be home before that.'

She smiled but her reply seemed weary: 'I will, child, I will.'

I leaned forward to give her a kiss on the cheek. She was dropping off, so I tiptoed to the door. I looked back at her, now serenely sleeping. I owed that woman so much.

The next morning, as I was making the beds, there was a knock on the door. It was Rose.

'Why are you knocking, for God's sake?' I said, laughing. 'The key is in the door like always.' The smile left my face when I saw the strange look on hers. 'Mrs Cuddihy died last night,' Rose said quietly.

'She can't have. I was in with her yesterday. She looked okay.'

'She died during the night. A heart attack. That's all I know.'

What would I do without my lovely neighbour? No one could begin to appreciate the relationship I had with that good woman. I would no longer be able to stand on the top step and call her at all hours and know she'd be there. She had never let me down, never had a bad word to say about me and she knew me better than my own mother had.

Mrs Kelly was a great one for the guards. The barracks were right beside her shop and they were encouraged to go in whenever they liked, to make a cup of tea or look at television. It was a good arrangement. They kept her informed of everything going on, which gave her a lot of satisfaction and power in the village. The relationship always paid off. Once Michael was found asleep behind the wheel of his car, parked in the middle of the road. The guards were called and there was talk of prosecution until Mrs Kelly had a word and the whole thing was dropped. But the incident had given Michael a fright and now he wanted me to pick him up from the pub every night. It was around the time the law started to take drink-driving seriously. White squad cars were constantly around the village. Male drinkers all over Ireland were in fear of losing their licence and were teaching their wives to drive like never before.

It didn't seem to matter if I was caught drink-driving: I was now making a habit of going into whichever pub Michael was in and having a couple of drinks myself. At first, I wondered how they could stay there night after night. 'Consultant Gob-shites' my father would call them — not, of course, including himself — but I was beginning to feel comfortable in there. Now that Geraldine, with her new boyfriend, a nice lad, was at home with the sleeping children, why couldn't I go out for a few hours at night like everyone else? There were other women from the village who went out for a drink.

Michael could be in any of the three pubs in the village. I would try Paddy's first and have a stout, followed by a whiskey or two. This would be on the house, from Paddy, as his sister watched disapprovingly. Maybe she thought I shouldn't be there without my husband, or shouldn't be drinking at all because I was a woman. Her brother took no notice of her, and neither did I after a while, or rather after a couple of stiff ones.

If Michael wasn't in any of the village pubs, it meant that he had gone off somewhere else. In this case, I went home and found comfort in my own personal booze store — hidden in the wardrobe.

When I discovered that I was pregnant again — for the seventh time! — I thought straight away of Mrs Cuddihy. She would have been the first to be told. Instead of saying that I had enough children already and asking how I would manage, she would say something like, 'Another little one for you to look after.' She knew I loved having a baby to dote on.

She had always made me feel good about myself. I was not unhappy about the pregnancy. I had had a two-and-a-half-year break from childbirth, so I felt strong, and Mary was also pregnant with her third child. She would take the ten-minute walk up to me most days. Our time was spent knitting and choosing names. We were talking about Alison's plans to get married to a farmer's son from up the road.

My fifth baby, Ellen, was born in December 1970. She had green eyes and golden hair and was very lively. She was born two months before Mary's and it happened very fast, with hardly any labour. When she heard I had a girl, Mary, who already had two boys, was convinced hers would be another boy. She still came up to see me, but I would have to leave the fireside and breast-feed in the bedroom because she couldn't bear to see it, not having her own baby yet. I couldn't even talk about my baby without Mary getting upset. When at last she had her little girl, the pressure was off. But our pleasant period of bonding as expectant mothers was over. Our relationship as sisters was also strained because of Michael. My sisters disapproved of him not only because of his treatment of me, but also because he was such a flirt.

Chapter Fourteen

After Ellen was born, I felt I wanted no more babies. Philip was nearly three and I had been getting used to not having to turn continually and move the nappies that were hanging around the house to dry. And here I was starting all over again.

Around this time, there was a lot of talk about the pill in Ireland. It seemed that if you lived in a town, you could get it easily enough, but the rural doctors were different, and the country people were different too. I heard the women at the school gate talking.

'Can you imagine what the doc would think if I asked him for it? That I was going home straight away to do it, for God's sake! I would rather die.'

They would all roar with laughter.

All the Catholic Church had to say about the pill was that it was between you and your conscience. If you felt in any doubt about taking it, then it was a sin. The bishops were dead against it, in other words. None of this helped me to make a decision. Supposing I could get the pill and that I took it: God might not be too happy with me. On the other hand, if I kept having babies every year, I might end up with twenty children. How would I feed and clothe them, never mind have time to love them all?

Mary came over to me at the school gate one evening, all excitement.

'Wait until I tell you what I heard. There's a lady doctor in Kilkenny giving out the pill!'

'What's she like?'

'She has children herself, and is very nice. But you have to pay for it.'

'How much?'

'A pound for a three-month supply.' She looked at me. 'Will Michael give you the money?'

'God knows.'

Next morning, lying in bed beside Michael, I started tossing and turning to make him wake up.

'What's up with you this morning?' he groaned.

'I have to talk to you.'

'You're always on about something.'

'It's about going on the pill, so that I won't be pregnant nearly all the time. It costs a pound.'

Michael sat up in the bed.

'A pound? Are you mad?'

The noise woke Ellen, who had just gone to sleep after her feed.

'No, I'm not, but I will be soon if I keep having children at this rate. Please, Michael!'

The baby was crying. He made a face, got out of bed and was gone in a flash.

That night, he came home in his usual state and I heard the money jingling in his trousers as he fell around the bedroom trying to get out of them. I jumped out of bed.

'Where are you going?' He was groping blindly for me in the dark. 'Get into the bed, woman. I'm freezing.'

'In a minute. I have to make a bottle for the baby.'

It was a lie, but he didn't know. In no time, he was asleep and snoring. I took his trousers down to the kitchen and I stuck my hand into his pocket. I pulled out a fistful of silver, coppers and notes. I grabbed the first note I saw, shoved the rest of it back and left his trousers where I'd found them. I didn't worry about him missing the pound, but I certainly didn't feel good about what I had had to do to get it.

The doctor examined me thoroughly and said that because I didn't smoke or have varicose veins and was only twenty-six, she would be happy to let me have the pill. I thought all my worries were over. Ellen was a good-humoured and happy little soul, but the fun of the tin bath in front of the fire was long gone and I wanted an end to the pee-pots that had to be emptied and washed every day. Mary's house was like a palace with a big bathroom built on, a fine new kitchen and a room for their baby girl.

Our children were getting big. J.J. was ten. They were noticing other people's houses. They knew that there was no need for our home to be as it was. Michael had good wages — at least £20 a week. The garden was overgrown and wild since Mr Kelly had got too old to look after it. There were no vegetables now, only a few potatoes from the jungle of drills. Inside, the house was in a desperate state. The wallpaper was covered with spots of mildew, the curtains were black around the edges, and there was a damp furry fungus on the floor in the bedrooms. I found it so depressing. Now I seemed to spend what little money I got on alcohol to help me relieve the hopelessness, but instead I exchanged one negative feeling for another. I was full of guilt.

One or other of the children constantly had a cold. Then one winter they all got the measles together. When Katie got sick, she always thought she was going to die. She would ask me to bring up the mirror, to see her face covered in spots, and then have hysterics and be afraid to look. Her hands were kept firmly under the covers so that she couldn't see them. Long after the others were up and about, she was still in bed. None of this made any difference to her father's way of life. Mr Kelly, sounding enraged, told me, 'That fellow is a holy show, asleep on the counter nearly every night. And on Sunday evening at seven o'clock, he didn't know where he was.'

'What can I do about it?'

I felt that he regarded his son's behaviour as my responsibility. Mrs Kelly had always believed it. Sometimes I would almost burst with things I wanted to say to the Kellys about their precious son. It hurt me more that it was Mr Kelly saying these things to me because I thought he had been my ally in this battle.

Geraldine and her boyfriend Pat decided that they wanted to get married. I was surprised and thought that at eighteen she was too young, but within a matter of months they wed and moved in with my father. He was delighted to have one of his daughters back in his house again. Then Alison got married. She went to live with her in-laws and kept her job. I often wondered what my mother would have thought of her daughters, all married and living within ten minutes' walk of each other. Would she be proud of us and her eight grandchildren? Had she lived to see them, she would still have been only forty-nine years old in 1971.

Because my sisters seemed to be so happily married, I felt more isolated, especially because they didn't often call in. I thought they wanted to leave this part of their life behind, and create new families and homes for themselves. I didn't blame them one bit, but I felt deserted. I'd stopped going to the pub because my father made a remark about me being out drinking every night, but I still drank, in secret, at home.

Michael soon recruited other people to take him home. I heard the rare sound of a knock on the door one night about ten o'clock. It had to be a stranger because, as usual, the key was in the lock. I opened it to a man who had my husband, his eyes half-shut and his mouth half-open, hanging from his arm. A Cortina was parked outside the gate.

'My God! I said. 'Where was he?'

'In the pub,' the stranger said. 'Where do you want him?'

He was quiet and matter of fact, like a delivery man.

'In here,' I said, holding open the bedroom door. The man hoisted Michael through the hall and dumped him on to the bed, as if he were a sack of coal.

'Well, that's him home safe,' he said, looking me straight in the face. I blushed and glanced quickly away. He had a full black beard, a twinkle in his brown eyes, and smelled faintly of diesel oil.

'Thanks very much,' I mumbled.

'No problem at all,' he said. 'His car is down in the village. Will it be all right?'

He had a deep and interesting voice, exactly right for a black-bearded man. And he was good-looking, in a Spanish sort of way.

'His car's down there as much as it's up here,' I said. 'It'll be grand as it is, and thanks again.'

I felt I shouldn't let him go straight off, and he seemed in no particular hurry. But I couldn't think of a thing to say and nor, apparently, could he, so we stood silently in the hall for a moment.

Then I heard Katie calling me. This brought me back to earth. She was tucked up on the couch in the kitchen, looking at television with J.J. and Jackie.

'Coming.'

I turned to the stranger. 'I must go. She isn't well.'

'Is she yours?' he asked, giving me a surprised look.

'She is. I have five children.'

'That's a good one,' he said. 'You only look about fifteen yourself.'

I was stuck for an answer to this. I didn't really like it when people thought I was young. I wanted to look my age.

'Well, I'd better be off, and let you back to what you were doing,' he said. And with that, he was gone.

Standing there in the hall, I breathed the diesel smell into my lungs as if my life depended on it. Somehow I wanted to stay and let it into my clothes and my hair, and all over me. But then I shook myself and looked into the bedroom. Michael had not moved a muscle since he'd been dropped on the bed. I covered him with a coat from the back of the door, and went down to the children.

They moved close to me. I took Jackie on my lap, Katie slipped herself under one of my arms and J.J. nestled under the other so that we were all entwined. I always loved this snug, warm feeling.

I let my thoughts wander. Who was the man who had brought Michael home? All I knew was that he drove a red Ford Cortina.

The next day, I asked Michael who had brought him home. He had no idea until I mentioned the make of car.

'That's Jack O'Meara. He's just come back from England. Why all the questions?'

He looked me up and down, and then laughed. 'He's a right one for the women, but he wouldn't be bothered with you at all,' he told me with a grin.

Chapter Fifteen

In the end, I did start going into Paddy's pub again. Paddy began to slip me and Michael more and more free drinks, though it seemed he did it only when I was there. Of course Michael was delighted with this and wanted me down early every night. Paddy took a shine to me all right and, when he was walking up the road during the day, he would pull out a large bottle of Guinness from his overalls and slip it to me.

'See you tonight.'

'Sure,' I'd answer. I would sit at the kitchen and drink my stout and the day would pass all the quicker for it. But I could not shift Jack O'Meara from my mind.

Then, one day, I was standing at the sink washing the dishes when I heard a strange car coming down the road. The sound told me it was not local and, the next thing, the red Cortina swept past. Maybe it had slowed down as it passed the house. I could not be sure, but I couldn't stop myself from running out to the gate to see if it had stopped in the village. Yes, there it was, outside the pub. My heart was racing, but my thoughts were even faster. Would he bring Michael home again later? What would I say to him? I must make sure I looked nice.

My God, I thought, what am I doing? I remembered what Michael had said about the man being a womaniser. And here I was, going to wash my hair. I'd cut it myself in what I'd hoped was a curly Audrey Hepburn style. But now I decided to straighten it. I put rollers in and covered them with a scarf, knotting it at the nape of my neck. It suited my face like this, I thought, as I stood at the mirror, dabbing some Ponds Vanishing Cream on my face. Then I got my foundation and put that on lightly, which I had to do because I was trying to save it. Finally I put my blue eye shadow on, which brought out the colour of my eyes, and a little touch of mascara.

It was just past midday and, as the afternoon dragged on, I sipped some port. I was in and out of the house like a woman possessed, checking that the red car was still there. The next thing, Michael came in. It was six o'clock and he had already a good drop taken, but he'd driven home himself. He bent over the fire as he always did, stretching his hands wide in front of it, like a priest saying Mass. I thought bitterly about all the times I had wanted him to come home. I couldn't stay looking at him, so I asked him if I could have the car keys for a few minutes.

'Okay,' he grunted.

I picked Ellen up and caught Philip by the hand.

'Do you want to go for a spin with Mammy?'

'Yes, yes,' Philip shouted, all excitement. So off we went.

I thought I would go as far as Mary's, because to get there I would have to pass the Cortina. I desperately wanted Jack O'Meara to come out and see me with my face made up. But on the way through the village, there was no sign of him.

My face was, of course, the first thing Mary remarked on.

'My God! What's with the glamour?'

'Oh, it's nothing,' I said quickly. 'I was just trying some stuff on, that's all.'

We talked about this and that, then she told me that she was pregnant yet again and was hoping for another little girl. I didn't stay long. I took the children for a short spin. Then, just as we got near the pub, out he stepped. He looked at us and waved. I thought I was going to run into the wall.

Rose's younger sister, Carmel, now baby-sat for me. She didn't have to be paid because they had no television and to look at ours for a couple of hours in the night was payment enough.

Carmel would come up about nine and we'd watch something together until I went down to the pub about half-past ten. I had seen nothing of Jack O'Meara since he'd waved at me, weeks before, but that isn't to say I hadn't thought about him. I did, all the time. If I could have asked someone about him, I would have, but I was afraid there would be talk at my interest in this stranger.

One night, Michael and I were in Paddy's pub when in Jack walked and suddenly I hoped he wouldn't notice me. I wondered how I looked. I could never look good enough for him.

He didn't see me until the crowd started thinning out, and the usual clique was settling down for an after-hours session. I had almost finished my drink when Paddy came over to wipe the table.

'Would ye like to go into the back room?' he said. 'The fire is lit.'

Jack O'Meara was in there before us and, as we went through, he looked steadily in my direction, as if he had been waiting for me. I looked up, our eyes met and he gave me a flash of a smile that made my legs melt. I all but fell over a stool and managed to spill the remains of my Guinness. Oh my God, I thought, he'll think I'm a complete fool.

Immediately he came over, all concern.

'Are you all right?' he asked, his eyes twinkling.

'Yes,' I said, so faintly that I could not even hear it myself. Was he laughing at me? I wondered — a thought that took the silly smile off my face. Right beside the fire was a seat that used to be kept for me; I was a regular by now and I went and sat down. Was I imagining it or was Jack O'Meara watching me? The effect he had on me was something I had never experienced before.

'Well, Michael, how are things?' I heard him say, in that deep voice that I could never mistake for anyone else's.

'Grand, Jack,' said Michael casually. I thought, for God's sake, say more, but he didn't; instead, he stood up and went out to the toilet and, when he came back, he sat away from me. So now I was sitting with an empty seat beside me. Don't let Jack O'Meara sit beside me, I prayed, or I'll pass out!

My prayer was answered almost immediately. He said his goodbyes and left. There seemed to be no point to anything once he was gone, so I went over to Michael and told him I had to go home.

Ellen was still awake and I took her in my arms and hugged her to me. We watched the rest of a programme with Carmel before she left. The fire had gone out, and I was aware of the heat of my baby as I cradled her. She looked up and stopped drinking from her bottle for a second to smile at me.

'Well, you have no worries, thank God,' I told her. 'And I hope you never have mine.'

I became obsessed with looking out for Jack O'Meara. I was going down to Paddy's pub five out of seven nights. I felt guilty about it, but not enough to stop going. For three weeks, I saw no sign of the man. Then one night, when I picked up Michael from the pub, there it was — the red Cortina. I was about to see him again! My heart was pounding, I was sure everyone there would hear it when I went through the door. As soon as my eyes got used to the dim lights, I realised that Jack was dancing with one of the women from the village. I felt like running back out. It was torture to see someone in his arms. Just then, the music stopped and they cleared the floor. I looked around for my husband.

A woman said to me, 'Are you looking for Michael? He's over here.'

She walked me to the bar, where a familiar figure sat slumped at the end of the counter, fast asleep.

I shook his arm. 'Michael!'

Everyone was looking. I felt ashamed and embarrassed, squeezing my eyes shut, forbidding tears. I shook him again. 'Michael!'

The next thing, I heard a voice above the murmuring crowd. 'Do you want a hand with him?'

I turned and said to Jack O'Meara, 'Would you mind?'

'Not at all.'

He lifted him with ease off the high stool. Michael half-woke and began grumbling, but when his feet hit the ground, his legs would not hold him up. A couple of other men came to help and I followed as they half-carried him to the car. There was a great deal of swearing because he was awake now and wanting to go back inside. His father appeared out of the darkness.

'What's going on here?'

'I'm trying to get Michael home,' I said.

'I'll go up with you,' Mr Kelly suggested. But when we turned back, Michael was staggering off towards Paddy's pub.

'Ah, to hell with him,' his father said, walking away.

I wasn't sure what to do. I followed my husband into Paddy's. When I got there, he had already ordered his pint of Guinness. Paddy saw me and he gave me a half-pint of the same. It made me feel bad that there was no offer of money from Michael, that he just took it for granted that it was free. I had no money, but I asked Paddy all the same, 'How much is that?'

'Don't worry your pretty head about it,' he said. 'Enjoy the music.'

The Clancy Brothers were playing there, as they often did.

By then, Michael was slumped on the long seat in the bar, with his pint on the table before him. I stood there, feeling awkward. Then the door opened and in came Jack O'Meara.

'Well, Michael,' he called out. 'Will ye live to fight another day?'

He turned to me and then back to Michael.

'Have one with me. What will ye have?'

Michael went on the shorts; he was too full to drink another pint.

'A Power's Gold Label, and she'll have a small stout,' he said.

Shame and anger surged through me. I didn't want Jack O'Meara seeing me with my drunken husband. And, besides, when Michael was like that, he never put his hand in his pocket. He could sit there all day and let others stand him one drink after another.

'No thanks,' I said. 'I'm going home.'

'Right,' Michael said.

'Are you coming with me?' I asked him.

He shook his head.

'No, it's too early. I'll get a lift.'

I drove home. People were spilling out of the pub as I passed. The gate to the driveway was closed. As I put the handbrake on, someone pulled up behind me and jumped out. Quickly I realised that the gate was being opened for me. It was Jack O'Meara.

'Thanks very much,' I said. I was so scared, it was almost pleasurable; so thrilled to be alone with him, I could not bring myself to look up into his face.

'Do you know, you're always saying thanks?' he said softly.

We were now standing at the side of the car in the privacy offered by the copper beech. I didn't want to move in case he left and went home. Eventually I looked up at him. He had that wonderful smile and I felt this was a time when anything was possible. He caught me by the shoulders and kissed me full on the lips — a short, sharp kiss. He pulled back and looked questioningly at me. There was no smile on his face as he bent and kissed me again. It was a deliberate and serious kiss that lasted a long, long time.

Chapter Sixteen

When Jack O'Meara kissed me that night, it changed my life for ever. I lived just to see him. To know that he was thinking about me was enough to make me happy. I was twenty-seven years old, had been married for eleven years and was the mother of five children.

He pulled up outside the house early in the evening a couple of nights later. From the window, I saw him helping Michael out of the car. I blushed scarlet and didn't know which way to turn. How was I going to face this man, having kissed him? We had not spoken that night. He had just got into his car and driven off. Now I would have to look at him and act normally.

Leaving the children playing in the kitchen, I went to the front door.

'I have a present here for you,' Jack said, looking me in the eye. 'Where do you want him?'

'Would you mind putting him on the bed?' I was now staring at him as I had been longing to do since that kiss. He was as handsome as I had remembered.

He tried coaxing my husband into the bedroom but Michael

was having none of it; he knew the bed would be freezing. So down he went into his usual position in front of the fire.

'What will you do with him now?' Jack asked.

I shrugged. 'If he stays there too long, we'll go to bed — myself and the children.'

'That's a terrible state of affairs.'

'Thanks for bringing him home.'

'Not at all. He asked me to.'

We were standing in the kitchen, facing each other, with my husband on his hunkers in front of the fire, seemingly unaware of anything.

'I feel like I should take him back where I got him,' Jack said.

'Don't worry about it. Would you like a cup of tea?'

'That would be lovely,' he said, sitting down on one of the kitchen chairs.

I made the tea and sat opposite him.

'Where do you come from, if you don't mind me asking?' I tried to make it sound casual.

'Not at all. Myself and my family have come back home from England to make a fresh start.'

'How do you mean?'

'Me and the wife were split up but we got back together again. We thought we might have a better chance here than over there.'

So that was it — he was married.

'I have two children,' he said as if he had read my mind.

'Do you think it will work?' I asked him, and then I could have kicked myself. It was a stupid question.

'Who knows?' he said, giving me a flash of that devilishly handsome smile.

Jack began talking about himself. He was a machine driver and had a couple of JCBs of his own. His father was a big farmer, and lived nearby, but Jack was machine-mad. He was the oldest son and would probably inherit the farm one day, but this did not seem important to him.

'What are you two talking about?' Michael said, rousing himself.

'Nothing,' I said quickly.

'Well, O'Meara, I don't know about you, but I'm off to the pub.' Michael struggled to his feet.

'Sure I'm only after bringing you home to your wife and family, for God's sake, man,' Jack said, looking at me to see what I was going to say.

'Sure you can just bring me back down again now. Never mind her.'

Off they went, Jack saying on the way out, 'Will you be down yourself?'

'I might,' I said.

I did go down — and spent a long time getting ready, washing my hair and carefully putting on my make-up. I had a couple of small stouts before Carmel came to stay with the children. It was near ten o'clock and they were all in bed except Ellen, who was in good form for playing.

I got a warm welcome and a free drink when I went into Paddy's.

'He's in at the fire,' he said.

There were about ten or twelve in the room. Most of them said, 'Good evening.' The musicians were strumming away, getting in tune, and you could tell it was going to be a late night. Michael was slouched in my chair at the fire.

'Let her in there, Michael,' Paddy said.

'She's all right where she is,' Michael replied. I sat down on the nearest seat, and then I saw Jack coming in. A wave of delight ran through me. He gave me a big smile and started to come over, which was when I realised he was drunk too. A neurotic fear took hold of me. How would he be when he was drunk?

But when I had downed a few more drinks, I didn't care how he would be. Every time I looked at him, he gave me a wink. Then I noticed Mr Kelly watching us.

Oh my God, I thought, what will he think? I finished my drink quickly and left.

When Jack passed the house in the daytime, he would beep the horn. Sometimes he would stop, and I would sit in his car and we would talk about our lives and families. When I think back on the insanity of it all, I cringe. My thoughts and feelings were not rational at that time. I was so jealous of his wife: I longed to be her, the mother of his children, never thinking of her hurt and pain. I genuinely believed that I should be able to have what ever it was that I wanted at this hour in my life. To have my children and Jack's and live as one big happy family was one of my favourite fantasies. I would sit and drink and dream every chance I got.

I became so desperate to see him that I didn't care what I did, or who knew about us. One night in the pub, Jack asked me to dance, which was like a dream come true. We did a slow waltz, with everyone in the pub watching. Tongues were soon wagging.

'There's something going on between them two,' people in the pub would say, just loud enough for me to hear.

'His car is around Michael Kelly's a lot. You wouldn't know what's going on, but you can be sure it's nothing good.' Jack did come into the house when he brought Michael home, but never came in on his own.

I was mad about him, but I did not know how Jack felt about me until one night at the front door after Michael had fallen asleep.

'When God made angels, it's a wonder he didn't keep you for himself.'

Nobody had ever said anything so lovely to me before. He would say things such as, 'Every time I close my eyes, I can see your face.' Every word he uttered, I would relive again and again in my head.

J.J. was eleven. He stayed at Kellys' most nights now, but he would come home for his dinner. I knew they were keeping an eye on me.

'You're going out a lot, aren't you?' Mr Kelly remarked one day.

That really stung me and I thought: why does he not say this to his son? I stopped going out again after that and, when Jack brought Michael home a few nights later, he asked me what was wrong. When I told him what Mr Kelly had said, Jack looked at me hard.

'I have to see you. Walk over the road about nine o'clock. I'll wait by the bridge.'

The bridge was only a couple of minutes' walk from our house; it came before a cluster of narrow lanes that in springtime were covered in bluebells, primroses and buttercups.

On this particular night it was inky black. I was trembling as I hurried along the deserted road. Then I saw his car. I thought: he must love me to do this. It felt strange getting into his car in the dark of the night. But after we had met a few times, we made love. My life until now had completely lacked affection. I could not get close enough to this man; every minute that we were not physically joined was a waste of time. He became an obsession.

I seldom went to the village in the daytime now. I could not face the whispering. J.J. and Katie did the shopping for me. Meanwhile, the lads in the pub would joke with Jack: 'I see your car in some quare places lately, O'Meara.'

He told me what was said and we decided to meet every second evening; other nights we would write letters to each other and put them in a jar under the hedge in front of the house. I had hundreds of letters from Jack, and he had hundreds from me.

Paddy from the pub called me out to the gate one evening as he went for his stroll.

'First I must give you something,' he said, handing me a naggin of vodka.

'Thanks. I'll enjoy that.'

I turned to take it inside before anyone passed by, but he called after me. 'Don't you let anyone stop you doing what you want to do. There's more people at it than you around here.'

'Thanks for saying that; sure I know there are.' This remark made me feel slightly better about myself and Jack.

But Mr Kelly was angry. He would call to the house now and look all around it, even going up into the bedrooms. I thought if anyone knew how bad our marriage was, it would be Mr Kelly.

Geraldine said that her husband suspected that something was going on and had told her she should stay away from me.

'And what about my father?' I asked her.

'Well, he drinks with Jack O'Meara. He knows everything that's going on.'

So it was all right for her husband and my father to drink with Jack, but she was to stay away from her own sister.

My father never came near me. I desperately needed him to say that I deserved to be happy with someone who loved me. In fact, I was more unhappy than ever now. I could not stand my husband touching me at all.

Our problems were getting worse. Jack and I decided we would stop seeing each other. He said to me, 'You would never leave your children and come away with me. You love them too much.'

I agreed with him and we cried in each other's arms that night.

I got out of his car. How was I going to live without him? My heart was brimming over with hopelessness and despair as I went home and sat with my children for comfort. Eventually I put the children to bed, except Ellen. Then I got out my vodka, turned off the television and sat there. I needed alcohol to get me through almost everything now, day and night.

Jack did not pass by the house any more.

It was two weeks since we had made the decision not to meet and, instead of getting easier, every day was worse. I was just about functioning for the children's sake. Every chance I got, I would sit sipping my drink and thinking of all the times Michael had told me that no one else would be bothered with me. Was it true? To reassure myself, I re-read Jack's letters. A man like him would not write those things unless he meant them. Tears ran down the sides of my nose; surely he would not have gone to all that trouble to see just any woman?

Then Michael came up from the pub one evening and said, 'O'Meara is gone to hell on the drink. He's drunk morning, noon and night.'

He must be in a bad state for you to notice, I thought. I also wondered why Michael had mentioned this to me, since he never told me anything that went on in the pub. Jack must be heartbroken too. He was making sure he was drunk all the time.

Three weeks later, Jack brought Michael home from the pub around midnight. I was sitting on the couch, with Ellen crawling all over me, wearing an old candlewick dressing gown and not a scrap of make-up. Hearing the sound of the Cortina coming up the road, I was paralysed. Then I could hear their voices, as Jack tried to get Michael out of the car. I told myself to let them at it. Jack might not come in at all. Then they were in the hall. I stayed on the couch with the baby. When they came into the kitchen, I looked up at Jack and the expression on his face was terrifying. His eyes were as black as soot.

'You knew I would come in eventually, didn't you?' he said in a low voice.

Michael was swaying in front of the fire and I could not make out what state of consciousness he was in. Putting my fingers to my lips, I stood up to take Ellen into her cot in the bedroom. Then I beckoned Jack to the front door. We stood looking at each other without speaking. He seemed to be fuming. In the end, he said, 'I meant what I said inside. You knew I'd come in.'

I looked him directly in the eye. 'I thought it was over between us. This is no game to me and that's the truth.'

'How could it be? I love you.' He pulled me into his arms.

In my recollection this was the first time anyone had ever said that they loved me. My heart swelled from the sheer joy of those words. We stayed out on the steps until four in the morning, in between me making bottles for Ellen and checking on Michael, who spent most of the night sprawled out on the floor. We talked about our feelings for each other, how life was not worth living unless we could meet. Jack said that he could not sleep, eat or work when he was not seeing me. It was why he was drunk all the time. We decided to start meeting at the bridge again, and an odd night I would go to the pub and we would have one or two dances. We both felt happy with this and thought people would soon get tired of talking. As Paddy said, there were more people than us having affairs.

I hoped this would satisfy me and I would not be living just for the time I could be with Jack. I wanted to enjoy my children like I had before.

I was not sure what game my husband was playing. One evening, he was at home when we both heard the Cortina coming up the road. I was dying to look out and get a glimpse of Jack. When it had passed, Michael started laughing. 'How did you stop yourself from looking out at O'Meara?' he said.

Jack could never understand Michael leaving us without firewood or coal. One Saturday, he brought us down a tractor-load of wood, cutting it up with a chainsaw so that it was small enough to fit in the fireplace. Michael never mentioned it.

One morning, Jack called to take Michael to pick up his car from wherever he'd left it the night before. I gave them both a cup of tea, which must have been a first for Michael; he never drank tea. As I went over to the table to pour it, Michael said to Jack, 'You should have seen her this morning, O'Meara.'

Jack went white and I stiffened. I knew nothing had happened, but who could tell what Michael would say? Holding my breath, I turned my back on them. Michael carried on. 'I was getting out of the bed and I pulled the blanket with me; well, she went berserk. She thought I saw a bit of her bare skin. I'm married to that woman over ten years and I have never seen her naked yet. What do you make of that?'

What a conversation, and what a person to have it with! It was perfectly true, though. I looked over at Jack to see how he was taking this. He seemed okay. The colour was back in his face. Will they ever go? I wondered; why is Michael sitting there? He normally gets up and is straight out the door. He must know something; he's laughing at me, tormenting us.

Jack and I had our signals. If the curtains were pulled in the kitchen, it was not safe for him to come to the front door. When they were open, he would knock gently on the kitchen window and I would go out to him. The arrangement worked well until one night when Jack was walking up to the window he sensed that there was someone behind him. He turned quickly as a man with something held up over his head came from the shadows. Jack caught the thing and threw it with all his strength into the next field. The man lunged at him. Jack hit him right in the eye. I opened the front door and saw Mr Kelly lying in the middle of the path, blood streaming down his face. I ran to help him to his feet. He gave me a look that would shrivel you. I said, 'I'm sorry.'

Jack jumped in. 'What are you sorry for?' he said. 'This bastard was trying to kill me. He had a garden rake and was just about to bring it down on my head.'

'I'll get you yet,' Mr Kelly said over his shoulder as he went down the road. The next day, he came up to show me his black eye.

'I'm sorry,' I said once more. It was the only thing I could think of.

This incident was the talk of the village, but Michael never reacted to that either.

Jack and I carried on meeting until one evening when he came down to say his wife had found a bundle of my letters under the seat of his car.

'I'm such a fool,' he said. 'But I couldn't throw them away. They were all that kept me going when we didn't meet.'

'Is she very upset?'

'She is.' He had a faraway look in his eyes. 'I don't think it would ever have worked for me and her, even if I had never met you. There was too much damage done already.'

Chapter Seventeen

'How do you stay sane?' Mary asked me. I'd gone over to her one evening and told her about the awful things that were happening: the incident with Mr Kelly, and Jack's wife finding my letters.

'What do you think is going on with Michael?' I asked, without answering her question.

'I don't care about him. I'm more interested in what you're going to do.'

I thought for a minute.

'I would love to know if Michael knows about us and just doesn't care.'

'Why worry over him? He doesn't give a damn about you or the children.'

I could hear her frustration. She could not understand my guilt, or that I didn't want to hurt Michael. No matter how much he ignored me or what humiliations he had imposed on me, I could not bring myself to inflict deliberate pain on Michael, but I did think that perhaps he would be killed in a car crash when he was very drunk, and not feel anything. What was happening to me? How could I think such a thing?

Then I took the plunge.

'Jack has asked me to go to England with him.'

'Well, would you?'

'I don't know. If it was only me, I'd go in the morning, but the children — five of them...'

'Yes,' she said thoughtfully.

'If you and Geraldine would look after them for a couple of weeks until we got some place to live, then I could bring them over and make a fresh start.'

'I would take two,' she said.

'Thanks.' I felt sick at the thought. 'I can't talk about it any more now, but thanks.'

I told Jack about the conversation and said I was thinking about it.

In bed that night, I could not rest; my whole life was tearing at me. I prayed to God to direct me and give me some peace of mind. The drink was not working for me any more. My head was full of madness. I used to think to myself that J.J. could stay with his grandparents because he was practically living there already, and they thought the world of him. In my desperate need to justify my thoughts and actions, I would even feel a certain anger that he had abandoned me for the Kellys.

Geraldine said she would take Ellen and Katie, which left Jackie and Philip for Mary. And it would only be for a couple of weeks. Sometimes it seemed quite rational and I would be convinced that it was the right thing and that indeed I must do it, to give my children a better life away from all this madness. At other times, I would jump out of the bed and get violently sick with dread and fear at the thought of it.

Weeks later, at around two in the morning, Jack and I were standing on the top step of the house when we heard footsteps coming up the road.

'Get in behind the front door, quick!' I whispered, thinking it was someone going home late from the pub. Nothing unusual in that, but they had enough to gossip about without seeing us outside our door at that time of night.

There was not a sound in the house, and it was in darkness. Michael had been in bed since twelve and the children were asleep. The next thing I heard was the front gate opening and someone walking up the path. The steps were brisk. My heart was pounding as the door was pushed in against our bodies. We flattened ourselves against the wall.

'I know you're there. Come out and face me.'

It was Mrs Kelly.

I did what she told me to do. I came out from behind the door. She was red with anger and loathing. She caught Jack by the arm, moving him into the kitchen. I followed them in. She stood between us with her back to me.

'Why don't you go home to your family like a good man? It's not worth losing them over this one: she's only a tramp. Your father is a respectable man. What would he say if he knew about this carry-on?'

Neither Jack nor I said a word. He was calmly standing there. I wanted him to react, to defend me. I felt degraded that he was witnessing her onslaught on me. She started up again. 'She's no good. She's a whore.'

Then I noticed Mr Kelly standing in the hallway. 'Are you all right?' he asked his wife.

'I will be when this good man goes to his home,' she said. 'I'm not leaving my house until he does.' She crossed her arms defiantly.

'Where's Michael?' Mr Kelly asked, walking towards the bedroom where his son was dead to the world. He looked in at him and shook his head in despair at the sight of him. Then he protectively closed the door.

Suddenly Jack walked out without a word. Mrs Kelly looked frustrated. I wanted to scream after him, but more than anything I wanted the Kellys to place some of the blame for this mayhem on Michael's shoulders. I was dying to say, 'What do you think of your precious son in all this mess?' If I had only had the courage.

Mrs Kelly went up to the bedroom; seconds later, she came down, looking defeated, and then she flounced out the front door. I stood there, fighting back tears of defeat. I could hear her footsteps fading away down the road, her husband struggling to keep up with her.

The next thing I saw was Jack climbing over the gate across the road.

'Are you all right?' he asked me.

'I'm okay. Do you believe the things she said about me?'

'If I did, would I be here?' He was smiling. 'I'm going now in case she comes back. I'll see you tomorrow night.' He kissed me on the cheek. I wanted to grab him and never let him go.

I made a brave attempt to stand up to Mrs Kelly a couple of weeks later. There was a knock on the door early one night and I went out to find Ritchie, a neighbour, trying to keep Michael upright.

'Hello, missus. Sorry to bother you, but Michael ran into the ditch up the road there. He's not badly hurt as far as I can see, but the car is a write-off.' I looked at Michael lurching all over the place. I was suddenly aware of my beating heart, as I said, 'Let him go.' He looked at me in surprise.

'Are you sure, missus?'

'Yes,' I told him positively. My husband fell to the ground with a thud, as we both knew he would. Ritchie bent to pick him up.

'Leave him. Would you do me a favour? Call into the shop and tell Mrs Kelly to come up here now.'

'Of course I will.'

He ran out to the gate backwards, still looking at me with terror in his eyes. There I was, standing over this man who was now snoring his head off, on the doorstep. Ritchie took off in his car like a rocket.

The children were looking at television; this was normal behaviour for their father as far as they were concerned. Within five minutes, the Kellys arrived. Mrs Kelly ran up the path, all hustle and bustle.

'What do you want me to do with him?' I asked, pointing at her son on the top step. I felt a frantic nervous strength in me, a feeling of being in control. She was struggling to say something that would put me back in my place. She gave up; instead she battled to lift Michael.

'Give me a hand,' she said to Mr Kelly. Between the two of them, they got his dead weight on to our bed and covered him. I stood at the bedroom door, silently looking at them performing what they no doubt considered to be my job.

As they continued to fuss over him, I said, 'I want a doctor to examine him, and then I want him out of here. I'm not looking after him any more.' She was about to self-combust, and once more she turned her back on me. I walked around and stood in front of her. We looked at each other with nothing but pure hatred between us. Then I dared to say what I was thinking.

'You look after your wonderful son for a while and see how you like it.'

She was at a loss for words; she could not gather herself at all. Mr Kelly escaped to get the doctor and I went to the children. Michael's snores were echoing around the house.

The doctor came eventually. Just as I approached the room to hear what he had to say, Mrs Kelly closed the door in my face. Firmly I opened it and went in. 'Michael needs rest', the doctor was saying. I gave a sarcastic laugh.

'He is not going to rest here,' I said to the three of them. 'His mother can bring him down to her house and look after him.'

Mrs Kelly looked confused. She pulled herself up to her full five feet, hands on hips. 'I will have you know that this is my house, and you won't put anyone out of it, especially not my son.' She took a deep breath and continued, 'You are nothing short of a tramp.'

The doctor didn't know where to look and Michael was

unaware of it all. The Kellys walked the doctor to the gate, then got into their car and left.

The next morning, Michael wanted to know what had happened, because he was bruised and swollen all over. I told him to go and ask his mother or father.

'Where's my car?'

'You can ask them that at the same time.'

A couple of days later, Michael was driving around in his father's new Ford Escort. And he was still living with the children and me.

One night, he asked me to drive him into Callan. He wanted to meet someone and have a drink, but he was afraid of getting caught by the guards

'We'll have to go the back road,' he told me. 'If my father hears that you're driving his car, he'll go mad.'

'I don't want to drive it.'

But in the end I did, just to get rid of him.

'I'll get a lift home,' he said. 'Leave the car outside the pub when you get back. My father will think I'm in there.'

'Any more orders?' I asked him, but I did what he had told me to do.

Later on that night, our next-door neighbour called to say that Michael had rung to ask if I would go and pick him up. I would have to get Carmel to stay with the children and Jack would be calling. It was half-past ten. I thought if he came home with me straight away, I would be back in time. Driving his father's car made me nervous and I hated the back roads. But I got there just before official closing time.

Michael was at the far end of the bar talking to a woman.

'Hello,' I said as I approached them.

She said 'Hello' back.

'This is the wife,' Michael said. 'What do you want to drink?'

'Nothing,' I said.

'Why not?'

'Well, I'm driving, aren't I?' Something that usually didn't bother me.

'This is Sarah,' he told me with pride in his voice. Sarah and I shook hands and I agreed to have one small stout. She was drinking gin and orange. It was one in the morning when I got Michael to leave, he was so busy flirting with her.

It was a winter's night. I had to scrape the frost off the windscreen so I could see. As we left the pub, one of the men said, 'Drive carefully. The roads are treacherous.'

Michael was very quiet. He put his feet up on the dashboard and made himself comfortable. We were outside the town when he started to snore; the next thing, he slipped. I thought the door was opening and he was falling out: I tried to catch him and lost control of the wheel. The car turned over and over and ended up on its roof.

My next memory is of being trapped inside and Michael standing on the road. I could hear a woman saying, 'I'm a nurse. Is she conscious?'

'Help me, please,' I said. At last the doctor came and said, 'Get her out now in case the car goes on fire.'

I would not go to hospital. I had to get home to my children. The doctor took me to his surgery. He spent a long time scraping the glass from my jaw bone, and then he had to stitch me. I had gone through the windscreen. It seemed as if my whole face were cut to pieces. My legs were badly bruised, too. There was not a scratch on Michael.

The next morning, the children were afraid to look at me. Michael got up and walked to the pub. His father's car was beyond repair. Carmel stayed with me.

I decided to tell her about Jack. 'You're not telling me anything I don't already know,' she said. 'Everyone knows.'

She went and looked in the usual place for a letter. There was a note saying, 'See you tonight, love Jack.'

Later in the day, I heard the Cortina coming down the road.

It pulled up at the gate. Jack ran in and asked Carmel where I was.

Carmel pointed to the bedroom. He stormed into the room, saying, 'That bastard Michael walked into the pub and said, "You can have her now, O'Meara. Her face is gone. You're welcome to her".'

Chapter Eighteen

Michael had known about us all along, but he chose this moment to admit it and to let me go. Jack had his permission to take me now and it had been given deliberately. Apparently, he had got one of the lads from the pub to drive him around until he found Jack.

'Now will you think seriously about going away with me?' Jack asked. 'We could go to London. I know plenty of people there and I'll have no problem getting work and a place to live.'

I started to cry.

Jack was on his knees by the side of the bed, holding my bandaged hand. It was too hard to think about leaving my children, even for a minute. Through the tears, I said, 'I will have to do something. I can't go on like this.'

He said he would call in and see me the next day.

When Michael came home that night, he was so drunk, he just fell in the hall and stayed there.

Carmel came up in the morning to get the children ready for school and to look after Ellen. When they were gone, she made me some toast and sat on the side of the bed, her eyes full of pity.

'They're saying terrible things about you in the village.'

'What kind of things?'

'That you were trying to push Michael out of the car to kill him. That's how the accident happened.' How could anyone have said such a thing? This was the end.

Jack came that night. He parked at the gate; there was no need for any more hiding.

'They all know now,' he said.

I told him I had my mind made up: we could leave as soon as I was able. I asked him if he was sure that he loved me enough to go away with me, not knowing what my face was going to be like. He assured me that he did, and always would. He had brought me a half-bottle of whiskey and I immediately had some.

He left, and, when the children were asleep and the house quiet, except for two-year-old Ellen chatting away to herself in her cot, I made myself get out of the bed. The drink had made me brave and had deadened my physical pain. I went up and looked at my sleeping children and prayed, 'Dear God, help me.' I ran my fingers through J.J.'s curls. My firstborn was twelve now. He made a little noise like a cat purring. He is content, I thought to myself. I went up to the girls' room. Katie with her big, long, dark lashes like spiders on her cheeks. Jackie's blonde hair on the pillow; she was like a Swedish child. Philip was in bed with me, not caring what my face was like because he knew I was still his Mammy. There are no words strong enough to describe how I felt or how my heart ached that night. I remembered my own mother. Did she go through this pain every time she had to leave me?

Getting back into bed with Philip, I looked at his lovely fair hair. He moved closer and I could feel his little warm body nestled beside me. Ellen was standing up in her cot, her golden hair shining, green eyes flashing with devilment. I reached over, picked her up and tried to cuddle her but, like J.J. when he was little, she was too busy for cuddles. She wriggled around in my arms and I had to put her back. She returned to her play world, perfectly happy.

I wondered where Michael was. What pub was he in? Would he ever know what it was like to hold his own flesh and blood in his arms? That feeling of contentment and achievement, knowing that this child was part of you.

As I lay there, it occurred to me to try to talk to Michael and ask him if he would leave the house himself, and let the children and me stay together. It would mean that we would not have to be parted from each other at all. The more I thought about it, the better the idea seemed. Even the thought of Mrs Kelly didn't bother me. The next question was: when would he be sober enough to listen? I made up my mind that I was going to stay awake, and put it to him.

Jack came back later that night and I told him about my plan. He didn't think Michael would agree to it and thought I was changing my mind about going with him, but I had to try everything. I didn't want to leave my children for a minute if I could help it. Jack told me he had a buyer for his JCB, that he wanted to leave enough money to keep his family going, until we got sorted. Then he would send some more. I got out of bed again. Just then, we heard footsteps coming to the front door and held our breath. It was Michael. In he came and eyed us up and down. Jack and I were standing beside each other at the kitchen sink. I could not hold back any longer.

'Michael, I can't live with you any more. I was thinking, would you leave and let me and the children stay here?'

I moved closer to Jack and put my hand in his.

'Jack and I love each other and want to be together.'

Michael bellowed, 'You are going nowhere, do you hear me? And neither am I.'

'But you said in front of everyone in the pub that Jack could have me now.'

'Neither of us is going anywhere,' he hissed.

'Yes, I am! You don't own me.'

'We'll see about that,' he jeered. 'You'll never see them children again if you go.'

'I'm taking them with me; you can't stop me. They're mine. You never cared about them.'

With that, he went up to the room, took Philip out of bed and went out the front door with him in his arms.

'Bring in the child, for God's sake! He'll catch his death.' I tried to go down the steps after them in my long nightdress and with my bandaged legs.

'He'll come back, don't you worry,' Jack said, bringing me into the kitchen. And after a couple of minutes, he did, with Philip crying in his arms. I took the child and soothed him.

Michael looked at me. 'That's what will happen if you don't stop all this carry-on. Go home, O'Meara, before I kill you.'

I indicated to Jack to go, and he went.

'Michael, will you sit down and talk to me?' I asked.

'What the hell good will that do?'

'We have to do something. I can't bear this any more. It's driving me insane.'

'Don't be so stupid. I'm going to bed. You should grow up.'

And off he went.

From then on, he watched me like a hawk. He never went to work, just sat at the kitchen table with a bottle of whiskey. I was determined not to grab the bottle and join him, even though it might stop the constant churning of thoughts in my head. I wanted to scream at him, tell him about the pain and rage that lurked beneath and was sapping all my energy. I was aware that I was in no fit state mentally or physically to care for my children.

I had left a letter in the usual place for Jack, asking him to stay away for a while. My bandages were coming off slowly. I had one long scar on the right side of my face, just under my jawbone. The rest of my face and head were full of cuts, some worse than others.

Sometimes Michael would want to talk, but his way of

thinking was so far removed from mine. He saw me as his property; he truly believed that if he said no to anything I wanted to do, that meant I couldn't or wouldn't do it. He never thought that I had a mind of my own, dreams of my own; he thought I was simply his.

During one of these conversations, he asked me if I'd go out for a day with him, just the two of us.

'Why?'

'We can talk in peace,' he said, smiling. 'And you can decide if you still want to run away with O'Meara.'

I had nothing to lose. I wanted to try everything.

'Okay,' I said wearily. 'I'll go. Do you know this is the first time you've ever asked me out since we got married?'

'You see, I'm not all bad.'

I ached with sadness for him.

About two weeks later, the day came when I felt strong enough to go for our heart-to-heart. My face was still grotesque, but that was the least of my worries.

Geraldine took the children.

Michael said he knew a pub that had an open fire lit all day. We sat there, me with a small stout, Michael with a pint and a whiskey.

'Don't get drunk, please,' I begged him.

'You're not still thinking of going away with O'Meara, are ye?' he asked, breaking into my thoughts. No matter how I felt about Michael, I did not want to cause him pain deliberately, but sometimes there is no level path leading up to what has to be said. I was determined to be honest, even though I knew it would hurt us both.

'Yes, I am,' I said quietly. Michael had his drinks finished, so I gulped mine down and he went to the bar and got the same again. I was not sure if he'd heard my answer or had chosen not to. He chatted with the barman about the weather for a few minutes. How could he act so normally when I was sick to my guts?

'What are you thinking of?' I asked when he came back.
'Nothing.'

I was getting irritable. 'If you think I'm going to go out with you and sit in a pub all day, you can think again,' I said.

'You know your problem? You're never satisfied. If I take you out, I'm wrong, and if I don't, I'm still wrong.'

'I don't want to stay here all day and that's that.'

'If you were with O'Meara, you'd sit here all day,' he said, eyes as still as stone.

'Yes, I would, and that's the difference, you see.'

He downed his drinks in one and went to the bar again. After several shorts, he returned. He handed me a stout, and looked me right in the eye. 'Do you really think that O'Meara will be bothered with you, and your face like that?' he said.

I took a deep breath. For the first time ever, I felt I had his undivided attention.

'Yes, I really do think he will,' I told him with great certainty. 'And you told him he could have me.'

'You know that I only said that. I didn't mean it.'

'I believe you said it to hurt me, and because you thought he didn't care enough about me to take me with my face like this. But you can't harm me like that any more because you don't have that power over me any longer.'

We sat there, glaring at each other.

Sitting in the corner was an old man contentedly sipping his pint of Guinness and making no attempt to hide his curiosity. Every couple of minutes, he would rearrange himself in his seat, to get a little closer to us.

Then his pal came in, a man about the same age, which appeared to be around ninety.

'How the bloody hell are you, Ned?' the man asked.

'Can't complain, Pat. Whisht now, there's some crack going on here with these two,' he replied, rubbing his hands with glee. Then he loudly related every word we had said.

I stood up.

'I'm going. I've had enough of this madness,' I said. I left and stood at the car door until Michael came out.

'What the devil is wrong with you now?'

'I want to go home. This is a waste of time.'

'We'll have one more drink first. Come on, there's a nice quiet pub nearby. We can leave the car here.'

He was off around the corner, and me after him. But when we got to the other pub, his mood had changed.

'You're telling me you want me to leave the house, so that you can meet O'Meara whenever you like. Is that what you want?'

'Yes. I want to be honest with you, like you are with me about the women you see.'

'Well, you'd better think again,' he said sharply. 'Because I will never let that happen as long as I live. So are you going to settle down and behave yourself or what?'

I heard myself say, 'Yes I am.'

He looked at me with a smile. 'Good girl. Now we'll have a proper drink.'

I could have screamed. What had I said? Michael went up to the counter and got two large whiskeys. Smiling triumphantly, he placed them on our table.

I played along. When he said we would go away together for weekends, just the two of us, I agreed with him. Our children were not in his plan at all, but then they never had been. Michael would believe whatever he wanted to, no matter what was staring him in the face, and I knew of no way to get through to him.

We were both drunk when we got back home; and I was disgusted with myself. He drove me to pick up the children at Geraldine's. I whispered to her that I definitely had to leave Michael. When we got home, Michael went to the pub. I was glad. I needed time to myself. I carelessly gave the children their tea and put them to bed.

Totally dejected, I sat down with my whiskey. By now I was

drinking a lot of spirits: whiskey, vodka, whatever I could lay my hands on. It deadened my fears and helped me to think. There was a terror in me that I did not want to surface. Perhaps I was meant to be with Michael, though I couldn't even tolerate the thought. I knew I had to get out or go mad.

In Michael's mind, everything was as usual; there was no way he was going anywhere. I knew that for a fact. So I would have to leave Michael, my sisters were going to look after the children until I got organised, and then, after a few weeks, I would come back to Ireland for them. We would work out a whole new life together in a different country with people who knew nothing about us; who thought I was capable of pushing Michael out of a moving car. I would have a man I loved by my side. We would go places and do things together; it would be heaven. As I sat there, one minute I was full of hope, the next I was heartbroken. How would I live until I actually had the children with me?

When I allowed myself to think about Jack's wife, I would rationalise everything to myself. She must have known that it was over between them. A woman does. Naively, I thought his children would have their mother and what more could they want? God knows, my own children never seemed to have any feelings about their father.

Jack came down that night around nine, bringing me a Baby Powers. He asked how the day had gone. I told him that Michael thought everything was back to normal.

'I have to go. I can't stay here any longer,' I said. 'Are you sure it's what you want?'

'You know it is,' he said.

We put whatever clothes I had that were any good in his car. I had to believe that things were going to be better from now on or I would come asunder.

We planned to go the next day so that I would not have too much time to think. As Jack said, the sooner we left, the sooner we would be fixed up. Then I could send for the children.

When he left, I had to have more drink to collect myself. I

wanted to take all the children into bed with me and hug them to bits. How was I going to live without them, even for one day? I had to try to believe I was doing the right thing, but the more I thought about it, the less it seemed like the right thing. It was so wrong for the mother I wanted to be to do this.

Chapter Nineteen

When the four oldest went to school, I put Ellen in her pushchair, much against her will, and started out. I took a drink from the quarter bottle of vodka in my shopping bag to give me the courage to walk through the village.

I went to Mary first and told her that Jack and I were leaving that evening. She wished me well and we arranged that I would ring her at a nearby phone box that night at eight, to see how everything was; she had no phone herself. This was another problem: because Mrs Kelly manned the telephone exchange, she heard every call that went through her switchboard.

I walked back by the school and could see the heads of the children, including mine, sitting at their desks. I started running, past the church where I had got married, past Kelly's shop — I would never have to ask her for anything again — and I did not stop until I got to my father's house where Geraldine was living. She was feeding her baby.

'This is a surprise,' she said. 'I don't usually see you this early.'

'I know, but I'm going away today, with Jack. I don't want to think about it any longer. I just want to get it over with.'

'Sure, you have no life with Michael. Tell Katie to bring Ellen down after school.'

'Will it cause problems for you?' I asked, remembering that her husband didn't approve of me and might be angry. 'I'll get sorted out as quickly as I can.'

'You can only do your best,' she said. 'Don't worry about me.'

We parted before we got emotional. It all seemed so unreal. I took another swig from my bottle and thought: I have looked after my younger sister for years and this is her way of repaying me.

The children came home from school and I wondered why I hadn't told them to go straight to my sisters' homes. Looking at them sitting at the table, eating and chatting, I wanted so much to be able to tell them what I was going to do, and to say I would be back for them in a short time. But I didn't have the courage to see their pain, and so I said nothing. I handed them over to God, and to my sisters, to look after until I saw them again. I promised myself that it would be a few weeks at the most. The children went without question to Mary's and to Geraldine's, and J.J. to Kellys', and I was on my own. Pouring myself another drink, I stared out the back window, imagining myself, at seventeen, hanging out the endless washing, digging the potatoes for the dinner, and I remembered the baby I had miscarried at the clothesline. Did anyone care about me or that baby? I seemed to get strength from this feeling of abandonment. Then I went around and touched the children's beds, picked up their pillows, hugged them to me, breathing in their smell. It was as if someone had reached inside and pulled out my guts.

I heard the Cortina coming. It was early. I ran out to the gate. 'Thank God you're here,' I said to Jack. 'I felt I wasn't going to be able to go.'

'I knew that would happen. Get in.'

I grabbed a few things, shoved them in an old suitcase, and didn't look back. Jack turned the car so that we wouldn't have to go through the village. He drove to the station in Kilkenny, where we left the car with the keys in the ignition. We were just in time for the train to Dublin.

I rang Mary at eight on the dot. She had had a terrible job getting to the phone, and then we had to be careful what we said. The whole village was watching her and they knew already that I had gone away with Jack. I told her I didn't care about them, only about my children.

'They're not too bad,' she said. 'I told them you'll be back for them in a couple of weeks.'

'Thank God.'

We arranged that I would ring her two nights later; it seemed like a hundred years away.

Jack and I booked into the Ashton Hotel in Dublin and went to the bar. We were able to sit together and hold hands. Amid all my emotions of pain and sadness, I had the feeling of being loved by this man. Here I was with my face and body scarred, and he wanted me regardless, and told me so. After a good few drinks, we went to bed and fell asleep in each other's arms.

The next morning, when I awoke, I was hit by a powerful panic at the thought of my children going to school from three different houses. My God, what had I done? I didn't deserve happiness. I must get away this instant and start looking for a house for us, for schools, and for a job for myself. What kind of job could I do? I was not qualified for anything. I could look after children maybe, do housework, things like that. When I started to think about practical matters, I felt better, but it was almost impossible to keep my mind on the future.

I cannot remember one thing about how we got to London except that we ended up at a B&B in Shepherd's Bush.

'You're coming back to yourself,' Jack said.

'What do you mean?

'You've been out of it. I've had to lead you around by the hand.'

I rang Mary again at the agreed time. She assured me that the children were all right. They were going to school and eating. I tried to feel relieved but inside I was pining for them. Michael was staying at his mother's, and he had my sisters driven mad, asking where I was. He knew that I was ringing them. We agreed to change to a different phone box in the next village about five miles away. This meant that I could not ring as often as I'd have liked, because Mary would have to get there. I told her I would give her my address as soon as I had one, and we could chance writing to each other. By the time the call was over, I had a knot of pure pain in my chest.

We were in the B&B for about four days. Jack bought a car for a couple of hundred pounds to get us around. We went to a pub where he used to drink before he had returned to Ireland. Nearly everyone in there knew him. The landlady, a flashy blonde, was being very friendly with Jack. I was so jealous of her knowing him, I couldn't hide it. I asked him to sit down with me at one of the tables, but he said he preferred to stand. I felt lost.

After a couple of gins and tonic, I started to listen to the band. I loved the sound of the reggae music they were playing. They stopped for a break and one of the singers came over because he knew Jack. Jack introduced me and then returned to talk to his other friends. The band started to play again. The song was 'I Can See Clearly Now' and, as it went on, the man said to me: 'You're a very sad young woman.'

'How do you know?'

'By looking at you. So can you see clearly now?'

'Not really. I just got a flash of something.' It was of myself sitting in this pub, my children so far away in Ireland, Jack not paying me any attention. Then I heard Jack talking to a man about somewhere for us to live. He was a big Irishman called Billy, in his early thirties; he had a couple of houses and, yes, he would fix us up.

The following day, we moved into All Souls Avenue, off the

Harrow Road in west London, where Billy lived on his own. He had a girlfriend called May and they were thinking of getting married.

This house had everything: carpets, a vacuum cleaner and electrical gadgets of all sorts. And it had central heating and a bathroom. My children would think they were in heaven if they lived in such a house.

Jack got a job straight away, driving a JCB. May had her own place but sometimes stayed at Billy's at the weekend, and she and I would chat. I told her the truth about my children and it felt good to talk to another woman. It was May who told me that Sainsbury's in Kilburn was looking for staff, and how to get there by train. I knew I had to learn to find my own way around or I would end up as I had been when J.J. was born, afraid to go anywhere. So I found Kensal Green station and got the train to Kilburn High Road, asking there for Sainsbury's.

God be with me, I said to myself as I went in the door. I asked a girl in uniform if they were looking for staff. She said she didn't know, but just then a middle-aged man came by.

'My name is Mr Doyle,' he said, putting out his hand to shake mine. I thought he had a kind face. 'Would you like to work on the tills?'

'I don't know much about handling money. I'm just after coming over from Ireland and I've had very little to do with cash.'

'Okay, I'll find you something else.'

I followed him as he went through a pair of plastic swing doors. Two women were sitting at a table, weighing all sorts of fruit and vegetables. They smiled at me.

'Betty and Flo will show you what to do,' said Mr Doyle, 'if you would like to work in here.'

I could not believe it. I had a job in the first place I'd tried. So I was not useless after all.

'I would love to. Thank you so much. I won't let you down.'

'You can start on Monday.'

My feet never touched the ground leaving there. We had not been gone a week and were both working. We would save every penny and get a home and I could have my children with me.

I couldn't wait for Jack to come home that evening to tell him I had a job. I thought I would explode with relief. He was delighted for me.

'Didn't I tell you everything would be all right?' he said, with one of his big handsome smiles.

I rang Mary and told her my exciting news and that it wouldn't be long now until I came and collected my babies.

On Monday morning, I started my job. I was given a blue and white overall to wear. The two ladies I was working with were nice to me but they asked a lot of questions. How long had I been married? Did I have any children? I didn't know if I should tell them the truth or not. They were so friendly and I didn't want to tell them lies, but I did. I told them I had been married for three years and would love to have a family. I think they knew that something was not right.

I was stocking the shelves. This meant that I had to make sure they were full and looking good at all times. It was heavy work. I had to push big trolleys of produce and lift crates of apples and bags of potatoes, but I got £20 a week and I didn't care what I had to do as long as I got the money to have my children with me soon. It was February 1973 and I was earning as much as Michael was at home. Apart from the phone calls once a week to Mary, I was saving every penny towards a deposit to rent a house for us.

Straight away I started looking for a home for us all to live in as a family. My search was disappointing, but then May and Billy mentioned that they had a house; the people who had been living in it in Kensal Rise had just gone back to Ireland. It had four bedrooms, a sitting room, and a big kitchen. We went to see it and it was perfect. Jack was very generous, never taking any of my wages from me so that I had nearly £100 saved for the deposit.

Having looked at the house, we went straight to the phone to ring the Kellys. I thought it was only right to let them know I was coming home for the children. I was carried away with happiness and relief. I was going to see my children shortly. My hands were shaking so much, I could not dial and Jack had to do it for me. The next thing I was talking to Iris, Michael's sister; she had moved back to Ireland to live.

'I'm ringing to let ye know that I'm coming home for the children. We have a house got in London for us all.'

'The guards are watching out for you. You gave up the right to your children when you walked out on them. They are back in their own house with their father,' she said coldly before cutting me off.

I was stunned.

'How dare she? They can't do that! I'm going to ring back again this minute,' I said to Jack. We got through but when she heard my voice, she said, 'Don't ever phone here again. If you come near the children, you'll be arrested. I promise you that.' And she hung up for a second time.

I had never thought, not for one second, that anyone could take my children away from me. They were mine and always would be mine. I was on the floor of the phone box and wanted to stay there forever. Unnatural sounds came from me as I sat there rocking. Everything was going through my mind so fast, I could not grasp any one thought.

I stayed in a catatonic state for a couple of days.

Jack rang work to say that I was sick. He would tell me things and I would nod to let him know I had heard, but I couldn't bring myself to talk, fearful that if I started, it would come out all garbled. Then Jack said quietly to me, 'Tonight's the night you ring Mary.'

That caught my attention.

'What time is it?'

'We have an hour before you call her; I very nearly forgot

about it,' he said. I could see that he was delighted that I had spoken and he was determined to keep me talking.

'I think I'm going to be all right now,' I said.

Jack got me a glass of brandy. I sat there sipping it, wondering what Mary was going to tell me.

'Please, God, don't let me lose my mind. Help me to cope with whatever it is,' I prayed.

We got through to Mary, who was waiting in the phone box. My voice went again. Jack quickly took the phone from me. I could hear him saying, 'Is everything all right?' He sounded as nervous as I felt.

With a surge of desperation, I took the phone from him and said, 'What's happened? I rang the shop and Iris said the children are gone back to that house with Michael. How could the Kellys do that to them?' Somewhere in my mind I knew I was not giving Mary a chance to answer, but I couldn't stop talking. 'We were planning on coming home next week for the children, but after what Iris said, we don't know what to do. Why did the Kellys put the children back in the house with him? And how are the children going to look after him?'

'Carmel is being paid to take care of them,' Mary said. 'They're his children, and that's that.'

'But they're my children too.'

'Yes, but the Kellys are saying that if you want them, you'll have to come home to Ireland permanently. You can't take them out of the country. They'll never let you do that.'

'I'm sorry for all this. I'm coming home and I'll go and see the guards and hear what they have to say. I'm sure they would think it better for the children to be with their mother.'

'No harm in trying,' Mary said.

'What'll we do about the house?' Jack asked me when I'd put down the phone.

'We'll wait and see. I'm sure the Kellys won't want the responsibility of five children. I'm going to talk to the guards.

We'll see who is entitled to my children.' I was in fighting form now.

I could not believe that Michael would want to keep the children, but I knew that I could never live like I had before.

Chapter Twenty

The next day, we flew to Dublin and rented a car. We had been out of Ireland for four weeks.

Jack's father said we were welcome to stay at the farm. I couldn't believe how good he was being. As we drove through the gates, I was extremely anxious. It was a big concreted yard with hens, chickens and two dogs. Out came an older version of Jack, his hand extended.

'Come in, come in,' he said, shaking my hand. He led us into the house. The place was spotless and welcoming.

'I know your father well,' Mr O'Meara said. 'All of us around here used to tell the children, "Keep in near the ditch. The post office van will be along any minute now, and it will be flying." He was always on time, never a minute late. A great man altogether.'

Jack came into the kitchen. 'You make the tea, son, and I'll set the table.' As we sat down to eat, he made the sign of the cross. There was a big pot of tea and a huge loaf of brown bread, cold roast beef, ham and tomatoes.

'How are all your mother's family?'

'I'm sorry to say I lost touch with them when she died,' I said.

'Well, these things happen. She was a beauty and young when she passed away, God rest her.'

After we had finished eating, we washed the dishes as if we had known each other all our lives. Then he said, 'I'm off out to the fields now. Ye have the room at the back tonight, in case I don't see you until morning.'

'Thank you,' I said, blushing.

'Not at all.'

He put on an old overcoat and his wellington boots and left. I sat beside the Aga listening to the kettle gently humming. I thought how understanding and loyal this man was towards his son. He must be such a good person. If only my father had been like this; he had never even come to see me after my road accident. There was no way I could fool myself that he hadn't heard about it.

We waited until it was dark to go to Mary's, travelling by every back road that Jack knew.

Mary seemed delighted to see us. She said my children had been in school every day since they had been back to Michael, but they had not come over to see her. I suppose they'd been told not to.

'What are you going to do?' Mary asked.

'I'm going into the barracks in Kilkenny tomorrow to find out if what the Kellys are saying is true.'

'That's a good idea. Then if it's okay, you can take them back with you, and no one can stop you.'

The thought of having my five children with me made my heart race. We stayed talking well into the morning and I felt very hopeful by the time we left. Jack and I were up bright and early. As we drove along the familiar winding roads, my mind was twisting with every bend. When we reached the barracks, I told Jack I would have to do this on my own.

I asked to speak to whomever was in charge. Eventually a sergeant appeared and told me to step into his office.

I told him everything.

'I can see it's a heartbreaking situation,' he said, 'but that's the law. You would have to get your husband's permission to take the children out of the country.'

I started to cry.

He didn't know where to look.

'He is not a fit person to take care of them,' I said.

He shook his head. 'Sorry. There's nothing I can do for you.'

'But there must be.'

'If there were, don't you think I would tell you?' He held the door open and put out his hand.

I went out to Jack.

'I don't know what to say to you,' he said. 'What more can you do?'

Jack dropped me off at Mary's and drove away so that no one would know we were around and cause trouble.

Mary's house was just over the road from the school and we heard the children coming out for their morning break. I ran up to Mary's bedroom where I knew I would be able to see into the school playground. There they were: Philip playing ball and Jackie walking around the school yard with her friend Rita. The urge to hold them and run to the end of the world was all-consuming, but Mary put her hand on my arm and brought me back to reality.

'Come away from the window. You can see they are okay.'

'How can they be?'

'Children are very resilient. Come on, we'll have a cup of tea.'

I did my best to concentrate as Mary talked about my father and my sisters. I vaguely heard her say that my father had signed over his house to Alison and her husband, Ray, and that my father had gone back to live in Thomastown in a mobile home. This would have shocked me if my overriding feeling wasn't a longing for physical contact with my children, to hold them, to touch them.

Jack returned before Mary's children came home from school. The three of us knew I would agonise if I saw them, and I didn't want them to tell my children, 'Your mother was in our house.' I went out to the car. I was raw inside.

Jack had our bags in the car because we were going directly to Dublin Airport.

'Do you think is there any point in going to see Michael or the Kellys?'

'What do you think, after all his threats?' Jack said.

'But how can I leave without them?'

'Well, you could go back to Michael. That's another choice.'

I gazed out the car window and the fields looked greener than I ever remembered. Wisps of cloud floated across the sky, the same sky that was over my children and over me. Was this all we had to share now? I felt numb right through to my heart at the thought of what I had done, but I could not find it in me to go back to Michael.

I knew I could never survive living with him again. I would go out of my mind. Even if I had gone up to the door, it would have caused havoc and the children would have been in the middle of it. And I was sure that I could never move back to Ireland and live there with Jack. I would be in fear of my life. I could not silence the sobs any longer.

Jack pulled over and stopped the car. 'Let's go back to London and give it a bit of time,' he said. 'Maybe if the Kellys thought that you didn't want the children, they would let you have them.'

This could happen, I thought. I would try and hold on to that belief.

When we reached Kilkenny, Jack said, 'We'll go into Delaney's pub and have a drink.'

He got me a large brandy. 'Drink that and you'll feel better,' he said. I drank it in one go.

'I didn't mean that fast,' he said, looking at me in amazement. He went and got me another, and a small stout.

Then I remembered that this was the pub where my father had spent every evening after visiting my mother in hospital, while the four of us were left at home like orphans.

Jack was at the bar, talking to the owner, and I was sitting away from them at the open fire. If my father had walked in then, I would have told him that he had abandoned his children just as surely as I had mine. At least I could see what I had done and admit it. I was not so deluded as to think I was the best parent in the world. How he had terrified us with his ghost stories! We had to become thieves to get Christmas presents for our sisters, though his wallet was bursting at the seams. I would give him something to think about. It was easier to dwell on his wrongs than on my own.

On the plane back to England, I consumed miniature brandies. I was desperate to pour them down my throat, one after another. I struggled to get the tops off the tiny bottles, but they were hard to budge. Jack took one from me and I heard the crunch of the cap as he twisted it. He handed me brandy in a plastic cup.

I was near to madness. We went to the pub on the way home from the airport. The drinking went on.

Later, we got into bed and wrapped ourselves around each other, but nothing could satisfy the hollow emptiness inside me.

Chapter Twenty-one

I'm writing this over thirty years later and my stomach tightens in pain. I have to get up and do something, wash the dishes, sweep the already-swept floor, anything, until I can allow myself to think about it all again. I constantly ask myself what I could have done. What stopped me fighting for my children? My fear of what I thought of as a powerful family, the Kellys, my fear of the law, and my lack of belief in myself. These are the answers I come up with and they sound feeble in the light of what was at stake.

At the time, the whole thing gnawed at me as I tried to function in what appeared to be a normal way. Jack wanted to let the house go. I worried that we would never get something so right again, but I did what he asked.

The landlord would now convert the entire house into bed-sits, so we took one of them. We were not moving in for a month or so.

Meanwhile, Billy and May were going to a dinner dance and they asked if we'd like to go with them. A group of them were hiring a minibus. Jack said we'd love to.

When he saw me ready to leave, Jack said that I looked

beautiful and that he was proud to be with me. He looked very handsome himself, in a suit, and I told him so. I was nervous about meeting new people, so he poured me a glass of vodka. I loved him so much.

By the time we left, I was much more relaxed. There was a great deal of talking and joking in the bus. I was sitting beside Jack. He had my hand in his and was stroking it.

There must have been twenty tables reaching from one end of the room to the other. Everything looked so appealing. We went to the bar first and I had a couple of drinks. Then we were called in for the meal, which smelt and tasted wonderful. We had coffee to finish, which I had never drunk before.

Jack and I sat side by side. We had wine with the meal, another first for me. After the food, the music started and it was as if there was no one else in the room as Jack and I got up for a slow waltz. When we finished and were going up to the bar, one of the men asked me to dance. Jack told me to go ahead. It was a fast one. This man, Mickey, grabbed my hand and started to jive. I would have sworn that I couldn't do that, but by following his lead, I did. When it was over, he walked me back to Jack. I was beaming and just about to say, 'Did you see me?' when Jack turned and poured his pint of Guinness over my head. I stood there, drowned in stout.

'You bitch! I thought you said you couldn't jive.'

His face was ugly with anger and his eyes clouded over with rage. He turned on his heel and walked out the door. I went to run after him but May caught me by the arm. 'Let him go and cool off. There was no need for that.'

She took me into the Ladies' and tried to clean me up. It was no use; my top was destroyed.

May wanted to talk about Jack. 'Has he ever done anything like that before?'

'No.'

'What came over him? Mickey is one of his mates from work. Sure, he can't be jealous.'

I told her what he had said to me about jiving.

'For God's sake, is that all he has to bother him?'

It was a couple of hours later when we got on the bus. There was no sign of Jack and it was very embarrassing. No one knew what to say.

The next thing, we saw him walking along the road, head down and collar up. He ignored us as we drove slowly along beside him for several minutes. Then, without warning, he got into the bus, sitting as far away from me as possible. As we came nearer home, Billy said, 'Will we all go and get a few more drinks for ourselves and round off the night the right way?'

'Take us home first,' Jack said.

We went in and I sat on the side of the bed.

'I'm sorry,' I said.

He sat beside me and started to cry. I put my arms around him gently and asked, 'Why did you pour your drink over me?' He made no effort to answer me. I let go of him and for over half an hour he sat there as still as a statue, as if he had stopped breathing, tears dropping onto his hands which were resting on his lap. In the end I had to break the silence.

'What's wrong with you?'

'I'm just terrified of losing you to someone else.'

'I love you. How could I leave my children and come away with you if I didn't?'

'I don't know what I'd do if you ever left me. Do you hear me?'

'Yes,' I said. After that brief conversation we lay in each other's arms, not saying a word. Then he fell asleep. I wondered how he could without even saying that he was sorry. Maybe I deserved it. All the men in my life had treated me badly. But no one had ever loved me enough to be jealous of me before.

The following morning was a Sunday, and when I went into the kitchen, Billy and May were there. There was no sign of Jack. I thought it was because he was ashamed of the scene he'd made the previous night. The next thing, in he walked.

'Nice morning,' he said. They muttered something and left us.

'Come on,' Jack said. 'Let's get out of here.'

But before we left, May called me aside. She said she would give me the money to go back to my family that very minute, that she didn't want Jack treating me like that. I explained to her that he'd just got jealous and that he really did love me.

'Have it your own way,' she said. 'Men like Jack don't change.'

Jack didn't ask me what she had wanted. He was taking me to the pub. I didn't have to drink much before I felt drunk.

I started each day with a drink. It numbed the yen inside me and made going into work easier. If I didn't go, I knew, I would spend the day agonising about my children and I could not bear that.

A week later, I got a letter from Katie. She had got my address from Mary. I was terrified to open it. Eventually I got the courage.

'Dear Mammy...'

Having read that alone, I felt as if I were suffocating; my eyes were swimming in tears. Katie told me that she missed me but she understood why I had gone. She was eleven years old and she was trying to console me. She said she would write when she could and that they were all okay, and not to worry. She signed off, 'Love Katie' and two kisses.

I was so relieved to be told that she loved me, and that everyone was grand. But it stirred the deep hurt inside me. By now, I knew people in London who had split up, but it didn't mean that the children had to make do with one parent. I wrote back to my little daughter telling her how much I loved and missed them all.

Most of my time was given to my thoughts and memories and I seemed to be constantly drained. Whatever kind of love Jack had for me, even a jealous love, it could not wipe away my children and the only time I was not thinking about them was when I was in a drunken sleep.

I wrote to Katie twice over the next couple of weeks, but got no reply.

Then Mary, who had the phone in by now, told me that Katie had never received my two letters. Mrs Kelly, being the postmistress, knew every letter that went through. Mary said, 'Well, what can you do about it? And you might as well hear what else she said to the children. She told Philip and Ellen that you were dead and they were never to say your name again.'

Quiet tears ran down my face.

'I'm sorry,' Mary said. 'But you have to know.'

'Promise me that you will tell Katie that I did write to her,' I begged Mary.

'Of course I will.'

What was I up against? Was there that much bitterness against me? Did I have any chance of seeing my children again? My life was almost unbearable.

Chapter Twenty-two

I didn't feel like myself any more. I went around having fictitious arguments with the Kellys, Michael, my father and anyone else who entered my head. I would spend hours trying to explain to my imaginary children what had happened, even though I could not fathom it myself. This always ended with me dissolving in drunken tears.

I gave up the job in Sainsbury's because my workmates were asking awkward questions. I wanted to feel safe and removed and not have to explain things. But I had to get work immediately to keep my mind occupied.

Then I saw a sign in a bakery window, advertising for an assistant.

The manageress, a small, slim, Dublin girl, asked, 'When can you start?'

'Tomorrow.'

'Great. I'll show you where everything is when you get here.'

This job paid more than the other, but I wasn't sure if how much I earned really mattered. I quickly got into a routine, however, which involved a lot of drinking and seemed to make the time pass less painfully. Another girl and I used to keep a bottle of vodka constantly at hand. She would bring it one day and I would the next, and between serving the customers and drinking, we would definitely empty that bottle before we went home in the evening. I never told Jack that I drank at work and he never seemed to notice.

On my days off, I would sit in the empty bed-sit, my mind back with my children. When my grief got too much, I would stop it the only way I knew how. I would take a mouthful of neat vodka and a shiver would rush through my body. I would crave sleep, oblivion.

One night, Jack did not come home at his expected time. I knew by now that when he departed from his routine, it always ended badly, with him getting into one of his jealous rages, imagining all sorts of things that weren't true. I started getting uneasy, downing a lot of vodka to help me stop worrying. It was well after midnight when the door opened. I looked up, faking a smile. Jack's face was white.

'Did you have a good night?' I asked.

There was no reaching him. He was in one of his black moods. Soon the insults flew. There was not a glimmer of the man I thought I knew. The tirade continued and in my fragile state of mind I allowed him to carry on insulting me.

The next morning, first thing, I pulled my dressing gown on and reached into the airing cupboard. Having taken a quick drink, I held the bottle away from me to look at it. Thank God, it was nearly full. I took a big gulp and waited for that feeling of remoteness, before making my way back to the bedroom.

Jack was lying with his hands behind his head, his expression icy cold. He looked straight at me as I crawled along the wall, his expression icy cold. The fear of more hostility made me end the suffocating silence.

'Jack, what's happening to us?'

'I'm sorry. Will I take you out for a nice meal?'

I nodded mechanically, but I was raging inside.

The alcohol scorched my throat as I topped myself up once

more in the bathroom. We had nothing to say to one another in the car, or at least I had lots to say, but, just as I was with Michael, I was afraid to. We went and got something to eat. Not hungry at all, I tried some soup and we had a bottle of wine. After we had eaten, he said we'd go to a quiet pub for a couple of drinks. I had four or five double brandies, which made it harder to keep my wrath at Jack's behaviour from surfacing.

'I'm not going to work tomorrow,' I told Jack that night. I yearned for an argument on my terms, to be able to express the seething violence inside me. He just sauntered into the bathroom.

I started to get undressed. How could I make him feel as bad as I did? Jack knew that I was unhappy, but he said nothing. He came back in and got into bed beside me. I could feel the tension in his body. Eventually I fell asleep.

The next morning, Jack went to work, kissing me on the cheek as usual. The minute I heard the front door bang shut, I was out of the bed and the search was on for the nearest bottle. There it was, standing straight and proud in my upright hoover. I had hidden it there in case Jack was in the bathroom and I needed a drink immediately.

Once more, I set about convincing myself that Jack loved me. We had been together for ten months and I thought he would not be jealous or want me with him if he didn't love me. He very seldom went anywhere without me and he was generous when we were out. When I had lulled myself into a comparatively peaceful state, I went back to sleep. Later I rang work to say I had a cold.

Having spent the day alone with my bottle and thoughts of my babies, I desperately needed to feel close to someone. So when Jack arrived home, I was prepared to do or say anything to achieve this bond of attachment.

'I'm sorry for being touchy,' I said, clinging to him for dear life, when he came through the door. I felt that he was all I had in the world.

A couple of days later, Billy, the landlord, came over to the house. Jack said, 'Well, Billy, how are things?'

'Not too good,' he answered, with not a flicker of a smile or his usually pleasant face. 'I will have to ask ye to move out. I'm thinking of selling the house.'

Jack was expressionless. 'Fine!' he said cheerfully. 'We'll do that as soon as possible.'

I wondered what the truth was. Had the people downstairs complained? I felt so ashamed. I could tell Jack wasn't pleased. His chin jutted out the way it did when he was angry.

Within a couple of days, we got a place on the Harrow Road. It was huge. There were long dark stairs with bare boards, and the rooms were enormous, with high ceilings and big windows. Immediately, my thoughts were of having my children with me. I was all excited. You could walk from the kitchen out on to a balcony, with a canal flowing by underneath. After months of sleeping and eating in one room, it was a luxury. It was still near enough to the Catholic school that I had looked at, and the doctor with whom I was going to register. God is good, I thought.

But before I got to do anything about the children, I was on my way to work one morning when I collapsed on the street not far from our front door. I had been complaining about a pain in my leg, but the doctor had said it was nothing to worry about. Now I was in Saint Charles's hospital in Ladbroke Grove, surrounded by nurses and doctors. I had deep-vein thrombosis in my left leg and, because they could not disperse the clot, they were considering amputation. The next thing I heard was Jack's voice; as he was my common-law husband, they needed his consent to amputate. He would not give it.

I remained in hospital for two months while they tried various drugs, which eventually worked. During this time, no one could have been better to me than Jack. He never missed a visiting time, always bringing flowers and chocolates. He even came in to see me before he went to work in the mornings. I had my bottles of smuggled Guinness hidden in my locker, and I loved the feeling of being taken care of. I quickly became institutionalised.

When I eventually left hospital I was on a lot of medication and was worried about my drinking; I could not seem to live without it. I didn't go back to work for months because I was so weak, but when I did, I was given promotion. They asked me if I would like to be manageress in a bigger bakery in Kilburn Square. I said I would try it.

Once more, hope of getting my children pounded through me. I rang Mary and told her that I felt I had been given a second chance at life, after my thrombosis ordeal, and that something good was bound to happen. That meant only one thing to me: being with my children at last. She cautioned me by saying the children had settled into a routine, and I should wait another while.

I was empty inside. She went on to say that Geraldine had a lovely baby boy and that Alison was expecting her first child. How I yearned to be there for my sisters. I remembered when my babies were born and how I had longed for my mother.

Then Mary asked me if she, her husband and their four children could come over for a holiday. I was delighted and said that they could, of course. Now Mary and I together would be able to think of a plan towards my getting the children.

But when Mary eventually came, she was very nearly the ruination of me. They arrived in the summer, for two weeks. I wanted to do everything for them. I thought it was only right, because she had been so good to me since I had left over a year before. But Mary's attitude towards me had changed completely. I felt that she had forgotten why I had left home in the first place, and that now she was judging me.

'How can you go on about work and jobs when your children are lost at home without you?' Mary said the first night.

'But you said on the phone that they were settled and to leave them for a while.'

'What else did you expect me to say?'

'The truth.'

'Mary, you must understand that I never realised when I was leaving home that I would not be able to go back and get my children.'

She stood up, left the room, and went to bed.

It did not make sense. Mary must know how much I missed my children. Her four children were her life, and she had a husband by her side who felt the same way about them and about her. I didn't envy Mary any of this. Still, in my eyes she seemed to despise me and I felt yet another loss in my life. Then I thought: she sees me in a job, having money and being able to buy things that I never could have when I was at home. And yet she didn't see me in Marks and Spencer, asking women what age their children were and comparing them with my own. She did not feel the hunger in my heart to cradle them in my arms or to look at them sleeping warm and peaceful in their beds. When one of her children called her 'Mammy', my heart missed a beat with pain. She was my sister and I couldn't understand why she no longer showed compassion towards me in this dreadful situation. I needed her understanding and blessing, but it seemed that I would no longer get it.

One evening, I got the courage to ask Mary if my children had liked the clothes I had sent them. She told me that they ended up flying around her garden and Mrs Kelly saying not to bother sending anything else to ease my conscience. I was sickened. I wanted Mary, someone, anyone, to tell me what to do next. I felt so alone in the world.

'Why didn't you tell me this before?' I asked Mary. 'I've sent a couple of parcels since then.'

'I don't want to be the bearer of bad news all the time.'

'I sent them £50 each for their birthdays and the same at Christmas to buy what they wanted for themselves. Please tell me that they got that.'

'Not as far as I know. The children told me that they got nothing from you.'

'How can the Kellys do that?'

I burst into tears and fled. She just left me to it. What was happening to Mary and me? We had been best friends. I always felt that we would support each other in any crisis, but now I felt I didn't know her any more and perhaps she felt the same way about me. Did she resent the fact that she had had to give up her schooling when I married Michael? She was definitely angry with me and, no matter what I did to try to get close to her, it was no good.

Before Mary went back to Ireland, she reluctantly said that she would have a chat with Katie and Jackie and ask them to write to me or make some kind of contact. I was relieved that she was going to let them know that I was thinking of them at least. Perhaps they thought that I didn't care at all. When she'd gone, I was taken over by incredible sadness.

I tried to keep busy. My bottle of vodka was my closest friend.

Whenever my thoughts started to ramble, I would go into the toilet with it. I went in one person and, in a matter of minutes, came out another.

Jack would pick me up from work most evenings. Sometimes we would go to the pub and stay there until the early hours. I would feel so sick in the morning, I would throw up at the bus stop. But I never missed a day, because I knew that when I got into work, I would be able to drown my sorrows.

This life in Kilburn went on for two years and I was never sober. I drank from the moment I opened my eyes in the morning until last thing at night. In the summer evenings, if I got home before Jack, I would put on the dinner. Then I would sip away at a vodka and orange as I wandered out on to the balcony to watch the boats going up and down the canal. I had planted flowers in window boxes and tied them to the railings. I liked being out there and it was also handy for getting rid of my empty bottles. I would watch and drink as the people sailed by. Some of them would look up and wave to me. If you knew the kind of person I was, you wouldn't wave, I used to think. 'You people don't have a care in the world,' I would mutter as I stood there draining my bottle and waiting for them to disappear around the bend so that I could sling the bottle with all my might into the water.

I had three flat half-bottles which were easier to hide from Jack, because he didn't approve of my drinking at home. I would pour the large bottle of vodka evenly into them. Then I would fill them to the top with juice, and I had my drinks mixed for the next three nights, or so I told myself, but they never lasted as long as I intended them to. I went to great lengths to hide them. I felt that everyone needed a couple of drinks during a hard day.

One evening, I realised that it was getting cold on the balcony. Jack was late. I went inside and looked at the chops, curled up at the edges under the grill. The water had boiled off the potatoes and the tin of peas was still on the worktop, waiting to be emptied into a saucepan. Food never bothered me. I ate only because Jack would want to know why I wasn't eating. I turned on the television and sat down on the settee with my drink, trying to focus. Then I heard him coming in.

'How ya?' I shouted.

No answer. He just stood there, swaying and staring vacantly at me. I shifted nervously in my seat. What was the matter with him? Then the abuse started, the taunts and the insults used to keep me in my place.

Many times I would think about leaving Jack. He would be well aware of the change in my behaviour. I would be distant and quiet, and he would threaten me by making statements such as, 'If you ever leave me, you'll end up in the gutter.' I would think a lot about what he'd said.

The next morning, he said, 'Sorry about last night. I was knocking down a wall yesterday and it fell the wrong way on to someone's car. I just lost it.'

'I see,' I said, though I didn't see at all. I knew it was a waste of time saying anything, and I couldn't be bothered fighting with him. I sat there in silence. After a couple of days, it was as if nothing had happened.

The landlord in the Masons' Arms had mentioned a couple of times that we should get a pub to run ourselves. It was easy in the 1970s to get places to manage for the breweries. I hoped that Jack's moods would not be as unpredictable if there were people around all the time. So, I agreed to give up my job in the bakery and start my pub training. I was full-time behind the bar, while Jack was still working on the demolition by day and doing a few nights' training for pub management. The landlord said he would pretend to the brewery that Jack was there full-time. We got an interview a short time after and passed it without any problem. So we were put on a managers' waiting list until a suitable place became available.

After a six-month wait, we were offered a pub, the Prince of Wales, in Hillingdon in Middlesex.

Chapter Twenty-three

Every morning when I awoke, my first thought was of my children, quickly followed by heartrending sorrow. Then I would have to have a drink to drown the feelings and help me focus on something less painful. It was now three years since I had left Ireland. J.J. would now be fifteen, Katie fourteen, Jackie twelve, Philip nearly eight and little Ellen five. In that length of time, I never had the courage to go to Mrs Kelly or Michael's door and demand to see my children. The only contact I had with my children was the one letter from Katie.

But even in the haze and insanity that was my life, I had the rooms chosen for my children the minute I saw the place. This was going to be where I would have them with me at last.

Ours was a country pub, not too big and in no way like the ones in London. It had a garden at the back with apple trees, shrubs and flowers. There were five bedrooms and a huge sitting room covered from wall to wall with white shag-pile carpet. The free-standing bath had gold taps. It had a family kitchen with everything you could ever want in it. The first thing I did was tell Mary. She said she was pleased for us and asked if she could come over for a week and see the place. Of course she could. This time I would really talk to her about getting my children back.

We were doing a good trade. Many nurses came in because Hillingdon hospital was right beside us. Most of them were Irish, so it was a home from home. There were no staff to start with, and we did the cleaning ourselves before opening up, and then took turns to serve in the bar.

The pub became my world. I never went out shopping or visited anyone. I would go down to the bar where, if someone offered me a drink, I would never say no. The customers were friendly, and there was after-hours all the time.

We'd been in the Prince of Wales about six months when one day I decided I needed new clothes. When I mentioned it to Jack, he said he would take me into Uxbridge. I'd used the car occasionally when we lived in London but now I found my nerve had gone and I could no longer drive. I felt that I needed a drink before I left, but I was afraid to say it. We were just about to go around the shops when I started to dry-heave. I was shaking all over. Taking big gulps of air, I grabbed Jack by the arm. 'Take me home,' I said.

'My God, you're white in the face.'

He took me back to the car where I pulled down the vanity mirror and looked at myself. My face had no colour and my lips were purple. 'What's the matter with me?'

'Don't worry, you'll be okay.'

Back at the pub, he sent me upstairs, saying he would bring me a drink. I lay down on the settee and he came up minutes later with a glass of brandy. I wanted him to go away quickly so that I could drink it in one go.

Then it was as if I had flipped a switch. I felt drunk immediately but I needed more, so I looked around for some upstairs. I had to have spirits close to hand at all times, just to feel normal. Frantically, I searched every cupboard in the place until I found a bottle of Martini. I walked around the bed-rooms, the drink in my hand, and imagined to myself what my children were like now. Pouring some of the Martini into a glass, I had a conversation with each of them as if they were with me. I went to the top of the stairs to make sure that Jack was not coming back up to interrupt my dream world.

I was in the bathroom now, sipping away. I looked at myself in the mirror and smiled. 'They'd love it here,' I said. 'And as long as they are with their mother, they'll be happy.'

My glass was nearly empty, but I felt good. I thought I should let Jack see that I was feeling better, but I finished the bottle first and then had to hide it. Having tucked it in the wardrobe under my jumpers, I ran a comb through my hair and went downstairs, hoping Jack would not send me back up again; the bar looked so warm and cosy. Some of the regulars were at the counter talking to him. They called me over. 'Would you like a drink?' Of course I would! But Jack said to me in a low and threatening tone, 'Why don't you go upstairs? You look tired.'

I knew that I'd better do as I was told. On the way up, passing through the public bar, I managed to grab a half-bottle of vodka. I was quite happy then. With all my clothes on, I got into bed, clasping the bottle tightly. Settling myself against the pillows, I was determined not to let myself think of anything that would make me sad. I was becoming an expert at that.

It was dark when I awoke. I must have slept for hours. Straight away, the search was on for my bottle. I was petrified in case Jack had found it and taken it away. Thank God, there it was under the mattress! I took a big swig and felt at ease. Getting out of bed, I checked the kitchen clock: it was ten at night. I could hear the murmur of voices downstairs and the sound of ABBA singing 'Waterloo' on the jukebox. A feeling of emptiness and desperation swept over me. I took a deep gulp from my bottle and it shook my body as if it had been struck by lightning. I struggled into my nightdress and, when Jack came in, pretended to be asleep. He was snoring in a matter of minutes. I envied him. After a while, I slipped out of the bed and crept downstairs. I went into the bar and looked around.

The light from the street was shining in and everything looked different. I went to the optics and held a glass up again and again, making it a treble brandy. I sat up on a high stool and drank it slowly, like a solitary customer.

I rang Mary now and then, but most of the time I would not be able to remember what we talked about. Yet I knew I never asked about my father. And I had lost touch with Alison and Geraldine. I didn't want it to be this way, but it was as if I couldn't reverse the circumstances. I felt as if I had lost a set of instructions telling me how to be normal.

There was nothing good in my life. I felt and looked desperate, and this made me jealous of every pretty female who came into the pub. I would watch Jack and, if he were looking at another woman, I would say something which would end in a row. Jack had now put a bolt on the bedroom door and would keep me in there for days. Then I'd be sorry and could not do enough for him.

However, I had made two good friends. One was an Irish girl called Lily, who had lived in London for years, and whom I had met in the bakery. The other was a man called Arthur who drank in our pub. He was only about five feet tall, and used to be an acrobat. When I knew him, he was still agile although he was then sixty. He used to pick up the glasses and polish the tables. I don't know if he ever got paid for it. I would slip him a couple of drinks when I could because he was my loyal friend. We called Jack 'the O'Meara'. Arthur had worked out the situation between us. He would say, 'Try and stay on his good side.'

'Which side is that?' I would joke.

Arthur was there every day and, if I were missing, he would ask about me. Jack hated him doing that and would get furious with me over it.

Lily came out a few times from London with one of Jack's mates she was going out with. She had witnessed a couple of things that had gone on between us and told me I should get out before I lost my sanity.

I asked her if I could send her some money to save, so that I would have it if I ever did leave Jack. She said it was no problem, and that she was glad I was thinking about it. Because of my lack of belief in myself, and to gauge her reaction, I casually mentioned to Lily that Jack would sometimes lock me in the bedroom, quickly adding that he was ashamed of me when I over-indulged. I wanted to see if I was making a fuss about nothing. She was shocked. 'For God's sake, why don't you go back to Ireland and try to salvage something before it's too late?'

Months went by and I couldn't get my head together to do anything. Lily could not understand that and neither could I.

A priest, Father Pat, a friend of Jack's family, came to visit. I asked him if I could have a word.

'To be sure, go ahead,' he said kindly.

I told him about leaving my husband and not being allowed to have my children. Then I asked him if he could give me something to do that would take away my guilt. He took my hands in his. 'You are doing your penance every day of your life. I don't need to give you any more,' he said. He then asked me to kneel and he made the sign of the cross on my forehead and blessed me. That was all he could do. I went to bed and told Jack what had happened.

'Are you happy now?' he asked as he turned away to sleep.

Chapter Twenty-four

Where could I hide my drink? That had become my biggest worry. Jack had found bottles in the wardrobe and another under the mattress, and I had suffered the consequences. I was having to find new places all the time, and trying to remember where I'd put them was terrifying. All I knew was that I'd die or go mad without it.

Jack locked me in the bedroom, to keep me away from the drink, but eventually he would let me out and I would go for walks and buy drink from the pub next door because Jack was now counting the bottles. What the owners must have thought of me buying my vodka in their pub I will never know. Coming back, I would stick a bottle in the hedge and go out and retrieve it when I got the chance.

I tried to stay out of Jack's way and to be in some way sober, but eventually I would take that one drink too many and it would end badly again.

When the hopelessness really got to me, I would ring Mary or occasionally she would ring me. Talking to each other this way seemed easier than face to face. She told me that Michael had stopped drinking and was seeing a woman called Liz, who had just moved into the village. She was looking after Michael and my children now.

'How long is it since I left?'

'You mean to say you can't remember?'

'No, I can't. How long is it?'

'It's nearly five years since you last saw your children.'

I gulped my vodka. I could hear Mary's voice as if through cotton wool, saying, 'J.J. is living down at Kellys now, all the time.'

I flinched at that. Suddenly I had a clear vision of my children becoming adults without me. Soon they would be all grown up and never need me again. At that moment something stirred within me, and I knew I had to do something.

When Jack went to the bank, I rang Lily in London. 'I'm going home,' I told her.

'Good,' she said. 'Are you going to tell Jack?'

'God, no. He's going to the races in Cheltenham, just for a day, so that will be my chance.'

I sounded a lot calmer than I felt.

Every year, most of the Irish landlords whom Jack knew hired a coach to take them to the races.

'What about the money I have belonging to you?' Lily asked.

She posted it to Arthur's address and put a note in to explain what was going on. She said, 'Try and cut down on the drink and keep in touch.'

I promised her that I would do both.

Arthur gave me the thumbs-up sign a few days later, so I knew that he had the money. I was dying to chat to someone about what I was going to do but I didn't dare. If I went over to Arthur, Jack would want to know what we were talking about. If I rang Lily, he'd pick up the phone downstairs and listen.

The night before the races, one of the customers brought me a rose bush for the back garden and planted it for me. As a way of saying thanks, I gave him a free pint. Then I turned around and saw Jack glaring at me. I put my could-not-care-less face on and he was furious. God, I thought to myself, why did I do that? I went over to him and tried to make the peace. 'I gave Kenny a pint for the plant. Is that okay?'

He looked past me, greeting someone who had just come in. Arthur saw the whole thing and turned his eyes towards heaven.

Eventually all the customers went and only Jack, Arthur and I were left. Jack said to me, 'You go to bed now.' I jumped to attention, saying goodnight to Arthur. A strange smell met me as I went up the stairs. I could not put a name to it. When I went into the dimly lit bedroom, it got stronger. The bedclothes looked as if someone were underneath them. 'Don't be silly,' I told myself as I pulled them back. Slowly I realised that it was the pungent heavy odour of wet earth. I gave a weak, stifled scream, realising that it was the rose bush, smelling like a freshly dug grave. I ran out of the room.

Arthur met me halfway down the stairs. 'What's the matter?'

I dragged him into the room, and turned on the light to show him what was on my side of the bed.

'It's only a rose bush,' he said, winking furiously at me and squeezing my hand very tightly. It was a signal to stop me saying too much; Jack was listening.

'How could anyone do a thing like that?'

'Go to bed and stop thinking about it.'

I put clean sheets on the bed and looked around for one of my hidden bottles. Taking a couple of swigs, I slid in between the fresh linen. The smell in the room and in my nostrils was suffocating, but I was not going to mention any of it to Jack. He came up to bed after a while and we lay as far away from each other as possible.

Next morning, I was anxious. I drank the last of my vodka. I didn't go to the bar until Jack called me. He went to the cellar, telling me to do the bottling up. Arthur was there.

'How are you?' he asked. 'I have the money here for you.'

He patted his pocket, and I leaned over and gave him a kiss on the cheek. 'You are one in a million.'

'I slept here last night, on the seat by the window; I was afraid something might happen with the O'Meara.'

Arthur often slept in the pub, and I was truly grateful that he cared for me.

'Thanks,' I said, tears in my eyes.

'Stop that, or he'll know something is up.'

I looked around for some drink to get me through the morning. It was only eight and Jack would not be leaving until eleven. There was a half-bottle of vodka. I had to have it. I dashed upstairs with it and put it behind the saucepans in the kitchen. The time passed slowly. I cooked breakfast for Jack and Arthur, which I avoided having in case it spoilt the effect of the gulp of vodka I had just taken. When they had eaten, they went back down to the bar. I restlessly paced the rooms with my drink in my hand. I thought of the dreams I had had when I had first seen the place. Now I would not miss one thing out of it and I was glad that my children had never come over. I would have hated them to have seen how I had been living, in fear. I looked at the lock on the bedroom door and saluted it with the bottle and a smile.

Mick, the barman, was in by ten o'clock. He was going to help while Jack had his day at the races.

At last, the coach arrived. They all made for the bar as if they had not tasted a drink for months when, in fact, most of them were already drunk. I knew that Jack wanted me to be there when they came in, looking good and being nice to everyone, but I was not going to do that ever again. He was in and out of the bedroom trying to intimidate me. I kept my head down, just biding my time.

Jack came up and had a shower.

'What are you going to do with yourself all day?' he asked irritably.

'God knows.'

His face was as white as chalk. He put it close to mine; his breath was warm on my cheek. 'Are you coming downstairs?' he hissed.

'No,' I said defiantly.

He started to walk away from me, then turned and came back slowly. I reached behind me and felt for a pint mug. I grabbed it firmly and raised it over my head.

'Don't come any closer,' I said, 'or I'll hit you with this.' He kept coming but I couldn't do it. He snatched the mug from my trembling hands.

'I'm glad that I'm not like you,' I screamed, tears spilling down my face. 'You bastard!'

He reached out to try to pacify me. I wouldn't let him touch me.

'Go away from me. I hate your guts!' I screeched.

'I'll see you later,' he said.

'You might,' I replied quietly. I didn't know if he'd heard. I went to the bedroom window and saw them drift out of the pub. They were carrying crates of beer. Jack was the last one out, looking grim as he got onto the coach.

The minute they were gone, I took a great big drink and started to go downstairs. I met Arthur coming up. 'Are you okay?' he asked.

'Yes.'

We went into the bedroom and started packing furiously. Then Mick the barman, who was now in on the secret, came upstairs. 'Do you need a hand? Take everything you can.'

'I will.'

There were empty bottles falling out of everywhere. Arthur and Mick never said a word. I was half-crying and half-laughing as I crammed things into my suitcases. Then I ran downstairs and got two glasses of brandy, one for Arthur and one for myself; Mick never drank until after six in the evening. I wanted to have a bath but felt too vulnerable, too afraid, in case Jack came back. I was starting to panic again, so Arthur got more brandy. I put on my make-up, and looked at myself in the mirror. I looked more alive than usual, I thought.

I went and got the keys to the safe. There was £400 in it. I took £200. Then I scribbled a note, saying what I had taken. I signed it and put it in the safe so that Mick and Arthur would not get the blame. I sat at the counter and had another drink, trying to persuade Mick to have one with me before I left. 'No,' he said. 'Not for any reason. You should ring for a cab.'

It arrived in no time and Arthur came with me to Heathrow. I had nothing booked, so I had to wait on stand-by. Arthur tried to get me to eat something but I could not have swallowed food to save my life. We carried on drinking and, after a few hours, my name was called. We stood there crying, with our arms around each other. Then we waved until he was out of sight. I went straight to the duty-free and bought myself a bottle of brandy.

On the plane, I rested my head against the window, closing my eyes. I felt exceptionally calm. I was going home and would soon see my children. I was sure that they would be delighted. The woman who had left five years ago was totally different from the one I was now. Nobody was going to push me around or ignore me ever again.

My thoughts changed direction. How full of hope and love I'd been when I had made the decision to live in England with the man I then idolised. I was so sure Jack and I were meant to be together forever. I remembered Mary saying to me, 'You are such an optimist.' I had asked her what that meant and she had explained, 'You always think that things are going to turn out great.' She was right. Now I would show my children how much I loved them and would prove to them that they were the most important people in my world. I would devote the rest of my living days to proving that.

It was seven o'clock, on an evening in March 1977, when I arrived at Dublin Airport. I piled five suitcases precariously on top of each other. Gathering myself as best I could, I got a cab. I asked the driver to take me to Kilkenny and I would direct him from there. Mary's, that's the first place I will go to, I thought to myself. I slept for most of the journey, with my brandy on my lap. As we were coming down the hill into the village, I sat up and took notice. We passed by the graveyard where my beloved grandfather was buried, then my father's house, everything about it changed beyond recognition. The lush green hedges that had surrounded it were gone, the orchard and my big tree that had been my whole world as a child, all flattened in concrete. We went up the road and past Kellys'. If they only knew who was back, I thought with a wicked smile. My driver asked me, 'Where now?'

'Turn left at the church,' I said in a posh voice, taking a drink out of my bottle.

By the Catholic church we sped. Then Paddy's pub. I wondered who was in there and what they would say if I walked in. Over by the school. Then I was at Mary's. I tried not to feel anything. I had spent my whole life trying not to feel. She heard the car door and stuck her head out of her kitchen window. I chewed on my bitten lip as I paid the driver and slammed the cab door behind me.

Turning defiantly, I said, 'I'm here now, so what are ye going to do with me?'

Chapter Twenty-five

Mary and her husband Tom came out to meet me. I walked ahead of them and let them struggle with my suitcases. When I got into her spotless kitchen, she asked me if I would like a cup of tea.

'No, thanks, but can I have a glass for this?' I said, holding up the brandy. It was ten at night and her children were asleep. I sat down and drank and poured as if no one were there but myself. Mary stood staring at me. Tom was sitting at the kitchen table, afraid to look at either of us. Not a word was spoken for ages. Then Mary said to her husband, 'Go to bed, you have to be up early in the morning.'

Obediently, he left us.

'I'll move Ciara and you can sleep in her bed.'

'Thanks. You don't seem very pleased to see me.'

'I am. It's just a surprise. What are you going to do now?'

'Go and talk to Michael, and see how my children are.'

'Just like that, after abandoning them for five years?' she asked.

I ignored her question. I knew in my heart that Michael would take me back. How many times had he told me that I was his wife until the day I died. His property. And I knew that it would help restore his injured pride that I wanted to come back. It would not matter to him that the real reason I had returned was for our children. He would be able to convince himself that it was back to him I came.

I stood up. 'Where's this bed?' I slurred.

She brought me up to her youngest daughter's room. In I got — clothes, bottle of brandy and all.

The next morning, I could hear Mary and her children talking in the kitchen. The bottle was beside me. I tried to get something out of it; about two drops fell into my mouth. Teeth chattering, I lay there until I fell asleep again. I awoke a few hours later, feeling worse.

After a while, Mary came up to me. 'I see you're awake,' she said, standing away from me as if I had something contagious. 'About time. It's two o'clock in the day.'

'Do you have a drink you could give me?' I asked her imploringly.

'No alcohol in this house. Water or tea only,' she said, nostrils flared.

'Would you get me a brandy?'

'I'm not going into a pub to buy booze for anyone.'

I pulled the blankets up around me for comfort.

She stood there, her arms folded across her chest. I told her that if I had just one drink, I would go and talk to Michael.

'You can't just go up like that after all this time. I'll go myself,' she said. So, without any discussion, off she went.

'Thanks,' I called after her. 'Don't be too long. Get me a drop on the way, please.'

After Mary left, I slept again. When she came back — it seemed like hours later — I still hadn't got up.

'He'll see you when it's dark.'

I stayed in the bed, drinking cups of hot tea. It stirred up the alcohol in my system and I felt better for a short time. Around nine that evening, I got up and washed myself as best I could. It was a hard job; I felt frail. Tom took me up to Michael. As I got out of the car, he said, 'Best of luck.'

'Thanks.'

I stood there, looking at the house. Michael had built on a big room at the end. The front door was at the side now, up a different set of steps. I looked down at where Mrs Cuddihy used to live. My top step was gone. I would never stand there again and look down over the village and at my father's house.

Michael was standing at the front door.

'Well,' he said — a word that was used a lot around this part of the country when we didn't know what else to say.

'Hello. Thanks for seeing me.'

'Come in,' he said. I went into the new hall. Michael pointed to a door where the kitchen used to be. There, playing on the floor with their toys, were Philip and Ellen.

'Who's this?' Michael asked them.

'It's Mammy,' Philip said quietly, remaining where he was.

Ellen jumped up, ran over and put her arms around my legs, saying, 'Mammy, Mammy, Mammy.'

I was overcome as I bent down and picked her up in my arms. I nearly fell.

'Sit down,' Michael said. I sat on an armchair at the open fire with my little daughter on my lap. She was talking non-stop and every second word was 'Mammy'.

'I always wanted to call someone Mammy,' she told me, looking up at me with her twinkling green eyes.

'Well, now you can,' I managed to say, giving her a hug. I felt overwhelmed and yet terrified. This seven-year-old girl and nine-year-old boy were striking fear through every cell in my wrecked body.

'I want to buy you a hat,' Ellen said. 'Daddy, can we go to Waterford tomorrow and buy Mammy a hat?'

It was all so unreal. This was my first recollection of ever hearing any of my children calling Michael 'Daddy'. He told her we could if she wanted to. This was a side of him that I had never seen before. I called Philip over to me and put my arm around him and gave him a kiss on the cheek. He blushed. 'Granny told us that you were dead but I didn't believe it,' he told me.

'Well, here I am. You're such a big boy now, aren't you?' My voice sounded so strange to me. He nodded. Then their father told them to go to bed, and off they went, giving me a kiss each.

'She'll be here in the morning,' Michael shouted after them.

I was trembling. I asked him if he had a drink in the house. He said that he hadn't because he had been off the booze for a couple of years himself, but that he would make me a cup of tea. He went into the kitchen and I looked around the room. It had a lovely stone fireplace, nice bright paper, and there were glass doors out on to the hall. I wondered if he had made all these changes for the woman he was seeing. He came back in with the tea and smiled at me. I felt uncomfortable.

'Did I hear right? Are you going out with someone?' I asked him, wanting him to know that I was aware of what was going on.

He nodded.

I told him I wanted to come back for the children and that I would not interfere in his life.

'Okay, but you will have to meet Liz and tell her that,' he said.

'I will.'

The door flew open and Katie and Jackie came in, breathless.

'Daddy can we go to a dance in the community centre?' Katie asked. She was a young woman now, with lovely big blue eyes, shiny brown hair and a smile that lit up the room. Jackie was taller than her older sister. She had the same blue eyes and long blonde hair. They were beautiful.

'Do you see who's here?' Michael asked them.

Katie said, 'We were told in the village that she was here. How ya?'

'I wouldn't know you,' I heard myself say.

Jackie said, 'Come on, Daddy, can we go or not?' without as much as a glance at me.

'Off ye go. Don't be too late,' he replied, and they were out the door. The children all seemed happy and I became desperately worried; had I done the right thing by coming back into their lives?

Michael broke my train of thought. 'Are you tired? Would you like to go to bed?'

He showed me the big room where we used to sleep. There was now one double and two single beds in there for four of the children. J.J. was at his grandparents' as usual. The front room had been turned into a bathroom and Michael slept in the back room. I didn't know if he expected me to sleep in there, with him.

I looked in at my youngest children. They were in one single bed, back to back. They looked like twins. They were the same size, with short fair hair. I touched their heads lightly with my fingers, just as I had dreamed of doing for five long years.

'Good night, Mammy,' Ellen's little voice said. I thought my heart would break or I would suffocate on the words as I said, 'Good night, sweetheart.'

I craved sleep but other matters had to be considered first. Michael led me towards his room. I dithered, my mind hurling miserable memories at me. Then I lay beside this stranger who was my husband, hoping he would not want sex. But that was too much to expect. It was in Michael's nature to feel that he deserved to have everything, and after all, wasn't he allowing me back? Equally, it was in my nature to try to please at all costs. So I went to that place of escape in my head and let it happen.

That night, because of the need for alcohol and the pressure I was under, every time sleep was near, I gave this unmerciful jump and was wide awake again. I heard Katie and Jackie coming in, laughing and talking as if they didn't have a care in the world.

In the morning, I felt Michael leave the bed quietly and heard the two eldest girls get up for school. Katie was nearly sixteen and Jackie fourteen and a half. They were going to the Convent of Mercy school with the same order of nuns who had taught me. Then Ellen woke up; she came and got in beside me, putting her arms around me. I felt so choked up, I could scarcely breathe as I held her tightly to me. I didn't deserve this. She told me all her news about the children she was in school with; how they teased and taunted her about having no mother, and would sing 'Where's your mama gone?' and how she would box them. She was a little fighter by the sound of her. She told me how she would punch anyone who said anything to Philip, too. Just then, he put his head around the bedroom door.

'Do you want to get into bed with us, Philip?' I asked.

'No. I'm going to have my breakfast.'

'We're getting up now anyway,' I said.

Ellen didn't want to; she would have stayed there in my arms all day, talking. I felt terrified being so close to this little child, with all her questions and expectations. I was afraid of letting her down again.

Michael was sitting at the kitchen table staring out of the window that took up most of one wall. He looked older than his thirty-eight years. He asked how we had slept. Ellen answered for the three of us,

'Fine. Are we going to town for the hat?'

'We will if that's what you want. But first your mother has to speak to Liz; she's coming up in a few minutes.'

He had the fire lit in the sitting room and said we should go in there when we'd eaten breakfast. I tried to get some tea and toast inside me but without much luck. I sat at the table, watching my children, my heart overflowing with love.

Ellen and I were in the sitting room when we heard a knock on the front door. She jumped off my lap. I could hear her saying, 'You don't have to knock, Liz. Come in and meet Mammy.'

A pretty brunette, in her late twenties, came into the sitting room, holding Ellen's hand. Ellen let her go and sat on my knee again. I could see the tears in the woman's eyes.

'You don't want me any more now you have your mother back,' she said to Ellen. I put my hand out; she didn't raise her eyes to look at me as we shook hands.

'Sit down. I'm glad to meet you,' I said to her. 'Thanks for looking after the children. They're mad about you, I can see.'

'Thanks,' she said, giving me a fleeting smile.

'I will never stop them from going down to see you or being your friend.'

'Ellen is like my own daughter.'

'I won't come between ye. As far as Michael and you are concerned, it's none of my business. I'm home for my children.'

'We'll see,' she said, and stood up to go.

'Nice to meet you,' I said as she left.

Michael was waiting for her at the front gate. They talked furiously for a few minutes and then she ran towards her own house.

The four of us were now ready to go to Waterford. Ellen was jumping up and down with excitement.

The bedrooms were shabby and neglected, so I bought bedclothes and bits and pieces for them. I asked Michael if he minded, and he said, 'Not at all.'

I couldn't walk around very much. I was unsteady and nervous in myself. So much had happened so quickly, it was hard to take it all in. Sometimes I forgot where I was and what I was doing. I would call Michael 'Jack', and get all confused. He didn't comment on my mistake and I was grateful for that.

When we got back, Katie and Jackie were home from school. We were uncomfortable and didn't know what to say to one another. How would I go about bringing unity to my family? Apparently Ellen had been down in Mrs Kelly's, saying 'Mammy bought me this in Waterford'. J.J. heard her and told Katie to tell me that he didn't want to be brought to see me: 'She can keep her money,' he had said.

I had so much on my mind, and after the initial shakes stopped, I hardly thought about drink. Two weeks went by and I was slowly settling in. I asked Katie and Jackie if they would come shopping with me. Ellen was going to make her First Holy Communion in a few weeks; I thought we should start looking for new clothes for the occasion, and Michael was going to lend me his car. Driving for the first time in ages made me nervous, and having two troubled daughters with me didn't help. Katie was friendly when I got her on her own, but Jackie was angry with me and was not afraid to show it. In Waterford, anything that either of them looked at for longer than a minute I wanted to buy for them.

When I had time to think, I would wonder how Jack was and hope that Arthur and Mick hadn't got the blame for helping me to take off.

Michael came home early in the evenings now. I was sure that if it had been like this, years before, I would never have looked at anyone else, but now it was too late. And, because I was so desperate for my children to feel secure and normal after five years of not being able to be a mother to them, I was being a wife to Michael in every sense of the word, as hateful as this was to me. In my mind, it was prostitution: allowing my body to be used so that I could be with my children. Liz's house was only two minutes from ours and I knew Michael went in there every time he passed, but still he wanted me.

Sometimes I wanted to ask him if he would stop seeing Liz. I had no right to ask him to do this and the fear of not being enough for him made me think again. I was terrified of making things worse and thought that if I made a big issue of Liz, I might lose my children.

The children were complaining about having to sleep in the one room. I asked Michael if there was any way he could build on some bedrooms. He didn't see why not. The girls were all excited about having their own space. Then I suggested that maybe we could ask J.J. if he'd come back home, when we had more space. They all agreed that it would be great. Michael and a few lads from the village started digging the foundations within a week.

Now the real work had to be done: J.J. and I had to try to make our peace.

I had been home three months and into the routine of washing, ironing and cooking. But there were times when inside me I wished I was dead. I never thought of a drink, since it had no place in my lifestyle, and yet, despite my alcohol-filled misery in England, I had not made the association that drinking was an escape for me.

I would see J.J. from a distance, and my heart would ache with longing to be close to my firstborn, but I was afraid he would turn away from me. He was a fine-looking seventeen-year-old, over six feet tall. I found out from Katie that he was a great bricklayer; he loved hurling and played in goal for the local team. I longed to tell him how sorry I was for what I had done, for hurting them all. I heard Katie and Jackie talking to Michael about him and how he had been involved in a row in the pub. It didn't seem to bother his father, who just said, 'He'll get sense sooner or later.' I would blame myself for J.J. being the way he was. I tortured myself with it.

Ellen and Philip were great. They were delighted to have their mother back and made no secret of it, but I felt that Katie and Jackie were merely tolerating me. I wanted the impossible: to have my children babies again so that I would have another chance to prove how much I loved them. The truth of the situation was that they didn't want to know. They were happy as they were.

I cleaned the house obsessively, one room after another. But what I really wanted to do was everything that my children and

I had missed out on: talk, laugh, hug, dance, sing. More than anything, I wanted to be called 'Mammy'. That would be my prize. But my two eldest daughters did not seem to want, or be able, to utter the word.

One day, as Katie and I were chatting about how we were going to decorate her room, she asked me why I had come back.

I knew that I could never describe to her the deep well of longing that had been inside me to see, feel and connect with my children over those shameful five years. So instead I lamely said, 'I loved you all. Ye were never out of my mind, night or day.' This was one of the many times I wanted to take her in my arms and hug her, but the fear of rejection stopped me.

The day of Ellen's First Holy Communion was getting closer. I asked Katie if she would talk to J.J. again and persuade him to come and see me. The next evening, I heard the long strides of my elder son coming into the yard. I couldn't think of anything except how much I loved him.

'Well, how ya?'

'I'm fine,' I said, fighting to keep the tears from my eyes. I felt that he would hate to see me cry.

'Will ya wash my hair for me?'

'Of course I will,' I said, nearly falling over myself to get a towel and shampoo. Immediately, he took off his jumper and leaned over the kitchen sink. I almost choked with the pure joy of this contact with my son. He felt and smelt so different from how I remembered — a mixture of cigarettes and beer. Thank you, God, for this, I said to myself.

'Are you going to town tomorrow?' he asked as he towel-dried his head of curls.

'I am,' I told him, even though this was the first thought I had of going.

'I'll come and get something to wear for the Communion.'

'I'll see you then,' I said as he put his jumper over his head. I reached out and pulled it down around him automatically, as I had done when he was a child. He fixed it himself as he went out the door with a spring in his step.

As soon as he had left, I wanted him back. J.J. had come to see me. I went over every look, touch and smell. I wanted to treasure all his words and lock them away in my memory.

Chapter Twenty-six

After a night of little sleep, Katie, J.J. and I set off for Waterford. I needed my daughter's light-hearted nature to cover up my nervousness with J.J. The first shop we went into J.J. chose a navy pinstripe suit, white shirt and blue tie. He looked great in them and my heart was full of pride.

The day of Ellen's First Communion eventually arrived. It was our first family outing together, all of us in our new clothes. I wondered if my father might take this opportunity to come and see me.

By this time, I had been back home for six months and I was still finding it difficult to go down to the village. The mere thought of all the locals who were going to be at the church was enough to make me feel ill. However, I was pleasantly surprised at how many people made the effort to make me feel welcome. After the Mass, we took photos, and some of the families went to the nearby pub. J.J. was heading that way and I said to Katie, 'Do you think we could go with him?' I wanted to be close to my son and Katie was my sounding board.

'Come on,' she said, and off we strode after him to Norris's pub. It had changed hands while I was in England. A couple around my own age, their early thirties, were running it now; they had built on a lounge and it was all modern and different.

Paddy's pub, which was across the road, had seen even greater changes. It was now closed. Apparently, Paddy had died, and his sister Nellie had given the pub and their land to the church, and had gone into a home for the elderly, which was run by nuns in the village.

That morning, I felt that I had been accepted back by most people, but, I felt, not by my sister, Mary. She spoke openly and freely to my children and to Michael, but hardly acknowledged me. She didn't go to the pub with her family and I was relieved.

'What are you having?' J.J. asked me.

'A small stout, please,' I said, looking up at him in adoration. When he left the drink on the table in front of me, I yearned to ask him how he felt towards me and if he could ever forgive me. I longed to do this with each of my five children but was terrified of what they might say. Earning their forgiveness was the most important thing in my life, but I knew somewhere inside me that it was too soon to have this conversation with any of them.

After about an hour, and a few more drinks, which made me feel more at ease, and helped me to grasp that my own father was not going to appear, the whole family went to Tramore, to the seaside.

As soon as we got there, J.J. took off to the pub with some of the lads from the village who had come down with their families. After the rest of us had had something to eat, the younger ones played in the arcades.

My thoughts that day were continually jumping from the past to the present. Did Michael ever think back? Did he ever think about the day in Tramore when he had left myself, J.J., Katie and Jackie sitting in the car, for five hours, in the lashing rain, while he sat in the pub? Looking at Michael now, I wondered if he had any feelings about anything that had happened in our marriage. I would never be able to talk to him about the past in case he thought I was making excuses for what I had done.

When it was time to go home, Michael had to go and find J.J. After nearly an hour, I saw them coming back. J.J. was walking way ahead of his father. I didn't like the look on J.J.'s face when he got close.

'Fuck off. I'll make my own way home.'

'Suit yourself, but we're going now,' Michael replied. Even as this conversation was taking place, J.J. was getting in the car. I revelled in the intimacy of being squashed in the back with my other four children.

My elder son and his father never stopped arguing all the way home. J.J. criticised Michael's driving and his father asked him what he knew about driving anyway. I talked manically to try to cover up the squabbling and to pretend that everything was normal.

When we got to the village, J.J. left us and went into the pub.

'He's a right tramp, that fellow. I don't know where he came from,' Michael said.

'Were you nervous when they were fighting?' Katie asked me when J.J. had left.

'Yes, I was.'

'I knew by you,' she said with a smile. 'You'd better get used to it if J.J. is going to come and live at home. Him and Daddy are always at it. They had a fight over Daddy and Liz seeing each other and that's when J.J. went to live at Granny's.'

'What do you think I should do about it all?'

'I don't know,' she said with a shrug.

Ellen said that she had had a great time and asked if she could go and show off her Communion dress to Liz and the other neighbours. She knew that she would be given lots of money for her big day. It was all part of the celebration.

Katie had started going out with a cousin of Liz's. He was a nice chap, and they were off to the pub that night. She asked me if I would like to go. I was delighted that they wanted me with them. J.J. was still in the pub when we arrived. He was drinking on his own and took no notice of us. He didn't seem to be too drunk, but he appeared to be in a dark mood.

My sisters Mary and Geraldine were there together. They barely acknowledged me. Was this because they were so annoyed with me for leaving my children, even though they knew why and had never tried to stop me, I wondered. I felt bitterly hurt by Mary doing this, but more so with Geraldine trying to be like her.

Later on, when I stood up to go to the toilet, I felt slightly drunk. How could I have forgotten this wonderful, warm, carefree feeling? I felt as if I could achieve anything. When I got into the toilet, I looked at myself in the mirror and thought I looked nice. I had my powder-blue jacket and skirt on, and a white blouse. As I came back into the lounge, one of the local lads asked me to dance.

'I'd love to,' I said, stepping on to the floor to dance the 'Blue Danube' waltz with him. I glanced towards the bar, catching J.J.'s eye. The look he gave me made me want to run and hide. I anxiously finished the dance and went back to Katie and her boyfriend. Eventually I looked up at J.J., but he stared right through me.

Slowly I realised that J.J. had a side to him that I found threatening. Whenever I saw him, I would look carefully to see what humour he was in. But I had it firmly in my head that if he were among his family, he would feel loved and wanted and that would bring about a change in him. I wanted to love him back to the person I knew was buried under all that pain. I asked Katie if she would approach him again about coming home.

Eventually she got the opportunity to ask him and he said he would. The three new rooms were built and ready to live in. We would all be back together as a family. I was prepared to do anything to keep us that way and felt positive that I would get it right one day.

I found it hard to fit in and to get used to the rows that went on between my children. When we were young, we were not allowed to fight with each other, never mind swear. When one of their disputes started, I would become a nervous wreck and found that if I had a little drink, it helped me to cope. Most nights, around eight, J.J. would arrive home from work having had his few pints. He would expect his dinner to be on the table, no matter what time he appeared. He might or he might not talk, depending on his mood. The sheer panic of not knowing made me drop things and be unable to think straight.

Sometimes I felt that in the five years I had been away, I had lost touch with how to behave around people, especially my own children. Every time one of them came into the house, I had to run and have a drink. I certainly could not face going to bed without my vodka, and I needed it once more to help me to sleep. It took the edge off everything.

My children seemed to be strong and independent, and I was in awe of them. I wanted them to come to me and ask me things, to help me feel useful and needed. When the girls and I started to decorate their rooms, I think we all enjoyed it. We bought carpets and new rolls of wallpaper. The rooms and the furniture were beautiful and the girls loved the privacy and the space. We did the big room up for J J and Philip but Philip did not sleep in there very much; he would doss on the floor in a sleeping bag beside Ellen's bed. They were very close and would chat well into the night.

For J.J.'s eighteenth birthday, I persuaded Michael to give him one of the cars he was doing up. This was a hobby of Michael's. He would buy one for little or nothing, do it up and then sell it. J.J. was delighted with his Ford Capri — not that he said it, but I knew.

Sometimes at the weekend, I would go down to the pub with

Katie and her boyfriend. I would have a couple of dances and a few drinks. They never drank fast enough for me. I wasn't getting the buzz I needed quickly enough. So I tucked a half-bottle of vodka into the lining of my handbag and would nip into the toilet now and then to have a sup. When they asked me what I wanted to drink, I would get a small stout because that was cheap. I would make it last for hours and Katie and her boyfriend would wonder how I had got so drunk. J.J. would never speak to me in the pub. I knew that he did not approve of my being there.

Then, out of the blue, Michael started drinking again. The children were really upset about it. After three weeks, he was back in Belmont Park Psychiatric Hospital in Waterford. He had been in there before and had stopped drinking for nearly three years after his treatment.

I was delighted that he had gone into hospital because since he had started drinking, he did not allow me out of his sight. It took two men from Alcoholics Anonymous to persuade him to go into Belmont Park. He was afraid that I was going to leave him again, and that he would run out of money for drink. He was a wreck. I used to visit him nearly every day and stop on the way home to get a bottle of vodka to help me to sleep. One of the AA men asked me if I thought I had a drink problem myself. I laughed in his face.

After a month, Michael came out of hospital, but he carried on drinking. It was like the old days, never knowing when he was going to come home, or what state he was going to be in. This made me feel that I had to drink more to survive. I had bottles hidden all over the house, in the cistern in the bathroom, in the hot press, wardrobes and stuck in the hedges around the garden. I needed a drink before I could do anything. I would have a panic attack if I could not get a drink the minute I wanted it.

One evening, when J.J. came in for his dinner, he walked over to the cooker to see what I was frying. Then he stepped back and looked at me. 'Why is there always a stinking smell of drink off you?' he said.

I nearly dropped dead. How could he say such a thing to me? One of the reasons I drank vodka was that I thought there was no smell from it. I didn't have an answer to give him, so I just put his dinner on the table and went to bed and cried. I was so hurt, but it did not stop me drinking.

If Michael came across a drink I had poured for myself, he would throw it down the sink, even though he was still drinking himself. Katie would have to get me more to stop me from shaking. The tension in the house was unbearable. Three of us were drinking to excess and I was in the worst state of us all. How could I get close to my children when I stank of alcohol and could not get them out of the house quick enough to have another drink?

One day, I took off in the car. I was supposed to be doing the shopping. The first thing I did was to buy a bottle of vodka and go somewhere quiet to have a drink. I went down a narrow road and into a graveyard and took out my bottle. I remember a wonderful feeling of freedom. Nobody was going to walk in on me, catch me, or take away my bottle. This started a twenty-four-hour cycle of having a drink, a sleep, a drink, a sleep. I have only a vague recollection of sleeping in the car, eating nothing, and having no concept of time. But it was a couple of days later when I got home.

When I walked in, Philip and Ellen were on the settee in the sitting room, looking at television. I sat in between them and put one arm around each of them and tried to focus on the screen. They snuggled into me and I was delighted. We stayed like that for an hour or two. I was quite content to sit between my babies. I really didn't feel that I had done anything wrong and the little ones were happy to have me there. Then the others started to come in from the pub: Michael and Katie and Jackie and their boyfriends. A feeling of unease came over me when I saw them all standing around the room, saying nothing. Then

J.J. came strolling in. He gave me an ultimatum: go to Belmont Park or he would not be responsible for his actions. No persuasion was needed. I agreed to go immediately. I was terrified. I dressed myself, falling all over the place as I was doing it. Then I said goodbye to my children. They all gave me hugs and said goodbye, except Jackie and J.J. I didn't go near him, and Jackie told me that she wished anyone else in the world was her mother besides me. Looking back at it now, I can understand why she said this.

I was sobbing my heart out as I went through the village. What was the matter with me? Was I mad? If I was, why was no one being nice to me?

Belmont Park was a lovely-looking place, beautiful grounds and the best of food. It was like a five-star hotel. When I got there, they medicated me and I didn't know where I was for nearly a week. I was wired to the moon, not able to think, feel, or hear anything that might help me face the reality of my life. I never missed my children. Alcoholics Anonymous meetings were compulsory in this institution, so I got my first introduction to AA. I went and laughed at everything they said. My denial knew no bounds.

After two weeks, I was discharged and given an envelope full of brightly coloured tablets. Coming out, I was no wiser about the disease of alcoholism that I was suffering from than I had been going in.

Ten days later, I was back in there again, worse than I had been the first time, because now I was dependent on prescribed drugs as well as alcohol. When I became conscious, nearly a week later, I found myself tied down in something resembling a child's cot — for my own safety, they told me. Gradually I was allowed up and about, and I learned how to make leather belts and baskets. We had relaxation in the mornings and dances at the weekends. They were generous with the medication, doled out three times a day, plus an extra one at night, to help me to sleep. It did exactly the same thing for me that alcohol had been doing. I was not able to think, feel, or hear anything that might help me to face the reality of my life.

Another girl and I used to sneak out of the hospital and stand outside the gate and thumb to the nearest pub. We would tell the drivers who picked us up that we were nurses on a break and needed a lift. We never had a problem getting one. On our way back with our vodka, we would hide it in the hedges of the grounds and retrieve it after dark. I had no intention of stopping drinking; it was what kept me going.

No one wanted me home and who could blame them? But after six weeks, they once again handed me my tablets — to help me to stay dry, so they said — and I returned once more to my unfortunate family. I have a poor recollection of things at that time in my life. The one outstanding feeling I recall was fear: fear of what I might do next, fear of not being able to get a drink, and the greatest fear of all, that I was going mad. Michael hid the keys to all of the cars, and the publicans in the village were refusing to serve me. I was finding it nearly impossible to get drink, but the medication prevented me from having panic attacks.

One fine sunny day, I started one of Michael's old cars with a nailfile and took off. The next thing, I found myself over at my mother's grave. That's how it was now. I never remembered planning to go anywhere, but I would find myself in many a strange place. Overcome with misery and wanting to feel close to someone, in my madness, I decided to go to my grand-mother's, in Ballintee, where my mother had died. I had bought a half-bottle of whiskey, and decided to explore the now deserted house. As I walked up that path, which had held such fear for me as a three-year-old, with its high hedges on each side, and the dreaded front door, the memory of the many rejections I had experienced at this place descended on me like a black cloud. My grandmother's resounding, 'No', when I asked her if I could come in, filled the air. Going round to the back of the house, I looked into the room where my mother had been waked. Taking a swig out of my bottle, I caught the reflection of a woman with her hair standing out around her head like steel wool and her clothes covered in stains. I looked bent and old. A shiver ran through my bloated body as the sun went behind a cloud. I began to run to the car, parked at the end of that long, fearful path. Then I heard someone call my name. It was one of the AA men who used to call on Michael. I jumped into the car, ready to drive away, but he had his hand on the door handle.

'What are you doing here?' he asked.

'It's my grandmother's,' I said, full of resentment. Two swollen eyes looked back at me from the car mirror; the whites of them were yellow and red in colour.

'Any chance of a cup of tea at your place? I'll follow you over,' this man said. Being the greatest people pleaser of all time, I said, 'Yes, follow me.'

I recall that as he drank his tea, he told me to take out my drink and enjoy it. I didn't have to be told twice. I sat there in front of him, supping away happily, not realising that this was a ploy they sometimes used in AA to get someone to go quietly to hospital.

My next memory is of being in St Canice's mental hospital in Kilkenny. I don't remember being brought in there, but I will never forget the experience. Michael had signed me in. The first night I was there, I woke up to an overpowering smell — a mixture of bleach, urine and faeces. I was in what appeared to be a men's ward; they had their heads shaven and the sounds that were coming from them will never leave me. When I allowed myself to look long enough, I realised that they were women who could not leave their clothes on they were so agitated in themselves. Apparently their heads had been shaved for cleanliness. These demented women hardly slept, day or night.

I tried to keep my eyes closed to avoid seeing what was going on around me. A nurse came with tea in a plastic bucket. She handed me a plastic mug and told me to help myself.

It was June. The heat was intense in this old grey building. The River Nore ran through the grounds and it was said that it claimed a life a year from the hospital. I swore to myself that if I got out of that place, I would never drink again.

Two long nights and days I waited until Michael came and signed the release form. As we drove through the well-kept grounds and out through the big grey gates, I thought of all the women who were still in there.

Within ten minutes of leaving that mental home, both of us were in the pub drinking as if there were no tomorrow. Even the fear of having to go back in there for the rest of my life was not strong enough to stop me.

Chapter Twenty-seven

A couple of dreadful weeks passed after I came out of St Canice's. I have only a vague recollection of them. There were lots of rows with Michael about my drinking. He hid my clothes to stop me going out, so I spent most of my time in bed. I craved alcohol. Katie took some time off from her hairdressing job, in town, to keep an eye on me. On one of those days, a neighbour called to the house for a haircut. When Katie left me to do the woman's hair, she locked me in the bedroom. There was a crater of thirst in me which overrode everything. I climbed out the window in my flimsy nightdress and walked to the village to get a drink.

What I must have looked like never entered my head. When I got to the pub, I went in as if it were the most natural thing in the world. A couple of men were seated at the counter. I had no idea who they were and I paid them no heed. I asked the owner for a bottle of vodka.

'I can't serve you,' she said.

'But you have to, or I'll die.'

She took a bottle of vodka from the shelf behind her, wrapped it in newspaper and handed it to me. I had no money to pay her. I dropped the paper to the floor and listened to the lovely crunch of the cap as my shaking hands twisted it. Taking a big gulp, which hit the bottom of my stomach like a brick, I staggered out. That is my last memory of that particular incident.

Another time, having stolen some money from Katie's purse, I once again took one of Michael's cars. A couple of hours later, I was arrested for drunken driving, and was taken to the Garda barracks in Kilkenny. I lost my driving licence for two years and was fined £85. This was a terrible blow to me. I would not now be able to get out of the village easily.

AA members called regularly; they were all men because there were few women in AA, in Ireland, at this time. I used to wonder why they wouldn't leave me alone.

'They're after opening a rehabilitation centre for alcoholics on the outskirts of Dublin,' Eamon, one of the men from AA, told me. 'Would you be interested in going in there?'

'Why not?' I said, thinking: it will get me away from all the rows in this place.

'I'll make an appointment for you to be assessed,' Eamon said.

He was back within the hour to tell me that he would take me there the following Wednesday, and that I was to bring a member of the family with me. None of this meant much to me at the time, but Katie was delighted that I was going.

The three of us set off for the Rutland Centre in Clondalkin in Eamon's Hiace van, a journey of about 80 miles. I was shaky and had taken a couple of Valium to help steady myself.

The Rutland Centre was an old monastery, with wrought-iron gates leading into a well-kept garden. Eamon knocked on the front door and a tall woman let us in. She took Katie and me into the office where she sat behind a formidable-looking desk.

'My name is Doreen,' she said. These were the first words she had spoken. Before we could say a word, she carried on, 'Tell me, Katie, what is it like to live with a drunk for a mother?'

I was stunned. My daughter looked at me in bewilderment.

'How dare you speak to us like that!' I said furiously.

'Will you be quiet, please, and speak only when spoken to,' she said to me.

'I'm not going to sit here and take that from you,' I told her, standing up to leave.

I thought she would apologise and ask us to sit down again, but I was wrong. She jumped out of her seat and held the door open for us to go. Katie went out the door first. I felt I could not leave without saying something.

'You big fat ugly cow,' I said as I stormed past her.

I got in the van fuming. How dare she ignore me and treat me like I was nothing?

Katie and I sat in silence as we waited for Eamon to come out. He was inside talking to that ignorant woman. How could he? He came out after about five minutes and never said a word either. The atmosphere in the van was stifling; you could nearly touch the rage between the three of us.

'It's true what she said about you,' Eamon said, breaking into the half-hour-long silence as we passed through Kilcullen.

'What did she say?' I asked.

'That you didn't have the guts to do it.'

'I'll show her.'

We had another hour's driving to do before we were home, and not another word was spoken until we stopped at the gate of the house.

'You're on your own from now on,' Eamon said. 'I have to stay away. You're a threat to my own sobriety.' I had no idea what he meant but it sent a shiver through my body.

Everyone in the house was furious with me when they were told what had happened.

'The Rutland will take you in on Sunday if you don't drink or take any more Valium,' Katie informed me the following day. Eamon had told her that the Centre had been in touch with him.

Something had happened to me in those two days. First, something inside me had sprung to life when the woman called Doreen had ignored me. The second thing was when Eamon had deserted me at our gate. Being ignored and abandoned caused me great pain and conflict.

I had no wish for food and craved sleep. I walked the floor of the kitchen for the next four days and nights. I was curled up in a ball, teeth chattering, perspiring from every pore in my body. Every time my eyes closed, I would immediately jump up in terror.

If anyone bothered to ask me why I was putting myself through all this, I did not have an answer. It was as if I had been possessed and the most important thing in the world for me was to be allowed into the Rutland Centre. I drank endless pots of tea and gallons of water to try to quench my insatiable thirst. I slept on the Saturday night for the first time in nights.

On the Sunday morning, Michael and our two youngest children, Philip and Ellen, brought me to the Rutland. I knocked on the door. A man answered and held the door open for me to go in, then closed it gently but firmly on my family. I stood in this huge hall. The man walked into the room opposite to the one I had gone into before. I followed.

'Did you take a drink or any drugs since you were here last?' he asked me as he shuffled some papers, with his back to me.

'No,' I answered, shaking like a leaf. He turned sharply and looked me straight in the face.

'Why should I believe you? All active alcoholics are liars,' he bellowed. Then more quietly, he said, 'You are not a patient in here. You are a client. The door is not locked; neither is the gate. You are free to leave whenever you want to. No visitors, post, or phone calls for the first two weeks. No radios, newspapers, or books at any time. No distractions. If we let you stay, these are our rules. I will introduce you to one of our clients now,' he said as he handed me a piece of paper with all the regulations spelled out. He must be going to let me stay, I thought to myself, as I watched him going through my suitcase and handbag without as much as a by-your-leave.

A woman called Eve came into the office. She was going to show me around. I knew that she was from Northern Ireland the minute she spoke.

'You and I will be sharing,' she said over her shoulder as we climbed the stairs. We went into a small room with a wardrobe and two single beds squeezed into it.

'That's yours,' she said, pointing to the bed behind the door. There was not much of the floor to be seen, but what I could see was a varnished wood.

'I'll introduce you to the others,' she said. As I followed her downstairs, I hoped the others would be a bit friendlier.

We went to the kitchen, in the basement. It was basic. A couple of people were writing away vigorously, while a few others were staring into space.

'We have someone new,' Eve said, leaving me. I stood there. My throat felt so tight I thought I was going to choke on my own spittle. I looked at the stone floor for a couple of minutes, then lifted my eyes. No one seemed to be happy.

'I'm Liam. Would you like a cup of tea?' an elderly man asked me.

He made us a cup each and beckoned to me to follow him. We went and sat in an enormous dining room.

'I'm a priest and an alcoholic,' he told me. 'Don't call me "Father". Just Liam. Let me give you a bit of advice. Don't ever run out of a group, no matter what they say to you. And another thing. You must not go to bed before eleven at night, not even to lie on the bed.'

'Thanks for telling me that.' How in the name of God is that going to help me to stop drinking? I thought.

'We must help each other. We are all here for the one reason — alcoholism.' I, for one, did not believe that I was an alcoholic.

In the end, Liam and I ran out of things to say. I wandered around the dining room; it had four long well-scrubbed wooden tables, with an array of chairs that looked more abandoned than arranged around them. There were more people at the tables with their heads down, writing as if their lives depended on it. They were nothing like the so-called alcoholics I had seen in Belmont Park or St Canice's. How could those dedicated-looking people be hard-drinking alcoholics?

Eve called me to get up just before seven. I had had a restless night. We went to a small room where there was a reading from the big book of Alcoholics Anonymous. I glanced around at the others and they all looked like I felt, half-asleep. Afterwards we went down to the dining room for our breakfast. We had a choice of cereals, and a fry. A woman sitting next to me told me that we had to do our own chores. It was called therapeutic therapy. Therapeutic was a new word for me.

After breakfast, I answered about six pages of questions, then I was told that I had been allocated a group. I was terrified every time I went to this group.

When I walked into the room, three people had arrived before me: Liam, Ann the woman I had been speaking to at breakfast, and a bank manager called Steve. I sat down and looked around at the others. There was no eye contact and no talking. They had six chairs in a semi-circle, and a chair at the top of the room — for a counsellor, I presumed. A clock was ticking loudly on the wall, and there was one lone picture, of a chair that had fallen over on its side. Underneath, it said, 'The truth will set you free, but first it will make you cry.'

Two women and a man came into the room. The man sat on the seat at the top of the room. The women seated themselves amongst us. The silence was intense. The seven of us sat in this room with only the tick of the clock. There had been no formalities: no good morning, or anything like that. I wished that someone would say something, anything.

The clock seemed to be getting louder. Every fibre of me wanted to run or scream. My head felt as if it were expanding, my throat contracting, as if a pair of hands were throttling the life out of me. We sat there for what seemed like an eternity. At last, Ann said in a strangulated voice, 'I can't take any more of this silence.'

'Neither can I,' I piped up to support her.

'Would you like to tell us how it feels not to be able to take any more?' one of the female counsellors asked me.

'I hate silences because we used to have them in our house when my parents had a row, and they would go on for weeks,' I said.

'How does it feel?' she said again. I sat there thinking: *what is she on about? I've just told her.* Silence was filling the room once more. It went on and on until Liam spoke.

'I can identify with Kay,' he said. 'It makes me feel like a small child again, afraid, helpless.' He had tears in his eyes. I thought someone should comfort him. I stood up bravely and went over to him.

'What are you feeling now?' the male counsellor asked me.

'I think someone should comfort this man,' I replied in a squeaky voice.

'I didn't ask you what you think. I want to know what you are feeling?' he said.

'Well that's what I feel — that we should be nice to this man.' I looked around to see if anyone else found all this strange. I was met with looks of cold disdain from the other two counsellors, and the rest of the group made no eye contact with me.

Dear God, don't let there be another silence, I prayed. A deep booming voice interrupted my thoughts.

'From now on, I want to hear how you're feeling, not what you're thinking. It is of no interest to me or anyone else in here what any of you are thinking. Tonight, I want you, Kay, to write out three things that you did when drunk that you are most ashamed of. We call them your "Worst Drunks". You can read them out in group tomorrow.'

With that, they turned their attention back to Liam, probing him about how he always managed to get sympathy from someone. After an hour-and-a-half of mental and emotional grilling, the three counsellors stood up and left the room. Then the others left too. Were they not even going to talk about what had gone on? Did they think the way I had got picked on was fair?

This is worse than any mental home, I thought as I wandered downstairs. Then a wonderful smell of cooking reached me. I was hungry and this was a rare feeling for me. My step quickened towards the dining room where everyone seemed to be gathered. On the table by the wall were dishes of all kinds of vegetables, trays of roast beef, roast potatoes and gravy. We helped ourselves. I ate until I was full. Then I proceeded to tell the young man who was sitting beside me what had happened in the group meeting. He didn't seem that interested.

'You're not supposed to discuss what takes place in the group,' he said.

'But I don't understand what they're trying to get at.'

'You'll get it after a while,' he said, standing up and walking away to get his custard and stewed apples.

It was half-past one. They all began to move in one direction, so I followed. I was not going to ask any more questions and have them look at me as if I were a madwoman. There were twelve of us gathered together in a room where one of the counsellors from our group, who I discovered was called Angela, was giving a talk on denial.

'Hands up anyone who does not believe that they are an alcoholic,' she said.

My hand was itching to go up, but I had learned something that morning: stay quiet. A new man called Tony, who was about forty, put up his hand.

'Why are you in here then?' she asked him.

'Because my wife said I'm one and told me that she's going to leave me,' he said, looking around at us with a grin. A couple of people smiled feebly.

'Why is she going to leave you?' Angela asked.

'You know what women are like,' he said, looking around for some support, but he didn't get any.

'You tell me what they are like,' Angela said challengingly.

'Never satisfied,' he said, rubbing his hands and smiling from ear to ear.

'That tells me absolutely nothing,' she said with a condescending look, then continued with her talk.

When this boring hour came to an end, I followed the others outside like a lost sheep. I felt alone, just tagging along. We climbed the stairs and went back to group for another ninety minutes. My mind was firmly made up that I was not going to open my mouth, no matter what went on.

So began my second session. I sat on the chair I had been sitting on that morning. Tony, the new client, had now joined us. I sneaked a look at him. He caught my eye and gave a big grin. I looked away immediately. I didn't want to encourage him.

When the counsellors arrived, they stood for a moment and looked at us.

'You sit on this chair over here,' Counsellor Deirdre said to me, pointing to a chair at the other side of the room. I went and sat where she had said, full of spite towards her. My slight feeling of familiarity and comfort vanished. I was afraid to draw breath in case I became the centre of attention. Then the silence descended on us.

'What the hell is going on? Will someone say something, for God's sake,' Tony said eventually.

'You say something,' Angela said in a quiet voice.

'I would like you to tell me how sitting here in silence is going to help me to stop drinking?'

'You tell us,' Angela said. 'I thought you were the expert.' We were sitting upright in our seats, feet planted firmly on the floor in front of us. We were all learning the same lesson, as far as I could see: don't move or talk and you will be safe. But for some of us it was more difficult to be quiet, than for others.

'Will I ever understand what is going on in here?' I asked.

'Basically it's about getting in touch with your feelings, learning to identify and express them constructively, so that we don't have to drink and bury them,' Liam said.

'Silence can help you to discover who you really are and stop you denying the only person you know how to be,' Angela said. After a few words here and there and a couple of bearable silences, we were free to go.

'Don't forget you have to do some writing tonight,' Liam reminded me as we left.

I didn't want to think about the couple of times I had drunk too much, never mind what I might have done.

Looking around the dining room, I saw the rest of them writing. Now I knew what they were writing about.

Then I saw Tony with his lopsided grin trying to get chatting to someone, without any success. I thought to myself, I have a choice: I can chat to Tony, or I can join the others. I joined the others. It was the first positive decision I had made in years.

Pen in mouth, I stared into space, trying to appear hard at work. I had to write something. I wrote first about the time I had borrowed money from my next-door neighbour, an old-age pensioner, to buy drink. Then the night I drove up from the village with no headlights on. I thought about the time I went to town to get the groceries and spent days drinking and sleeping in the car. I decided I was not going to tell them about that. They might say I was an alcoholic. Let me see, I thought, there must be something else. Yes, the time my daughter Ellen found a bottle of vodka underneath her mattress, where I had hidden it. When I had written briefly about those three things, I sighed with relief. Why was it taking the others so long to write theirs? Perhaps they really were alcoholics.

Chapter Twenty-eight

The mixture of people with drink problems surprised me. Besides the priest, there were two nuns, the bank manager, a chef, a farmer's wife, a nurse, two housewives, one unemployed man with a large family, a girl of eighteen, and myself.

After tea, people started to clear away the dishes, and I stood up to help. I was told that it was not necessary; that everyone had their own chores to do and I would be told mine soon. By now, I knew that there were twelve clients, eight counsellors and a cook who only made dinner. We did all the other cooking and housework.

We all went to the AA meeting at half-past seven in the evening, even though it was not compulsory. My mind wandered throughout the session. I had heard that four of the eight counsellors were alcoholics too. An hour later, when the meeting was over, I went back into the dining room. My eyes were closing but there would be no bed until eleven. The others were writing and reading again. I rambled upstairs. Eve was sitting on her bed, writing her most significant event of the day.

'Here,' she said, handing me a small notebook and pen, 'You'd better write yours.'

I sat on the edge of my bed sucking the end of my pen. Then I wrote quickly and closed my book.

'That was quick,' Eve said as she continued to struggle with hers. 'What did you write?'

'I wrote that the food was good.'

She buried her head in the pillow to smother her laughter.

'My God, woman, where did they get you from?'

I told her about all the writing and thinking I had done earlier.

'Show it to me,' she said. 'Eight lines — is that all?' She exploded into the pillow again. I had no idea what she found so funny.

The next morning, the same routine occurred: seven o'clock, a big book reading, breakfast and then the dreaded group. Up the stairs we climbed, looking as if we were going to our death. I sat on the first available chair with my eight lines of writing on my lap. Tony sauntered into the room and said he had nothing written. This made me feel superior.

The three counsellors arrived: Matthew, Deirdre and Angela. If there was going to be a silence again today, it would not be my fault. Before they had themselves settled in their seats, I spoke up. 'Do you want me to read what you asked me to write yesterday?'

'Do *you* want to read it?' Matthew asked.

'Yes, I do.'

'Go ahead.'

'I borrowed money from an old-age pensioner to buy drink, but I paid it back,' I said, looking up swiftly to see how he was taking this revelation. There was no reaction, so I proceeded to tell him about driving without my headlights on, and hiding the bottle of vodka under my daughter's mattress. I read it all as quickly and well as I could muster. Then I quietly folded the copybook over to hide it from everyone, but especially from myself. I had not felt one tiny bit of emotion when I had written it, but reading it out to those cold strangers, I was full of shame and guilt.

'Would you like to tell us how you're feeling now?' Matthew asked me.

'I want to cry,' I sniffled, lowering my head.

'Would you say you were full of self-pity?'

'No, but a bit of compassion would be nice after reading that,' I said with a bigger sniffle.

'Well, I refuse to accept that these are the three worst things you have done. I want three more tomorrow,' he said. I was now sobbing for all I was worth.

'I feel sorry for you,' Tony piped up.

'Thanks,' I said, giving him a weak smile.

Angela pounced on him. 'Tony, would you like to tell us what your three worst drunks are?'

'What's the point if you won't believe them, like with this poor woman?' he said, sounding pleased with himself.

'Try us. Bring them in the morning,' Angela told him.

The day carried on the same as the previous one, with lunch, then our daily lecture, which Matthew was giving. It was on the first step of Alcoholics Anonymous. 'We admitted we were powerless over alcohol — that our lives had become unmanageable.' I switched off when I heard this. It was of no concern to me. I began to think about what I was going to write for group the next morning. Things were coming in and out of my mind but I could not hold on to them.

'Are you all right?' It was Matthew glaring at me.

'Yes,' I said, shaking myself. *He misses nothing.* One of the group was asking him, 'How important is honesty to stopping drinking?'

'Very important. When people come in here at first, they will say that they get drunk only once or twice a year. Some will even say that they have never been drunk in their life, when the reality may be that they haven't been sober for years. They build a wall of lies around themselves and they repeat them so many times that they start to believe them themselves. It's part of their disease not to be able to see things as they really are. In here, we try to get the addicts to break down the barriers, to own their disease, and do something about it.'

I found all this vaguely interesting, but was sure it did not have anything to do with me and my drinking.

After that, a cup of tea and back to the therapy room for another hour-and-a-half. More writing before and after our supper, interrupted only for the AA meeting. There was not a minute to spare. What was I going to write for group the next day? I wondered as once more I sat down with pen and paper. The things that came into my head when I started to write were unreal. Many was the time I had gone and drunk in a graveyard in the middle of nowhere, so that no one could find me. The morning that I went into a supermarket in Kilkenny and pleaded for a bottle of vodka. The shop assistant said that she could not sell it to me until after ten, because of the licensing laws; I was not having any of that. The woman must have realised that I was desperate. I stood before her, shaking and begging. She went behind the counter and gave me a bottle. I paid for it, then promptly took the cap off and took a large mouthful of neat vodka. As I wrote about it, I could feel the sting of it going down my throat, only to be replaced by a warm glow. That's strange, I thought to myself: having a drink had never entered my mind since I had come to the Rutland. Well, that proves that I'm not an alcoholic. I felt a surge of relief.

Sitting there, chewing the end of my pen, I remembered the time I had gone to the pub in my nightdress and insisted on having a bottle of vodka. If I told them about that, they would definitely say I was an alcoholic. I didn't think it was madness to be drinking in a graveyard, or demanding bottles of vodka from people. I had my own logic about why those things were happening and it was not my fault. I drank in a graveyard because those AA members would just walk into our house whenever they felt like it and there would be murder if I had a sign of drink on me. When I went into the supermarket before opening time, it was because I had driven Jackie into work and

did not want to delay in town. The time I went down to the
village pub in my nightdress was because I was locked in the
bedroom without any clothes and had to escape out the back
window to get a drink. So none of it was my fault. I was a victim
of circumstances.

The next morning, I went into group very pleased with
myself. I had my copybook with my confessions and I waited
for someone to ask me to read them. Nobody did. I was
convinced that they were beginning to realise that I was not an
alcoholic.

The rest of the week passed and, in the end, I stopped
bringing my writings in with me. The counsellors were focused
on other members and I was determined to have no part in any
of it in case it rebounded on to me.

On Friday evenings, instead of the AA meeting, we had a
community meeting and we got our chores for the following
week. I didn't mind what I was asked to do as long as they did
not bother me in group. A man called Ben and I got the job of
washing up after dinner for the next week.

The weekend was here. What was I going to do for the next
two days? Tony and I were not allowed visitors because it was
our first weekend. Anyway, there was no one I wanted to visit
me. My husband and I did not get on, my children had no time
for me, my sisters didn't speak to me, and my father did not
know I was in here.

With nothing to distract me because of the ban on books
and papers, I had time to think. For many years, my sanity had
depended on my *not* thinking.

This was the month of October and I was sitting on a wet
wall in an old monastery, tears running down my face. I allowed
myself to consider everything. It was three years since I had
come back to my children and I felt further away from them
than ever. The sadness, the awful certainty that I had made
woeful mistakes, seeped into my very soul.

Monday morning arrived. I was glad in a way. Too much time thinking was making me feel more and more alone in the world. The three counsellors arrived and sat among us, having first asked Tony to move from the seat he was sitting on: it might make him feel secure. They wanted us on the edge of our seats, I was told. That is exactly where they had me, one hand holding each side of my chair, knuckles white. I felt I would break in two halves if I were asked to move.

I sat there in that unyielding silence, trying to stifle my breathing in case I drew attention to myself. I did not realise it then, but the counsellors would not break the silence. That was up to us to do. We sat for over an hour, the clock ticking loudly.

'If you want to sit there in your own shit for the rest of your lives, that's up to you, but I don't have to sit in it with you,' Matthew finally bellowed, standing up and walking out of the room. Then Tony jumped up, saying, 'This is torture', and walked out after him. Every fibre of me wanted to run after him and beg him to come back.

'You have a problem?' Deirdre said, glaring at me. She must have read my thoughts.

'I think someone should go and bring Tony back,' I said nervously. She pointed to the door to let me know I was free to go after him if I wanted to. I was afraid that if I went, I would not be let back into this group that I hated so much. What was happening to me?

'Would you like to read your three worst drunks for us?' she asked me coldly.

'I don't have them with me,' I said lamely.

'Bring them this afternoon.' She stood up and she and Angela left the room.

'I'm surprised that they reminded you of the drunks. Usually they wouldn't bother if you didn't yourself. It's their way of teaching us to take responsibility for ourselves,' Liam said as he caught up with me on the way downstairs.

'Thanks for telling me that,' I said. 'I'm in a trance — not sure what is happening to me. I'm afraid of staying, and at the same time terrified of leaving, or being thrown out.' My voice was shaking.

'I can't answer that for you. Maybe some day you will get the answer to it all.'

Chapter Twenty-nine

Nine days without a drink was a long time for me. My drinking career, as they called it in the Rutland Centre, was about twelve years, relatively short in comparison to most of the others. This convinced me even further that I was not an alcoholic.

I was so anxious about having to read my Worst Drunks in group that I could not eat my lunch. Then I realised that Tony was nowhere to be seen. He must have left the Centre. The thought made me feel sick. What would happen to him now?

After the lecture, which I did not hear a word of, I made my way to the therapy room. My heart was pounding. I waited for the counsellors to arrive, fiddling anxiously with the corners of my copybook. Now I wished that I had gone to the trouble of writing about three incidents as I had been asked to.

'I would like to read to the group the worst things I did when I was drunk,' I said in a weak voice. My throat was dry and my eyes misted with fear. 'I only wrote about two because that's all there is.' Before anyone could interrupt, I carried on. 'I used to go to a graveyard to drink so that no one would find me, and once I went into a supermarket and demanded a bottle of vodka before the off-licence was open.' I scarcely drew breath, I read it so fast, my face bright red. I struggled to control my trembling hands.

'I do not accept that those are your worst drunks. Write four more and bring them in to group tomorrow,' Deirdre said firmly. I held on to my chair with all my might. I hated the counsellors with a vengeance. How was I going to sit through the rest of the session? I lifted my eyes from the copybook and caught Liam's eye. He gave me what I took to be a don't-do-anything-you-will-regret look.

When we were finished, I waited outside for him.

'Why are they picking on me?' I asked.

'They're not. This is the method they use to get you to look at your own behaviour. It's the first step.'

'Okay,' I said, still baffled.

'Every time you write about one of those experiences, they are hoping you will see how insane you are and how unmanageable your life is.'

'What's the second step in AA?'

'We "Came to believe that a Power Greater than Ourselves could restore us to sanity".'

'I'm not insane,' I said with a weak laugh.

'Think about that,' he said, walking away.

After supper, I sat down once again with pen and paper. I asked one of the counsellors if it was all right to miss the AA meeting for that one night.

'That's your decision,' she said. I knew I had better go or it would come against me later on.

The meeting was on the third step.

'Made a decision to turn our will and our lives over to the care of God *as we understood him*.' That was a tall order. I didn't understand God. I prayed, but that was out of the fear that if I didn't, I would go to hell. That's what the nuns had taught us at school. The second the meeting ended, I left. I had two hours to think of four more things to write about.

I went into a corner as far away from everyone as I possibly could be. I thought about the time I had been let out of Belmont Park for a weekend and all I could think of was how I would be able to bring a drink back in with me, without anyone finding it. That was when I poured the vodka into my hot-water bottle. Then my mind flitted to all the different places I used to hide my drink: in the bag of the upright vacuum cleaner, in a rip in the sofa. I stopped writing for a minute. The panic of not being able to get a drink when I needed it surfaced. The desperation on my face when I demanded drink from the shop assistant and the woman in the village pub. I sat there immobilised, trying to rationalise all this to myself. Even as I sat there writing, more and more things were coming into my mind. How I used to send Philip and Ellen to the pub to get drink for me before they went to school. When they came home in the evening, I would still be sitting at the kitchen table where they had left me that morning. No meal ready for them, no housework done, the same clothes on me in which I had slept. I didn't want to be like that, but I seemed to have lost the book of instructions on how to live. This was the opposite of how I had been before I drank. Then I had taken great pride in my children, my home and my appearance.

It was half-past eleven when I went to bed. I wanted Eve to be asleep, so I wouldn't have to speak to her. My mind was in overdrive.

I woke at the usual time, full of dread. After breakfast, I climbed the stairs to group, my copybook clutched in my sweaty hand. When we were all seated, I said, 'I would like to read mine to the group if that's okay?' Deirdre nodded to me to start. It took me some time to get through it all: the trip in my nightdress; the supermarket hold-up; sending my children to the pub; and bringing the drink into hospital in a hot-water bottle. When I had finished, I sat back and tried to relax my shoulders, which were up around my ears.

'What kind of hospital were you in when you brought in drink in a hot-water bottle?' Matthew asked casually.

'A mental hospital.'

'I see. And why were you in there?'

'I had a furious, hurtful row with my son.'

'So the hospitalisation did not have anything to do with your drinking?' There was a silence. How was I going to answer him?

'Did you hear me?' Matthew asked.

'Yes, my son and I had a row because I had been missing for a couple of days and nights and I was drunk.'

'How do your other children feel about the amount you drink?'

'They don't like it.'

'Would you say you have a problem with drink?'

'Not really.'

'Why would you drink in a graveyard? Normal people don't drink in those places, or terrorise people into giving them drink, do they?'

'I suppose not,' I said reluctantly, wondering where this was leading, but that was the end of it. I was confused and agitated. What did it all mean? Before the end of group, Deirdre said to me, 'I want you to go and sit in the church for an hour every night and not pray.'

I had plenty to think about and, no matter how hard I tried, I could not put it out of my mind. I did admit to myself that I might have a drink problem but I was not an alcoholic. To me, an alcoholic was a man in a dirty mac with a bottle of wine sticking out of his pocket. I was not able to see how close I was to that, living in the same clothes for weeks, all stained with food, stretched out on a grave with a bottle in my hand.

Then I remembered something else. Waking up one night in a pitch-dark graveyard, searching frantically for my bottle, and, when I found it, it was empty. I remembered the terror that came over me, not because I was in a graveyard in the dark but because my bottle was empty. One of my shoes was lost and I didn't have time to look for it. I had to get a drink fast. Hitting both sides of the lane, I drove towards Kilkenny in my old Ford

Capri. With one shoe on, I drove as if the devil himself were after me. It was just closing time when I got to a pub near St Canice's Cathedral. The doors were being closed on the last few stragglers as I jumped out of the car and hobbled over to the man and asked him for a half-bottle of vodka. At first, he refused, said it was after closing time. I implored him and was just about to go down on my knees when he relented and let me have it. I could visualise myself back in the car, taking the cap off the bottle and drinking as if I had been in the Sahara Desert for a month. I had never thought about it since the night it had happened until that morning.

When we had our lunch eaten, it was time to go to the afternoon lecture. Deirdre was talking about the fourth step of Alcoholics Anonymous: 'Made a searching and fearless moral inventory of ourselves.' I would never be able to do that.

'This is the step that separates the children from the adults,' she said. 'The first three steps are about denial, acceptance and surrender. The fourth is an assessment of all of your assets and liabilities. The most important word in this step is, 'fearless'. It is meant to make you feel better about yourself, so don't be afraid to look and find.' I noticed that I was listening to everything she was saying and was sorry when she had finished.

That evening, I went into the chapel at about seven. My first instinct was to kneel and pray. It was dark and empty and I felt intimidated. I sat down. My mind started to go over the day's events. I became a different person when I drank. This thought frightened me. I would have to do something about my drinking. It seemed impossible that I would be able to change. I wanted to leave the church after ten minutes, but I sat there for an hour.

The rest of the week went by in a blur. I was taking in a lot of information but could not apply it to myself. I could not imagine living the rest of my life without a drink.

I had been in the Rutland Centre for nearly three weeks and it was family day. This meant that your family came into group with you and told everyone there what it was like to live with you. My hair had started to fall out in fistfuls. I was extremely nervous. I didn't want to see anyone. All my strength and energy went to holding on to my own reality. I didn't want to hear about my family. My grip on the kind of person I was had just started to take hold, and I wanted to look at why I needed to drink and what I was avoiding by drinking and be as sure as possible that it was true. I was afraid that I would be shattered by someone else's version of my reality. By my children and husband telling me how disgusting I was when drunk, how unreliable, about the lies that I told.

Michael and Katie came on the first 'confrontation day'. Putting them through this ordeal made me hate myself more than ever. Whatever I had to do, I felt, should be my own hardship. It was humiliating to have to listen to my husband saying how he had found bottles of drink hidden all over the house and that I was not to be trusted with money to do the grocery shopping. I was glad when group therapy was over and they were told that they had to go to a separate discussion on what it was like to live with an alcoholic.

I went to another room to hear Ann, from my group, reading her life story. This was the Fifth Step exercise we had to do before we went home. 'Admitted to God, to ourselves, and to another human being the exact nature of our wrongs'. It was a harrowing story. How could she be so honest and humble? I wondered aloud. I would never have been able to do that.

'You will have to if you stick the pace,' Eve, who was sitting beside me, said.

'You would be bored to death listening to me.'

'We'll see,' she said with a wink.

I went for a cup of tea before I returned to group. Katie and Michael were there. They were like strangers to me. Maybe I was to them, too; it was all very strained. I asked about everyone at home. They just said, 'They're all right. Philip and Ellen are coming up for family day next week.'

My feet were unsteady on the way to group; the steps of the stairs were like cotton wool under me. My eldest daughter and my husband sat opposite me. The rest of my group had members of their family there and Fr Liam had his bishop.

Katie told everyone how she never knew if I was going to be at home when she got back from work. She told them that I had given her chips for dinner for two whole weeks. How I would try to go to the pub with her and her boyfriend. This was all news to me.

Michael didn't have anything to say. At the end of an hour-and-a-half, he was told not to come back any more, because he could not help me. Katie had been a great help apparently: she had painted a very clear picture of life with an alcoholic mother. She was crying and saying she was sorry for admitting all those things about me. I hugged her and cried with her, telling her not to worry, that I wanted to know how she felt, how all my children felt. I didn't realise that my conduct had damaged them so badly.

The rest of the day was spent on the others in the group. When it ended, I was physically exhausted. All the families left and we drifted around the Centre like the walking dead. After supper, I sat at one of the dining-room tables and thought about my eldest daughter. I wished I could take away her pain. I was aching inside at the thought of what my children were suffering, and I knew that I was the cause of it.

After supper, I was glad to have the chapel to go to. As I sat in the darkness, my tears brimmed over and an uncontrollable cry escaped from my throat. The sound of it echoed in the chapel. Drawing my cardigan tightly around my body, I rocked myself until I was empty of tears. Then I went to my AA meeting and to bed.

The next morning, I did a reading from the big book. I opened it at random. It was chapter 11, 'A vision for you'. It was the first time I had listened to one word from this book. This chapter spoke of hope and a power greater than ourselves. I had no problem reconciling myself to the idea of there being something greater than me.

Later in the morning, when we got to group, we were asked how we felt about what had been said to us the previous day. I said I had been amazed to hear that my daughter was afraid to come into my bedroom in the morning in case she found me dead, and also to discover how my actions and attitudes had affected my family's lives. It had never entered my head. I was told to write down everything that had been said to me. Then I was to read it out in group. The last thing I wanted to do was to go back into the humiliation and pain of such a detailed account, but that evening I sat down to write. I could see Katie's pretty face imploring me not to be angry with her for what she had said so bravely. I wished she was near to me at that moment, that I could hold her in my arms and reassure her again that she had done and said the right thing. I was a ball of hurt as I slouched over the table. How could I have been so blind? Now I was going to have to face myself. I wrote like a maniac. I wanted to rid myself of all my shame, regret and guilt, and pray that I would never again hurt my family.

Making my way slowly to the tiny chapel, I slid across to the centre of the pew and took in the moving mixture of smells: incense, candle wax and polish. Overwhelming sadness took me over. It was a freezing November night and I had felt icy cold in the chapel. Suddenly it was as if I were thawing, as if the moon were warming me, like a huge spotlight being put on my life, showing me all the amazing things that I had been missing. I thought, It's good to be alive.

This was the turning point in my recovery. I had been looking at the world through the bottom of a bottle. At that moment, the will to live, and a thirst for self-knowledge, were born in me. I went on my knees and said, *Thank you, God.*

I made the last quarter of an hour of the AA meeting. As I sat there and listened, it was as if my hearing had just been restored. Then, as on every other night, we were asked if anyone wanted to say anything before the meeting closed. I said calmly and firmly, 'I am an alcoholic. I came here to get away from my family and I feel I am changing in spite of myself.'

I went into group the following day, bursting with enthusiasm. Taking a deep gulp of air, I told them, 'I admitted for the first time that I am an alcoholic and I accept that I am.'

Trying to explain the experience I had is like trying to describe air. When I had finished speaking, one of the group said that she felt it had been a spiritual awakening. This was the first time I had heard this expression and I must admit that I was sceptical.

Chapter Thirty

I had been in the Rutland Centre a month when this took place and there was still a lot of work to be done. The job was now to see why I needed to drink myself into oblivion every chance I got and how mentally and physically dependent I was on alcohol. I realised that drink took up all my waking hours. I was hiding it, looking for it, worrying about getting more, afraid that someone would find what I had and throw it away, or I was drinking it.

Different members of my family came once a week to talk about what it was like to live with me. I was told many things that I had no recollection of and never wanted to hear about. Katie told me about the time that herself and her boyfriend had sneaked off to the pub to avoid me coming with them, because by now I was such an embarrassment. When I found out what they had done, I had thumped the table in front of her with a stick, when she was eating her dinner, until she ran from the kitchen. Jackie told me that she was afraid to come into my bedroom in the mornings in case she found me dead. The most difficult thing for me to hear was Ellen defending me. She said to the counsellors, 'Leave my mother alone, she has an illness.'

But no matter what anyone said, or what pain it was causing, it was hard for me to imagine my life without drink. I was terrified of hurting my children again, of letting them down. I thought that if Michael and J.J. stopped drinking, I might have some hope, but nothing would have changed when I got home. The same tensions and arguments would go on.

My biggest problem was my relationships — with my children, with my sisters, but most of all with Michael. I didn't want to sleep with him any more. I was told by the counsellors that if I didn't want to, I didn't have to. It sounded so simple. The Sunday before I went home, he came to visit me. I spent hours explaining to him how I felt about our marriage and was sure that he understood what I was saying.

After ten weeks in therapy, and having read my life story, the day for me to go home arrived. I was petrified. Would I ever be able to stay away from drink? Every second building was a pub, and there was an off-licence in most supermarkets.

My first test was when Michael arrived to collect me. He was on his own, although we had agreed that Ellen and Philip would come with him.

'I have a surprise for you,' he said before I got a chance to say anything.

I was anxious enough, so the last thing I wanted was a surprise. We got in the car and set off for home. A couple of miles down the road, he pulled into the car park of the Green Isle Hotel. *He's taking me for a meal*, I thought. Just as we reached the hotel door, he said, 'I have a room booked for us for the night.' I felt physically sick. How could he do this to me after I had explained how I felt?

'I don't want to stay the night. I want to go home now,' I said.

'Don't worry. I have them all told that we won't be back until tomorrow.'

'How could you do this?' I asked him, tears in my eyes.

'It's no big deal. If we go home now, the children will think there is something wrong between us.'

I knew he was using the children to get his own way; he knew that I wouldn't want to do anything to worry them. We had a meal, not that I was able to eat very much, but at least Michael didn't have a drink. This was the kind of situation I had needed alcohol to cope with. *Dear God, help me handle this*, I prayed, telling myself, I don't have to drink, or sleep with him. I held on to that thought for dear life. I wanted to go to bed and sleep to make the time pass quicker so that I could go home. I was only out of the Centre a couple of hours and here I was, wanting to escape from a situation. Was I a failure already?

The room had two single beds. I lay on one of them and he was on the other. We were pretending to look at television, when I said nervously, 'I'm going to go to sleep now.'

'Can I get in beside you for a minute?' he asked. 'I just want to feel close to you.'

'I suppose so,' I said irritably. Anyone would know by the look on my face that it was the last thing in the world I wanted. So he got in beside me. I closed my eyes and thought, I have done this for years; once more is not going to kill me. The sooner it's over, the sooner I can go home, but by letting him, I felt weak, and that was the last thing I wanted to feel.

When we arrived home the next day, the children were at school and work. I was disappointed. I needed my children to be there to make me feel that everything was worthwhile. At this early stage, I was stopping drinking for them, not for myself. That was a lesson I still had to learn.

Eventually they started to come in, one by one. I wanted them to be delighted to see me, to ask me about my experience in the Rutland Centre, to be proud of me and to support and encourage me. I would have to have patience.

Part of my agreement with the Rutland was that I would go to at least three AA meetings a week and, once a week for a year, attend a service called Aftercare, which was at the Centre. The Aftercare was a lifesaver. The group members understood when

I told them of my acute pain and loneliness at not feeling understood or approved of by my family. My vulnerability made the hunger in me for a family more intense than ever, but what right did I have to ask my children or sisters for anything, for support or compassion?

My nearest AA meetings were in Kilkenny, a 17 mile drive. Because I had lost my driving licence, AA members would pick me up and take me, or sometimes Michael would, even though he was still drinking.

Michael had once again taken to sitting at the kitchen table with a bottle of whiskey. He now added a Bible to the scenario.

'What God has joined together, let no man take asunder,' he preached to me.

J.J. was like a time bomb waiting to go off. When I bent down to kiss Ellen goodnight, she would give a loud sniff to see if she could smell drink from me. I was full of fear. When I went shopping, I had to take one of the children with me in case I bought a bottle of vodka in spite of myself. I was going to my AA meetings as suggested and that was one of the reasons J.J. was angry with me. He thought I should stay at home, now that I was all right, as he put it. Little did he know, or want to know, how close I was to the edge. I would hear people at meetings saying that, only for the love and support of their family, they would never stay sober.

One day, shortly after I came out of the Rutland, I was at home when I heard a familiar car coming up the road. I started to panic. It was my father! I watched the cream-coloured Volkswagen pull slowly into the yard. He's going to have a go at me now, for leaving my children, drinking and God knows what else, I thought.

I had not spoken to him for seven years. I saw him heave himself up off the seat while holding on to the car door. A sense of dread came over me. Even though I was thirty-six years of age, he still had the power to send a shiver through me. He straightened his shoulders and held his head high. He was wearing a navy suit, shirt and tie, his full head of silvery grey hair was immaculate, and the shine on his shoes would dazzle you. I decided that I'd better go out to him.

'This is a nice surprise,' I said, too cheerfully.

'Is it?' he asked, one eyebrow raised.

'Come on in,' I said.

'I didn't know if you'd be here or not.' There was nothing warm or friendly about his manner, not a trace of a smile.

'I'm glad I was here when you took the trouble to call.'

'I was down at Alison's,' he said, watching me closely. 'I thought I'd come and see how you were since you came out.'

By now, we were in the kitchen, and he had his Baby Powers in his hand.

'Would you like a cup of tea?' I asked him, the smell of whiskey turning my stomach.

'No thanks. No tea,' he said. 'I won't be staying long. I just wanted to know how you were since you came out.'

'Came out' sounded very strange to me. Why not say 'came home'?

'I don't know what you mean by coming out,' I said.

'Who do you think you're codding?' he snapped. 'You won't fool me, me lady. I know you were in prison in Limerick for the last couple of months for drunk driving.' A look of pure satisfaction spread across his face. 'I could have paid your fine, but I thought it would teach you a lesson, so I decided to let you do your time.'

I was speechless. To think that my own father would have let me go to prison before he would part with a few pounds.

'I was in a treatment centre for my drinking,' I said quietly. 'I was not in prison.'

'Oh, I see. So you're all right now, are you?' he said casually.

'I am, thank God.'

With that, he stood up and, straightening himself, made his way to the car. I stood at the front door. He looked in at me before he drove out of the yard and gave me a little wave, but no smile. I waved back at him before I ran into the bathroom and vomited for all I was worth.

After six months, I went to court and got my driving licence back. The judge said he was aware that I had gone for treatment for my alcoholism and that it was a privilege to return it. He wished me well in the future.

This meant that I didn't have to be picked up by anyone to go to meetings.

I continued to sleep in the same room as Michael so that the children would think we were normal parents. We had single beds but it was awkward at times.

I thought and hoped that my sisters would come around to wish me well to or offer me support, but I did not hear from them. I felt hurt. Katie was extremely kind to me, Jackie was indifferent, J.J. was J.J. and Philip was caring. Ellen watched me suspiciously.

Michael was still drinking, mostly in the house. He made it as awkward as possible for me to go to Aftercare in the Rutland. I had mixed emotions about him, alternating between great compassion and pure hatred. Knowing what he was going through with the drink, I found it hard to accept that I could not help him. When I tried to console him or persuade him to try the Rutland, it always came back to the same thing. If I were different towards him, everything would be okay; the whole family would be happy. The counsellors in the Rutland and people in AA advised me to keep my compassion for myself. All I was responsible for was me.

One of the many things that I had to look at in Aftercare was how my drinking had affected my relationship with Jack O'Meara. He was now back living at home with his father about five miles from our village. The counsellors asked me if I still had feelings for Jack. I didn't know how I felt about him. At times, I convinced myself that if I had not been drinking so much, he would have loved me more. I told myself that he was the only man I had ever loved, but that it was in the past. I had an overpowering fear that if I lied or didn't divulge everything, I would drink again. Most of the time, I talked about Michael: how demanding and claustrophobic our relationship was. The counsellors told me that I would have to learn not to encourage his dependency on me. They told me I was not doing Michael any favours. I would have to practise some 'tough love'. This was easier said than done. It would be another battle for me, on top of everything else I had to change about myself.

Michael was now infringing on every effort I was making to stay sober. He was insisting on coming to AA meetings with me. Sometimes he sat in the car until I came out, or he would come in with drink on him and tell me it was time to go home. I would have to lie down with him in the middle of the day when he was drunk, or stay up with him when he was afraid to be on his own. I would hold his hand at night from one bed to the other, so he would know I was there. He was full of fear and paranoia.

When I told them this in Aftercare, they said that they were in the business not of saving relationships, but of saving lives. They wanted me to move out of the house for six months and concentrate on my sobriety. They had been saying it to me for a while, but I could not bring myself to think about it. I couldn't make up my mind which was going to be worse: staying where I was, or telling my children that I was moving out again. I sat in group for months, telling them why I couldn't do it. They looked at me and said, 'It's up to you. No one else can do it for you.'

They knew that I had left my children for five years. I wanted them to say that they understood why I had left before and that that was why I couldn't leave again. Their answer was simple: I had to do it to save my life. One of the girls in the group, who was around my own age, piped up and said that I could share her flat in Tramore. She suggested that I could have the children for the weekends when she went to visit her parents. This had been another of my reasons for not going: that I could not afford to do it. I didn't have to worry about that, she said; I wouldn't have to pay any rent until I had got a job. This meant that I didn't have any excuses left. It seemed that this kind young woman had offered me more than any member of my own family had offered.

When I got home, and with the decision made at last, I said nothing to Michael. The first person I told was my rock, Katie. She suggested I get one of the AA members to tell Michael — that he would listen. I did as she said and I asked them to say it to J.J. too. Katie and I told Jackie together; she just looked at me and said nothing. I went up to the bedroom and told Philip and Ellen. I said that they could come down to me every weekend and we would go for walks on the beach and have great fun. They were wonderful and seemed delighted. Perhaps Michael would pull himself together when he realised I was gone.

Chapter Thirty-one

Tramore is a beautiful seaside place in County Waterford, with long clean beaches and crystal-clear water. It is also a place of nostalgic memories for me.

When Michael realised that I had left him, he was raging at first, but the AA people hung in there with him and slowly he grasped that there was nothing he could do about it. They even persuaded him to let me have an old car that he had been doing up to sell. I was grateful to him for that.

I got work straight away. Bord Fáilte, the Irish Tourist Board, was looking for staff. I was cleaning chalets. When one group of people left, the chalets had to be spotless before the others arrived. It was a hard job; the state some people left those chalets in was dreadful. They usually had an end-of-holiday party on the last night. I had to start at four in the morning when people left to catch the ferry from Rosslare to Fishguard. I got paid by the number of chalets I cleaned: £5 for each one that passed inspection. The woman who inspected them was very exacting. Everything had to sparkle.

When I left the flat for work, at about half-past three in the morning, there would not be a soul around. Having parked the car, I would look out at the sea and the wonder of it, and I would thank God that I was able to get up and do this without even thinking of a drink. The combination of fish and chips mixed with the smell of the sea gave me a ravenous and pleasurable hunger that I appreciated because of the years when I had had no appetite.

This job meant that I could now pay rent and feed myself. I had Philip and Ellen at the weekends and we had great fun together. None of my other three children came to see me. I tried not to make a big thing out of it, telling myself that they were busy teenagers. I went to a meeting every week night, except for my Aftercare at the Rutland Centre. After a few months, another flat became available in the same house, so I went and got it.

Then I met a man from our village, who was with his family in Tramore for the day. He told me about an insurance company that was training staff and suggested that I give them a try; the money was good. It was winter and the chalets were closed. I went right away. They paid me for the five weeks I was training.

I had now gone ten months without a drink. One evening, at an AA meeting, I heard that Michael had stopped drinking over a month before. When the younger children came down one of the weekends, they told me that their father was going away on a retreat the next weekend and had said that I could go home and be with them while he was away. The retreat was something that several AA members did every year, at Mount Melleray Abbey. I was delighted and thought it would be great to see what J.J., Katie and Jackie thought of me being sober. Would they be proud of me?

Katie was now doing hairdressing from home. Michael had put in a wash-hand basin in the front bedroom, and she was getting a lot of work.

I was excited by this change in Michael, letting me go home. Perhaps I might be able to go back for good soon. However, this was not to be. When I got home, Michael was sitting at the end of the table, his lecturing spot. Then he started. I was not going to come and go whenever I liked, to his house. I would not be welcome in his house until I decided to be a proper wife to him. And he was stopping Philip and Ellen from coming to Tramore to see me. I just listened to him. I didn't have any answers for him. Could he not see that whatever hope we had of being able to communicate with each other, moralising was not the answer? Was his fear of losing control over me that great, I wondered. Or was his pride dented once again to the point that he would rather see me drunk or dead than living a productive life away from him.

My spirits were very low after this episode. Did anyone understand what I was trying to do? If I didn't stay sober, I would either die or go mad. Perhaps they didn't care. My family was what I wanted more than anything in the world and it was the thing that constantly eluded me.

After this escapade, Michael stopped Philip and Ellen from coming down to me. I pleaded with him through AA members not to do this to the children. His answer was that if I wanted them in my life, I could come home. I felt heartbroken and hopeless. Then he said that he wanted the car back. If he took it, I wouldn't be able to go to work, to Aftercare, or to as many AA meetings. They were my lifeline. There was only one meeting a week in Tramore, and there was one every night in Waterford, about ten miles away.

One day in particular, I felt totally beaten. I couldn't motivate myself to go to work, or settle in the flat. My nerves were taut with uncertainty. I rambled around Waterford, trying to relax. I was walking along in a daze when I heard someone say, 'Long time no see.' I jumped and saw Jack O'Meara's sister Una.

'How are you? Would you like a coffee or something?' she said.

'Why not?'

We chatted about one thing and another, and then she said,

'He's always talking about you and saying that he never stopped loving you.'

That magic word 'love' caught my attention. Did Jack really love me? Maybe it was my drinking that had made him treat me as he had. I went off into a world of my own.

'Are you okay?' Una asked. 'You look lost. I come here to do my shopping nearly every week. Here's my number. Give me a ring and we can meet again.'

'Thanks,' I said. 'I'll do that for sure.'

I made my way back to the car. As I opened the door to get in, I noticed a note on the passenger seat. My hands were shaking as I picked it up: 'Hope you had a nice day. See you. Michael'.

I looked around the car park in a panic. Was he watching me this minute? What was he trying to do? Drive me mad? Drink came to my mind. It would stop me feeling afraid and help me to forget, I reasoned in my confused head.

'Dear God, don't let me do that,' I said aloud. I started up the car, revving the engine with rage.

'Come out, you coward, and face me. You say you want me back. For what? You bastard.' I felt braver as I put my foot down and drove defiantly out of the car park.

For a long time, I had needed Michael to treat me this badly. It had helped me to justify to myself why I didn't love him. But I was changing.

Back at the flat, I sat with a cup of sweet coffee and pondered. A feeling of gratitude swept through me. I was getting comfort from coffee. I hadn't needed alcohol to cope.

The next morning, I went to work and I didn't look around to see if Michael was lurking somewhere.

I had been sober now for over a year and we had an Alumni meeting at the Rutland. I had no idea what an Alumni meeting was until I asked one of the counsellors.

'It's for people who have finished their university education, and all of you have, in the university of life, at the Rutland Centre.'

Out of the group of five, two had taken a drink in that year. I was well aware that I was lucky. As each of us went up to receive a medallion, the tears of joy and pride from families and friends were flowing. Sitting there alone, I felt the stirring of old emotions: anger, self-pity, an urge to stand up and scream something, anything to shatter the celebrations. I wanted to draw attention to the rage and pain that lay close to the surface, the desperate need for someone to be proud of me and tell me how well I was doing. I would need to drink to show my family just how angry I was, how hurt, how out of place and how self-destructive I could still be. But would they care or was it just what they expected of me?

This was another turning point for me. The realisation hit me that to add alcohol to this mixture of feelings, instead of dealing with the feelings, was the difference between sanity and insanity.

It was around this time that the concept of staying sober for myself, and not for my children, suddenly made sense to me.

One day, on the spur of the moment, I decided to ring Jack's sister.

'Good to hear from you,' she said. 'Guess who's standing beside me?'

'Jack, I suppose.'

'Do you want to talk to him?'

'I might as well.'

'How are you doing?' he asked.

'Not too bad,' I said, with a shake in my voice. It was over three years since I had spoken to him. Hearing him had the same effect on me as it had the first time: it both frightened and excited me.

'Can I take you out for a meal tonight?'

'Yes,' I said without hesitation.

We arranged to meet at the Ard Rí hotel in Waterford, at seven. I washed my hair and put on my best clothes, telling myself we were just going to be friends.

Chapter Thirty-two

The Ard Rí stood high above Waterford city, overlooking the quays, shops and church steeples. I got out of the car and watched the lights flickering for miles around. It was a brisk, star-filled night.

Jack was pacing the lounge when I walked in. He seemed nervous. I saw him before he saw me, so I walked over and put my hand on his arm.

'How are ya?' I asked.

His face lit up.

'It's great to see you,' he said with a big smile. We sat down together and he took my hand in his.

'I never thought this day would come,' he said.

'Neither did I.'

'Would you like a drink?'

'I'll have a glass of orange, please.'

'So will I. I hear you're off the drink. Fair play to you.'

'You have a drink,' I insisted. 'Please. It makes no difference to me at all.'

We sat for hours and talked about things that had happened between us, and how things were in our lives now. He was back living at his father's. When he had first come back to Ireland, over a year before, he had gone to live with his wife and children, but he had had to leave again because of the irreparable damage that had been done to their marriage.

I told him where I was living and he said that he would like to see the flat. We left the hotel and took the two cars to Tramore. Within ten minutes of going in, we were in bed. We talked until dawn and decided that we would see each other once or twice a week, and I would go to my meetings on the nights when we didn't meet. I wasn't sure how I felt as we left for work the following morning.

When I got back to the flat that evening, I was tired and not taking much notice of anything. When I saw Jack's car parked outside the house, I immediately felt a surge of anger. Did this mean that he didn't trust me? How dare he! This was my meeting night. He appeared to be asleep when I approached the car. I tapped on the window and he opened his eyes.

'Oh God, I'm sorry,' he said. 'I just had to see you tonight. I couldn't believe that we were back together. Don't be cross with me.' We went and had something to eat, and he came back and stayed the night again.

Jack never went back to his father's. Without any discussion, we started living together. At this point in my life, I chose to believe that my drinking had been the cause of us splitting up. Then the insurance company I was working for moved me to Kilkenny. I reluctantly gave up my flat in Tramore. I had achieved a lot there — living on my own, for one thing.

Now we had to find somewhere to live in Kilkenny. We were lucky and got a flat straight away. A couple of mornings later, I went to the car to go to work but it was gone. I knew that Michael had taken it, and an AA member confirmed it for me later in the day. He also told me that Michael was drinking again.

Not having the car meant the end of my job with the insurance company but I was lucky to get work in a bakery within a couple of days.

Shortly after, Katie came into the bakery to tell me that she had left home. She and her new boyfriend had decided to live together, and they had a place in Kilkenny. How was everyone at home? I asked, desperate for information. She said that Jackie didn't want to speak to me, and Philip and Ellen had stopped asking if they could they come and see me, because it caused too many rows. J.J. never said anything about me, and Michael had stopped drinking again.

Katie got a hairdressing job and we would meet for lunch most days. I asked her if she would like to meet Jack, and she said that she would. Her boyfriend, Martin, was a nice lad and it was wonderful to have one of my children back in my life.

When Michael heard where I was working, he started ringing the shop, pestering me. Eventually I was asked to leave. Jack had decided it was a waste of money renting, so he bought a house in Kilkenny. We were getting on fine, but I was anxious around him when he had drink taken or when he went into one of his black moods.

I longed to see Philip and Ellen. A couple of times, I saw Jackie in the town but she remained distant from me. Katie felt as guilty as I did about leaving Philip and Ellen. She had been a mother to them when I was gone. She and her boyfriend decided that they would rent a house so they would be able to have Philip and Ellen for weekends, and I would get a chance to see them, without Michael knowing.

I was so excited at the thought of this that I couldn't eat or sleep. It was almost a year since I'd seen them. Philip was now thirteen and Ellen eleven. Since I was not working, I could spend all day with them at Katie's. My two youngest children were delighted to see me. One of the first things Ellen told me was that her father drove her around to different churches at night to pray for me and to save my soul. I was horrified. I said nothing to her to make her feel bad about it, but I mentioned it to Katie.

'Just be glad that you're getting to see them,' Katie said. 'Don't do or say anything to upset anyone.'

This time together lasted for only a couple of weeks, and then Michael found out I that was seeing my two youngest and stopped them coming in to Kilkenny. A woman in AA told me that there was a nun in the local convent who might be able to help legally, and because Michael seemed to be into religion at the moment, a nun might be just the person to get through to him.

Sister Loretto was wonderful. She came out to the house to me.

'It's disgraceful that you're not allowed to see your children,' she said. 'You're their mother and no one can take that away from you.'

When I told Katie what had been said, she started crying.

'Don't start anything or Daddy will drink again and then I'll have to go back home,' she begged. 'Please. I've never asked you to do anything for me before. I'm getting married in a couple of months. Will you wait until after that, please?'

I did what she asked. My eldest daughter was getting married. I didn't want to do anything to upset her wedding day. Martin, her boyfriend, was in the Irish army; he had been brought up in Birmingham but his parents were Irish. I had been saving in the Credit Union for a couple of years and so I borrowed £1,000 to get Katie whatever she wanted for her big day. We went everywhere to look at dresses and when she saw one she loved in Carlow, I bought it for her. The dress and hat looked as if they had been made especially for her.

Jackie, Ellen and a friend of Katie's were going to be her bridesmaids. They had blue fitted 'shower of hail' dresses. Katie said to Jack that he would not be able to come to the wedding and he understood. I thought a lot about how it would be between the rest of my family and me. Katie invited six AA people to help me feel a bit more secure.

About a week before the wedding, Katie came out to me in Kilkenny. I knew by the look on her face that there was something wrong, but I waited for her to tell me. We drank tea and talked about one thing and another. Then she blurted it out.

'Daddy said if you go to the wedding, no one else will.'

'I see,' I said, gently sinking back in the chair.

'Who does he mean by no one else?' I asked in as composed a voice as I could manage.

'Granny, J.J., Jackie, Philip, or Ellen — none of the family.' She looked at me imploringly. 'I don't know what to do. I'm only telling you what he said...'

'You and I must not fall out over this,' I said. What I really wanted to do was stand up and smash the place into a million pieces. Nothing mattered any more.

'This is not your fault, but does your father not care about what *you* want on your wedding day?' I asked.

'I don't know what he cares about.'

I went to Katie's hen party, to try to feel that I was taking part in some of the excitement. Jackie stayed away, I believe because I was there.

The day was drawing close and I was beginning to realise that I really was not going to be at my daughter's wedding. Jack wanted to take the day off work to be with me, but I wouldn't let him. I asked him if I could have his car for the day to help keep me occupied when the wedding ceremony was on.

Katie slept at our house the night before the wedding and left from there in the morning. She had her breakfast in bed, with a red rose on the tray, and we sat and talked as she ate. I prayed that I would not break down in front of her.

Her friend, who was one of her bridesmaids, came and did

her hair and make-up. We laughed and talked and I must have appeared normal, because nothing was said. It felt as if every word were wrapped in pain and had to be squeezed through my lips. In my head I was praying: *Please God, don't let either of them say that they are sorry that I'm not going or I will dissolve into a pool of tears.* When we were at the front door and they were leaving, I was shaking but I was not crying. They both hugged me and left.

Into Katie's red Mini they got and off they went. I stood at the front door and watched it all happen in disbelief. She was gone and I was still there. Suddenly I decided to get dressed and park where I would be able to see her and then I wouldn't have missed it all. I ran upstairs and jumped into the first thing I came across. I parked as near to the church as I possibly could without been seen. Somewhere in the back of my mind, I thought that Michael might feel guilty and let me go into the church. I was still hoping.

The wedding took place at St Patrick's Church in Kilkenny. The church is high above the road so I could look up and see everyone. There was no one around when I got there. Gradually they started to arrive. First the groom and his family. Then my sister Mary and her husband. I had not asked Katie who had been invited. I would have felt that everyone who was there was more important than I was and I couldn't bear that. Michael's mother and his sister were now on the scene. The three bridesmaids were there, looking gorgeous. Then I saw J.J. and Philip. J.J. looked angry and seemed to be speaking to no one. People from the village started appearing. Then I saw my father, and the tears began flowing freely down my cheeks. I didn't brush them away; they felt warm and real. My heart was breaking. The urge to rush into the middle of the guests, throw my arms around my daughters and feel the heat of their bodies against mine was excruciating. My father looked lost. Then Michael and Katie arrived. I wiped away my tears to see her better. My sister Mary went over to Katie and started to fix her hat, and a sound as if from an animal came out through my parched lips. 'I should be doing that,' I whispered to myself.

Then I noticed Ellen looking down at me. She ran over to tell Katie. Whatever was said, that was the end of it. They started to go into the church. I was left sitting in the car, on the street, thumping the steering wheel with all my might. After a while, I started the car and went back to the house. I collapsed on the hall floor, curled up in a ball of pain. I felt as if I were going to go mad. I crawled up the stairs on my hands and knees, into the bedroom and put my head on the side of the bed and prayed, 'Dear God, help me through this. Thank you for getting me this far and not into a pub. Give me peace, please.' I couldn't straighten myself to get into bed but instead fell asleep on my knees and didn't wake up for five hours, by which time Jack was home.

I was in a trance, but I knew it was over. They would be dancing in the hotel now, but I had survived it. We went out to get something to eat.

The next day, I was washing up in the kitchen when Katie and Martin arrived. They seemed so casual and indifferent, I just flipped. I screamed and cried and said no one cared about me. How could she have let this happen? I was trembling with rage and injustice.

'I missed you yesterday,' Katie said softly. 'Jackie asked me did I miss you, so she was thinking of you too.'

'Thanks for telling me that,' I said. The fact that my daughter had wanted me at her wedding made me feel at least something like a real mother.

After Katie and Martin had got married they decided to leave Kilkenny and buy a house in our village. She promised that she would come and see me as often as possible. The fear of losing her was like a physical pain.

Sure enough, when she moved, I seldom saw her. Michael had given her the deposit for her new house and I think that she felt guilty about taking the money and continuing to see me.

However something good happened after Katie's wedding. My father came to visit me and decided that he would make his peace with Jack. After that, we would meet regularly in Hoyne's pub, in Thomastown, and have a couple of drinks with him. He seemed proud of the fact that I was drinking a mineral. This was the first time in my life, I felt, that he approved of something I was doing.

One Saturday night, we had arranged to meet him in Hoyne's, but Jack was late getting home. My father was the kind of person for whom, if you said seven o'clock, it was a case of *Be there at seven on the dot or don't bother*. When I heard Jack's car in the drive, I had a feeling of panic. It was ten o'clock. The minute I looked at him, I knew he was very drunk. I just stood and stared as if I'd never seen him like this before. Part of me couldn't believe that he would have so little respect for my father. I didn't know what to say. He gave a careful stagger as he crossed the kitchen and sat down heavily on a chair. Rage and fear knotted themselves up inside me. I could scarcely breathe.

'I'm going to bed,' I said, putting a plate of sandwiches on the table in front of him. He took the lot and threw them at the wall as hard as he could. I carried on up the stairs. I got into bed and lay under the covers, fully dressed. Suddenly the house was in darkness, even the light from the alarm clock at the side of the bed faded away. It was the middle of winter, and the room was jet black. Jack must have switched off the electricity. It was as if he were trying to frighten me, just as he had all those years ago in London. Then I heard the stairs creaking under him. In a matter of seconds, I felt the bed sink under his weight.

Lying there beside him in the darkness, I knew that I couldn't go back to the way things were before. Staying with Jack would be like giving up everything that I had worked so hard to achieve since I'd stopped drinking. I was thinking all of this, but not a word was spoken. I was calm and lay there quietly. He fell asleep, but I didn't close my eyes all night. I knew that this was the end for him and me.

When he awoke in the morning, he went down on his knees, telling me how sorry he was for frightening me and how much he loved me. It meant nothing. In the end, he gave up and went to work. I started packing my things and left once more. I got a flat in Kilkenny later that day.

Chapter Thirty-three

I carried on going to AA but inside I felt I was a failure. I listened to others talking about their homes and families and this made me acutely aware of my aloneness. Why could I not stay in any relationship? Those people couldn't all have perfect partners, dutiful children, adoring parents, I thought, but they remained together. Was there something wrong with me? Self-punishment festered inside me as I wandered aimlessly around Kilkenny, living on the dole.

In my daydreams, one of my children or sisters would hear how unhappy I was and come and see if they could help. And in my nightmares, I was back drinking in that lonely graveyard again.

I spent about two months living in this mental hell when one day the doorbell rang. It was Katie and she wanted to talk. I felt hurt that she had not been to see me for so long. There was no way that she hadn't heard where I was living, or what had happened between Jack and myself. We behaved like strangers.

We had a cup of tea and she told me that she was pregnant and was delighted about it. But Michael was drinking again, and Jackie, now twenty, was also expecting.

'I don't know what you want me to say about all this,' I said.

'Daddy is going into hospital. Would you come home while he's in there and talk to Jackie?'

'Have you forgotten that Jackie's not speaking to me? It's not that I don't want to do something. I do.'

'Will you ring her and see what she has to say?'

'I will,' I said. I had a feeling that this had all been well talked over between the two sisters. Jackie was at work; she was a secretary for a company in Kilkenny. Katie gave me her phone number and I rang her.

'Jackie, it's me,' I said tentatively. 'Your mother.'

'I know who it is,' she said.

'Katie is here with me. She's just told me your news and I want to know if you would like me to come home.'

'I would,' she said immediately.

I was taken aback by how sure she was about it. We hadn't spoken for nearly two years.

'I'll have to get someone to talk to your father first. I can't just walk back in,' I said.

'I know that,' she said irritably.

'I'm going to be honest with you from the start. I will come home if it's okay with your father, but I'm not saying that I will stay forever. I'll have to see how it goes. Are you happy with this? If not, say so before I do it, please, Jackie.' I said this as gently and firmly as I could.

'I know what you're saying and, yes, I still want you to come back.'

'That's okay with me. I'll do what I can as soon as possible.'

I got in touch with an AA member to come with me to the hospital to speak to Michael. Once again, I wanted to make it quite clear to him that I was doing this not for him, but to help Jackie; there was no way we were going to live as husband and wife. I asked him if he understood that and agreed to it. The AA person was a witness to what I was saying. And so, after two years, I went back home once more.

Michael was out of hospital within a week, and we were once again sleeping in the same room, but in separate beds. When he was in the house, I felt I had to keep moving all the time in case he decided to sit down and start one of his lectures or quotations from the Bible. It was all a terrible strain. I kept wishing that he would go and leave me with the children so that I could be happy.

After a short time, Jackie and her boyfriend Tony got married. There were more or less the same people at this wedding as had been at Katie's. Katie and I chatted during the reception. She said to me that she frequently dreamt that she wasn't married and asked if it could be because I had not been at the service. I told her that we can't ever go back and change things. I hoped she would think about what I had said and not let her father have that power over anything else she did in her life. The only thing that got me upset that day was my father going on about my refusal to dance with Michael. I told him that if I did, it would give Michael all kinds of ideas. My father didn't know half the things that had happened between Michael and me throughout our marriage.

Mrs Kelly was there — distant, as usual, but it didn't bother me. I think J.J. respected me for not drinking at the wedding but we were not at ease with one another. He had a lovely girlfriend now; we got on well. All in all, it was a good day and I hoped that it might make it easier for Jackie to start to love me.

Waiting to become a grandmother was a joy. There was only a month between the two babies being born. Jackie's was first. Katie would have liked to have had the first grandchild. Her house was in the centre of the village; I went down to her every day for a couple of hours. We were getting close again and making great plans for when the babies were born. Jackie and Tony had moved into Michael's after the wedding, until they got a place of their own. Jackie didn't talk much about her plans, and worked to the end of her pregnancy. I think she was in denial about the baby, but it would become a reality soon enough.

One day, I took Jackie for her check-up to Waterford; she was having her baby in a private nursing home. After she had seen the doctor, she went into labour right away, so we went straight to the nursing home. I have never known anyone have a child so quickly. She went down to the ward and within half an hour the nurse came back and handed me this pink and perfect baby girl.

'Would you like to hold your first grandchild?' the nurse said, putting her in my arms. The baby snuggled into me and, as I touched her soft little face with my finger, I thanked God for letting me play a part in this wonderful day.

Ellen and I spent a week decorating Jackie's bedroom. We had a Moses basket for the baby and we lined it inside with white satin padding and a tiny mattress. Yards and yards of frilly pink material covered the outside. I couldn't wait for them both to come home. Jackie decided that she was going to go back to work and asked me if I would look after baby Shauna. I said that there was nothing I would enjoy more.

Nearly a month later, Katie also had a baby daughter. I went with her for her check-up and they kept her in. I rang her husband and we took it in turns to sit with her. Katie was in labour for six to seven hours and it was like it had been for me — hard work. When the baby was born, she was in a distressed condition and had to be put in an incubator, just like her mother twenty-two years earlier. She was a beautiful baby with a full head of dark hair, and deep blue eyes.

As they got bigger and their personalities started to develop, there was no likeness between the little girls. Katie's Amber was placid, quiet and easily amused. Jackie's baby girl, Shauna, was very different; she was needy and noisy but I loved her and she loved me back and that was all I wanted. I'd moved out of Michael's room and at night she even slept with me in my bed. My whole life revolved around her. Every day, either we went down to Katie's or she and Amber came up to us. I had taken over the daily care of the baby completely and was too busy even to go to my AA meetings. AA people said to me that what I was doing was dangerous, that I needed to get my priorities right and go to my meetings or I would drink again.

After about a year, a house in the village came up for sale, and Jackie and Tony bought it. I was apprehensive about them moving out, even though I'd still be looking after Shauna in the daytime.

I still dreaded J.J. coming home from work. The depth of his anger towards me frightened me and, of all my children, he was the one it seemed I could never reach. It was obvious to him and to anyone else around us that I would do anything for him if I thought I would get his approval. If I was just after cleaning up after dinner and J.J. came in, I would jump up and cook a whole meal again for him. Even though he wanted me to do this, it seemed really to irritate him. Perhaps it was himself he was annoyed with, but he took it out on me by not answering me when I spoke or looking at me as if most of the things I said or did were ridiculous. I needed to have Katie around in the evenings at the time J.J. was expected home. I felt stupid having to admit that I was afraid of my eldest child. Katie was the only one I could tell. It was something I felt that I couldn't talk about even in AA; it made me feel weak and vulnerable.

One evening, Ellen and I were washing the dishes when Michael pulled into the yard.

'Please, Mammy, don't let your face change like that when he comes in,' Ellen said. I told Ellen that I'd no idea that it had, and said I was sorry and would try not to do it again. She was coming up to fourteen — a big strong girl, very independent and popular, with a terrible dress sense, like most teenagers, but she was witty and full of fun.

Philip was just sixteen, a good-natured young man, with a great love for his mother. When he came home from a night out, he would lie on my bed and hold my hand, telling me everything. No one will ever know how much I longed for this intimacy and yet when it found me, I couldn't relax and enjoy it. In the deepest corners of my heart, I felt: if I cherish this, it will turn into something bad and I won't be able to bear the pain of losing it again.

I had been back home for a year-and-a-half. Michael's need to possess and control me was becoming sick — that's the only way I can describe it. Whatever book I was reading, he would keep checking it, to see what I was reading about. I would wake up in the middle of the night to find him sitting on the side of my bed, looking at me. It was as if he wanted to get inside my head, under my skin, and it made me want to run and run and never stop. I started drinking some of the baby's Dozol, after I had made sure that there was no alcohol in it. It helped babies to sleep when they were teething. It was harmless, but Michael told the AA members that I was drinking gallons of it. If I took as much as an aspirin, he would go and tell anyone who would listen that I was taking drugs. Some people in AA would look down on anyone who took any kind of medication; it was seen as a crutch.

Chapter Thirty-four

It was autumn 1983 when my sister Alison rang me to say that my father had had a heart attack and was in hospital. I went in immediately to St Luke's in Kilkenny and he seemed genuinely pleased to see me. One of the nurses told me that he would never be able to live on his own again. This was going to create some soul-searching.

Alison, who now lived in Daddy's house, said she couldn't take him; she had enough to do with six children and a business to run. Ray had built a garage at the side of the house; it sold tyres and had petrol pumps, and had become an established business over the last ten years. In our father's mind, Ray was the son he had never had; my father was so proud of him that he continued to live in a mobile home to let Ray have full rein in the house.

Neither Mary nor Geraldine were in a position to take my father in their houses either.

So, when the time came for Daddy to leave hospital, after a lot of persuading, he came to us. The children didn't want it; my father was sarcastic and contrary. Michael didn't care as long as it didn't affect him too much. My father moved into the room in which Katie used to do her hairdressing. It had a wash-hand basin and everything he needed. He took over the sitting room and the television and no one could look at anything he didn't want to watch. No matter who came on the screen, he hated them. It made me physically sick to hear him go on and on about people. J.J. and my father didn't speak to each other. When J.J. left the room, my father would say to me, 'Where did you get that whelp from?' When my father came into the kitchen, the rest of the kids would moan. It was a nightmare. If I went to a meeting, he would say to me in the morning, 'That was a nice hour of the night you came in at.' He would say this to me when I brought him up his breakfast on the stroke of nine: softly boiled egg, and brown bread with the crusts cut off. And a clean shirt every day. He would examine the shirt before he put it on and usually found something to criticise.

'Why didn't you iron the collar up?' or if it were up, 'Why didn't you iron it down?' The egg would be too hard, the bread stale, or the tea cold. Was it any wonder that none of us had an ounce of self-worth? We never did one thing right in this man's opinion.

He was with us for nearly six months and I was so delighted when he got a place in the community home for the elderly of the village. It was run by nuns and was a beautiful place. He had his own bedroom, and the toilet and bathroom were right next door. Not that he was in the least impressed with any of it. God help the nuns, I thought to myself. Before he moved in, I took him to Kilkenny and he rented a television and video from Sherwood's in the High Street.

Now there was plenty of room in the house and I started to worry about what I would do when all the children were gone. Katie was up with me one night. We were looking at *Dynasty* and when it was over we went to my bedroom, because there were some clothes that she wanted to borrow. Then I noticed that the bedroom curtains were parted in the middle.

'Look,' I said, pointing at the curtains, 'I'm sure they weren't like that when I went down from here. I'm really careful about closing them tight.'

She looked confused and I felt like a mad woman, but I carried on: 'Go and see is your father in the sitting room or in the garage.' I suspected that he was out the back, keeping an eye on me through my window. It was important to me that someone else witnessed all this. Katie came back and said that her father was nowhere to be seen, but that his car was still in the yard. I got a big safety pin and stuck it viciously in the curtain. I wanted Katie to ask me what was worrying me, but she didn't; she just went home.

I said nothing to Michael about my suspicions. These kind of invasions were an everyday occurrence; it was how I was learning to live my life. Sometimes I would feel so hopeless, I'd think it would be easier to let him think he had power over me, as he wanted. I set myself goals for the next week, but the closer it got, the sicker I felt. I decided that I would have to talk to someone about it, preferably a woman.

I rang the Rutland Centre and made an appointment with a wonderful lady who was twenty-five years sober. From what she had heard of my marriage, she said that Michael saw me as a conquest, and once he won, he would move on to his next, and I would be left feeling worthless again. By letting Michael control me, I would have gained nothing, but I would have lost myself. She got me to write down, 'To thine own self be true.' I was to keep the piece of paper in my purse and look at it at least once a day. It was one of the most rewarding days of my life. I felt strong, content and peaceful as I left the Centre to drive home.

But things came to a head one night not long after this. I had been talking to a couple of the AA people in the kitchen, and Michael came in. When they left, he asked me what we had been talking about.

'You know that whatever I say to those people is private.'

'I don't care. I want to know now.'

Philip and Ellen came in from the sitting room where they had been looking at television.

'What's all the shouting about?' Philip asked.

'Go away. I want to talk to your mother,' Michael said.

'I'm going to bed,' I said, as I made my way to my bedroom across the hall from the kitchen.

Within a minute, Michael was knocking on my door.

'I want to sleep.'

In he barged. I pushed past him and opened the kitchen door. I found Philip standing in the middle of the floor with the sweeping brush held above his head.

'There will never be peace in this house until one of them goes,' he said to Ellen, smashing the brush on to the floor.

'Thank you, God, for letting me hear that,' I said out loud.

I went to the bathroom and buried my head in the towels hanging on the back of the locked door. There was a surge of relief. This must be a sign from the man above to tell me to get out or we would all go mad. I would do it differently this time. God would give me the strength to be honest with the children and tell them one by one. My father would have to be told; I would not be afraid of his tongue. I couldn't bear to tell Michael and receive a lecture on 'what God has joined together', due to his on-off religious beliefs.

I told Katie first. She didn't put any pressure on me to stay. A couple of nights later, Philip was sitting on the kitchen worktop and I asked him if I could tell him something.

'Sure,' he said.

'I'm going to have to go again,' I said, watching him closely.

'Is it because I've started drinking? If it is, I will never drink in front of you again.'

'No, sweetheart. It has nothing to do with you at all. I love you with all my heart.'

'I know the real reason. I just wanted to be sure.'

'That's okay. You can ask me anything you want to, any time.'

I had an AA friend, Jill, in Dublin, who had always said that if I ever wanted to move there she would get me a place. I let her know and she got me a bed-sit in Rathmines.

When I told Ellen what I was doing, I said that she could come with me if she wanted to; she was fifteen now.

'I'll see. What about all my friends?' she said.

'You can make new ones. I'm not going to put pressure on you. I just want you to know that you have a choice.'

'I'll think about it,' she said, making for the door.

'Where are you off to now? I might not be here next Sunday.'

'Well,' she said, with a wicked smile, 'Which would you prefer? I can go where I was going before you said anything, or sit here crying because you might not ever be here on a Sunday again.'

As she left to go, she gave me a hug. That was one thing that Philip, Ellen and I did all the time.

Katie had told Jackie what I was going to do, so when I mentioned it to her, she just said that she already knew.

'How do you feel about it?' I asked.

'If it's what you want to do, there's no more to be said.' I knew she was hurt, perhaps more than the others. She had little idea how things were between Michael and me and would not thank anyone who tried to tell her. I wanted their blessing and understanding, but this was my choice. Did I have any right to ask my children for anything? I didn't have the courage to tell J.J., so I wrote to him. If he'd said something hurtful, it would have cut me to the core.

My father still had to be told. I usually went up to see him on a Monday night. He was sitting on the edge of his bed and I sat on the chair beside it. He seemed to be in good form, not too drunk and not too sober. We talked about this and that on the television as I awaited my chance. I couldn't leave it too long because my father would always say, 'It's time you were going', as the longing for a drink got too much for him. He didn't drink in front of me any more.

'Daddy, I have to tell you something,' I said cautiously. 'I'm going to live in Dublin. I can't stay with Michael any longer.' I held my breath.

'I knew that was coming,' he said.

'Really?'

'Yes,' he said quietly. 'I can see the way you are around Michael and I don't believe there is anything you can do to change that.'

I wanted to put my arms around him and hug him, but I hesitated. There were tears in my eyes as I said, 'Thanks, Daddy. It means a lot to me that you understand.'

The following week, I left. Ellen stayed home from school to help me pack my clothes into an old rusty Datsun car. She was cheerful. I took two knives, two forks and two spoons with me because I was hoping she would come up to me after a while. I gave Katie the letter for J.J. and put my trust in God.

I once again drove out of the village with my clothes in black bin-bags and my few kitchen utensils rattling around in a cardboard box. There was no way I could turn back, no matter how confused, alone and full of misery I felt. This was the only way for me at this time. I was forty years old, and no matter how many times I left home, it never got any easier. But I knew in the innermost part of me that for me to survive, I had to make a change. I was told in AA that no one can stand still in life: you have to grow or you will slip backwards. Backwards was something I could not allow myself.

Passing the graveyard, I made the sign of the cross and thought of my beloved grandfather. As I drove through all the familiar places on the way to Dublin, I felt as if I didn't belong anywhere.

Chapter Thirty-five

I arrived in Dublin around six in the evening and met my AA friend, Jill. She gave me my new address and I gave her the £90 that she had paid as a deposit on the bed-sit. That left me with £50 to live on. Jill had some cleaning jobs set up for me, starting the next morning. Two Arab students, who were studying to be doctors, needed a cleaner. They had an apartment each in Merrion Village and I was to clean for them once a week, eight hours at £2.50 an hour.

My new home was in Sunbury Gardens in Rathmines. It was a lovely setting: about twelve huge old houses, in a semi-circle, with a garden in the centre, and big old trees all around. My bed-sit was in number 5, on the second floor. It had an open fire, and everything I needed. The back window looked out on to a small garden and clothesline. As I looked around, I tried not to dwell on what I had done but concentrated on being grateful for what I had been given.

I hung photos of my children and grandchildren on the walls, kissing each one as I put it up. Eventually I got into bed and drifted into a restless sleep.

When I awoke in the morning, I got straight out of bed

before I had time to start going over in my mind where everyone at home would be and what they would be doing.

The cleaning was hard work, but I was glad of it. There was no way I was going to be able to live on £20 a week, though; the rent was £12. I would have to get more work. That night, I went to an AA meeting and met someone who wanted a couple of rooms in his house wallpapered. I said I was not a professional but that I would do my best.

It was a regular thing for most of the people at the meeting to go to a coffee shop in Ranelagh, called Pronto, and I soon became one of them. On this particular night, though, Katie was to ring me at the flat.

I had butterflies in my stomach as I waited for her call. She rang right on time. The first thing I asked her was if she had given J.J. my letter. She said that when she had given it to him, he had read it, folded it and put it carefully in his wallet. I was delighted to hear this. I'd imagined him tearing it up, or not wanting to know at all. Did this mean that he approved of what I had done? Oh, I wanted to believe that so much. I asked her how everyone was, and she said she missed me, and she thought Jackie did too, but she hadn't said so. Michael said that he had been expecting it and that I would never be let back into his house again unless I was going to be a proper wife. I asked Katie when she thought it would be okay for me to come down and see them all. She said, 'Give it a bit of time.' I told her that she was welcome to come to me at any time and that went for them all.

'Ellen is enjoying her holidays at the moment,' Katie said. 'She might go up to you later on, and Philip is in good form.'

I felt thoughtful after the phone call. I was consumed with guilt for not speaking directly to J.J., for doubting him. Did he have any idea how much I loved him? I wondered. I vowed to myself that the next chance I got to tell him, I would grab it with both hands.

After two months in Dublin, I had seventeen cleaning jobs.

They were scattered all over the city, from Blackrock to Ranelagh; a couple of hours here and there — it all added up. Only for my old battered Datsun I would never have been able to get around. Ellen came up to me for a weekend and decided that she would like to come and live with me, but not just yet. The ban on me going down to Kilkenny was still in place, in case I upset Michael and he went back on the booze.

One of the great joys to me at this point was being able to get closer to my sisters for a time, and also to Ellen. This was a source of great enjoyment and happiness. Ellen came to stay with me for a couple of days, and, out of the blue she said, 'I'm coming to live with you'.

'Great! I'd love that more than anything.'

My bed-sit was too small for both of us, so we decided to ask the landlord about one that was free in his house next door. Ellen felt grown-up at having her own little place, as well as going to Rathmines College. We went to see the bed-sit which was going to cost £10 a week. It was a garret flat with a dormer window from which you could see the lights of Dublin flickering. It had its own Baby Belling cooker, fridge, single bed, wardrobe, a big comfy armchair and a small table. We couldn't get over this and then we pulled back a sliding door to reveal a bath and toilet.

'We could jump for joy,' Ellen said, 'only the ceiling is too low.' We both fell on the bed laughing.

There was an intercom to the front door, a phone in the hall and her mother next door. It was going to be great. We decided that she could do a Saturday job at the weekends when she didn't go down home. I had a job cleaning in the Red Cross on Saturdays and Ellen said she would do it with me for pocket money. Everything was working out better than I had ever expected. I felt so grateful. We even went to meetings together. Ellen went to Alateen, which is for teenagers with an alcoholic in the family, and I went to my AA meeting at the same time.

Eventually I got a little bolder in myself and started going home. Michael would always know when I was around; he would see the car outside Katie's. My sister Alison, to whom I hadn't spoken for ages, came into Katie's on one of my visits.

'Why don't you call in when you're passing?' she asked.

'I wasn't sure if that was the right thing to do or not,' I said. 'I'll come in and see you next time.'

'The house is finished now. I'd love you to see it,' she said. 'Why wait? Call in today.'

'Right,' I said.

At one time in my life, I would have been delighted to be asked in. Now I was wary of getting pulled into a situation with any of my family. It provoked too many hurtful memories. None of my sisters had ever made any attempt to encourage me or to show consideration towards me when I came out of rehab. All this was so painful to me and I didn't want to get any more of it. Still, Alison only lived five minutes away from me at home. This felt like a time of positive change, so I called in.

The house had two entrances, one from the garage and the other from the road. I knew from the outside that not one bit of my father's house stood there any longer. It had been knocked down little by little and a new modern one had risen in its place. I stood at the front door, searching to see if I could recognise anything from the old days. No, not a thing to say that my father or grandparents had ever lived here. Suddenly the door opened and Alison stood there, beaming. 'Come in,' she said proudly. The hallway alone was the size of one of the old bedrooms. A staircase made of pine swept upwards to five children's bedrooms, each one nicer than the other, finished off by a huge bathroom, just for the children, at the end of the corridor.

We came downstairs and into the sitting room. The three-piece suite was big and comfortable. A marble fireplace set the whole room off to perfection. Then Alison took me down to a magnificent pine kitchen that must have been the size of the entire old house. They needed it with six children. Alison and her husband had their own bedroom on the ground floor with an en-suite bathroom. I was so pleased for her. I had a cup of tea and a chat and was delighted when she said, 'Promise me you will come in when you're around', adding, 'I mean that. I'm not just saying it.'

As I drove away, I felt great that it was not just a once-off invitation and told myself that I would be more relaxed the next time I went in. From then on, every time I was passing, I would bring a bag of sweets for the children and spend some time with my sister.

Alison was so different from me; she never talked about herself or her life. Sometimes I would try to steer the conversation towards our childhood or our parents, but to no avail. In the end, I gave up and instead we enjoyed long chats about some book we had read, or film we would love to see. She would never want me to leave and I often stayed until the early hours of the morning. This was a time that I treasure.

It was during one of my visits that I also bumped into Geraldine. I was on my way out of the nursing home after a visit to Daddy. She was working there. We both said sorry to each other automatically, laughing nervously. She asked how I was.

'I'm fine.' It must have been five years since we had last spoken.

'Were you up to see him?' she asked, with a God-help-us look on her face that made me smile.

'I was,' I said. 'I'm in his good books at the moment for some reason.'

'He's making my life a misery, so I suppose he might feel he has to be nice to one of us,' Geraldine said.

I felt a rush of anger towards him. My sister noticed the change in my expression.

'I don't take any notice of him,' she said quickly, to pacify me.

'What's he saying to you?' I asked.

'Whatever I do, it's wrong. No matter where I put the cup and saucer on the tray for him, it's the wrong side. He calls me the fool every time I go into the room to him. I stand outside his door shaking before I go in. Sometimes he comes down to the house to me. If I'm washing the dishes, he'll say, "Is the fool breaking them or washing them?" If I'm sweeping the floor, he'll say, "You missed a bit over there." You know what he's like.' She laughed anxiously.

'I'm going to say something to him before I go.'

'Don't, please, I beg of you. It will only make it worse for me. Sure I'm used to him.' Tears glistened in her eyes and I could feel them in my own. Then we both started laughing.

'Why are we laughing?' she asked me.

'Because it's better than crying.'

She nodded and said, 'I'll be all right. I don't want you worrying about me. You have enough problems of your own.'

'I don't see why the four of us can't all be friends and support each other.'

We stood there lost in thought. Then Geraldine broke the silence. 'Alison is the only one of us who's able for the father.' Then she said quickly, 'I must go.' It was all getting too personal.

'So must I,' I said, and off we went in different directions.

As I walked down the dark avenue between the high trees and precisely planted rose bushes, I wondered how many years would pass before Geraldine and I talked to each other again. I thought that if only people took half as much care of each other as they did of their gardens, the world would be a wonderful place. At one time in our lives, my sister and I used to snuggle up in the same bed together, eat from the same table, and now we were lost to each other.

Chapter Thirty-six

Ellen had a party for her sixteenth birthday. She invited all her new college friends and introduced me to them. She seemed delighted with it and said that it was a great success.

Shortly after this, she suddenly wanted to to go down home every weekend. I wondered about this. Did it mean that she was not happy in Dublin and that she wanted to leave college and leave me? It would seem so. One Sunday night, Ellen didn't come back from Kilkenny. I couldn't believe she was going to miss a day at college.

She rang me the next night, without any explanation, to ask if I would pick her up. She was at Heuston Station. Anger rose up in me.

'Get the bus. It comes right here to the door.' I wanted her in front of me when I spoke to her.

'Can I get a cab?' she asked.

'No, get a bus,' I told her in no uncertain terms. 'I'll be here, so come straight in to me.'

She never answered me, just hung up. I went down to the front door to wait for her. It should have taken her only ten or fifteen minutes to get home. An hour passed and there was no sign. She could have walked it in that length of time. Now I was worried. I got the car and went over to the station. Why had I not gone over and picked her up like I always did? I knew why — because I was so angry with her. Did she think I was printing money for petrol and cabs?

Anything could have happened to her. The station was closing for the night as I ran in. There were a few people there, sweeping and tidying up. No sign of Ellen.

I made my way back to the flat, praying that Ellen would be there by now, but no. It was over two hours since she'd rung me. She couldn't have gone back to Kilkenny because there was no other train until the morning. I went and waited at the bus stop. Three buses came and went and she was not on any of them. I rang Jill, and she came over and stayed with me. She made me a cup of tea and we tried to think what to do next. Should I ring the guards? I decided it was too soon. What would I do if anything had happened to her? Why hadn't she told me that she wasn't happy? I would have listened. I had no doubt about that. I sobbed with abandon.

The hours of that night passed slowly as we tried to work out where she might have gone. Then I became aware of the birds singing. At last, it was morning and we could do something.

I had made my mind up during the night that I would ring Mrs Kelly, Michael's mother, and ask if they knew anything about Ellen's whereabouts. It took every ounce of strength I could muster to do this. To have to admit to her that I didn't know where my daughter was made me flinch. I waited until half-past seven to ring, wanting to make sure that she would be out of bed.

'Sorry to bother you so early,' I said carefully. 'By any chance, do you know where Ellen is?'

'Her father picked her up from Dublin last night and brought her home, where she should be,' she said icily. I gathered my thoughts quickly.

'Will you ask Katie to ring me, please?'

'I will if I see her,' she said and hung up. I leaned against the wall with the phone in my hand and shook all over. Jill took the phone from me.

'She's safe,' I said feebly.

'That's the important thing,' Jill said.

'It is.'

But I wanted to kill Michael for not letting me know what they were doing. And how dare Ellen treat me like this.

I cancelled my work arrangements, and waited for Katie's phone call. Finally she rang.

'What happened with Ellen last night?' I asked, trying to control my rage. After all, none of it was Katie's fault.

'Daddy and I picked her up; she wanted to come home,' she said calmly.

'Didn't you think that it might be a good idea to let me know what was happening? I've been nearly out of my mind with worry.' What I was saying sounded so puny and feeble in comparison to how I was feeling, but I was afraid to say too much. 'Is she all right?'

'She's grand.'

'Good,' I said, defeated.

At the weekend, after a few AA meetings, I had the courage to drive down and talk to Ellen myself. I always went to Katie's first but this time I went straight to Michael's. It was early on a Sunday morning, and his car was in the yard. This meant that he was there and I was sure that Ellen would still be in bed. I walked boldly into the kitchen. Michael was sitting at the table, smoking a cigarette, calm as could be.

'Tell Ellen I want to talk to her now,' I said. He strolled casually up to her bedroom.

'She'll be down in a minute,' he said, resting himself against the kitchen cupboard. 'What's all this about anyway?'

'You know well what it's about,' I said. He inhaled deeply and looked at me with cold green eyes. Then Ellen rambled in, dragging her feet, head down, shoulders nearly meeting in the front.

'Are you okay?' I asked. She never lifted her head.

'Ellen, please answer me. Why didn't you tell me that you were unhappy? ' Ellen just shrugged her shoulders and looked at her father. I knew then that she felt torn between the two of us, and that there was nothing I could do about this. It seemed that I would always be the villain of the piece.

Ellen never came back to Dublin or to college. Nobody cared what was right for her, and what I wanted meant nothing; it was all about scoring points between Michael and myself. When I asked her what she was going to do every day, she said, 'I don't know.'

The following weekend, I brought down the rest of Ellen's things. I knew in my heart that contact was paramount at this point. If I didn't make the effort, no one would keep in touch with me, and that would have broken my heart. I stayed at Katie's and had to settle for an uncomfortable truce.

Ellen was civil to me, and I was pleased about this. She had got a job painting and decorating up at the nursing home where my father was living. When I went up to see him, he wanted to know why she was not at school. 'That's a man's job she's doing,' he said with disgust.

'I have no say with her.'

'You have no say with any of them.'

'You're right,' I said thoughtfully.

'I don't know why you bother coming down here at all.'

'I'm trying to make up for all the time I was not here,' I said.

'Mark my words, you're wasting your time.'

'I might as well go away altogether if that's the way.'

'Don't you ever come up here and tell me that you're going to that godforsaken country you were in before,' he said with fire in his eyes. 'Off you go now; I'm tired.'

I wasn't content any more; the good seemed to have gone out of everything. Passing the house where Ellen had been living tore at me.

Everything was a struggle. I was tired rushing from one job to another, especially now; it all seemed to be for nothing. Then I heard of a woman in Ranelagh who wanted someone to look after her two little girls. I thought it might ease my loneliness to have children around, and I was delighted when I got the live-in job. I decided that I would keep on Ellen's bed-sit, for when I had time off. It was cheaper than my own and I was not earning as much money now.

The night I got the job, I went to an AA meeting and then to the Pronto for a coffee, with the usual gang. There was someone there I had not seen before. He was different from the others; the men who were usually there were posers. I was introduced to this man, who called himself P.J. He was over six foot with dark brown hair and brown eyes. He had a great sense of humour, which seemed to pass over the others' heads. When he heard me say that I was moving into a cheaper bed-sit, he asked me if I would like a hand to move.

'Thanks a million,' I said, thinking what an obliging man he was.

'I'll be over tomorrow evening about seven,' he said.

P.J. came that evening to move me to Ellen's bed-sit. When we were having a cup of tea later, he asked me if I'd like to go to a dance with him at the weekend.

'Why not?' I said. I found him nice and easy to talk to.

In my new job, the family were very good to me. The two little girls loved me and me them. Sometimes I felt guilty for spending so much time with them. I would torture myself with the thought that I should have been with my own grandchildren.

I went to the dance with P.J. and enjoyed it. Then we started meeting nearly every night and would go to a meeting together and have coffee and a chat afterwards. I looked forward to it and began to like him a lot. And then, one day, he told me that he was married. I would like to say that I didn't meet him again, but I did.

A week later, I drove down to Katie's to think. I was surprised to hear Katie and her husband talking of going to live in Birmingham. Her husband wanted to be near his parents who were getting old. If they were to go to England, I thought, maybe I would too, but to London. I was taken over with this idea. I would have one of my daughters close to me and it would take me farther away from Michael. When I got back to Dublin, I told P.J. that I was going away and that I didn't want to see him again because he was married, not because I didn't care about him. He was good about it and we parted friends.

Now I had to tell Jackie and the others about leaving Ireland again. They would react in one of two ways. They might be terribly hurt and it would bring back powerful feelings of abandonment, or else they accepted my coming and going and had no strong emotions about any of it. Either way, I was apprehensive. The following weekend, I sped along the familiar road in silence. Philip came to Katie's and I told him what I was thinking of doing.

'If that's what you have to do, sure do it,' he said. I could touch his pain and wished with all my heart that I could explain to him why I was doing this. I had lots of reasons but they all seemed so pathetic. If I were being truthful, I would have said: I'm running away again because everything is too painful for me. Instead, I told him he could come over to me at any time.

Ellen didn't seem to mind. She appeared to be pleased, possibly because she knew that she could come over to me whenever she wanted to. She was just hanging around, doing nothing. When I extended the same offer to Jackie and her family, she avoided my eyes.

This time, I was not going to make the same mistake with J.J.

I was going to tell him to his face. He just said, 'Right.' I have no idea what he was feeling.

With a sense of grief, I tried to fit a lifetime's caring into a weekend. On the Saturday evening, I walked my two precious three-year-old granddaughters over to the corner shop. They chatted non-stop, one on each side; I could feel the warmth of their little hands in mine. This was how my grandfather and I used to be when I was their age, and I wondered if they would ever recall this moment in later life.

Six or seven customers were in the shop when we went in. People never seemed to know what to say to me, so I said 'Hello' to no one in particular.

'Hello,' they said back and busied themselves.

Amber and Shauna were having a great time picking out what sweets they wanted. Then I heard an unmerciful roar from the shop door.

'Don't you bother your head coming up to see me ever again!' I recognised my father's voice. 'Do you hear me? I know all about where you're going. I want no more to do with you.'

'Yes, Daddy,' I answered him as if I were a two-year-old. He turned on his heel and left. As the revs of the Volkswagen faded, silence filled the shop like a bad smell. Even the two little girls had stopped chatting.

Finally someone spoke. 'My God, what was that all about?'

Everyone jumped into action at the sound of the voice; it was as if we had all been on a pause button. We got served and went back to Katie's where I collapsed on her settee.

'What would you do with him?' I asked Katie. 'He made a show of me in front of everyone.'

Alison dropped in to Katie's later in the day. She asked me when I was going and a few more questions. Nobody seemed surprised or saddened about my decision. I had no definite plans made; it was as if I were waiting for someone to stop me or beg me not to go.

In retrospect, it seems as if I was afraid of being close to my children and to my sisters for fear of the pain of being rejected by them again. And perhaps they were equally afraid of getting too close to me, for fear of being abandoned again. In both cases, we accomplished what we were trying to avoid.

I gave a week's notice at work. My employer didn't ask me why, or say she would miss me. If she had, I probably would have stayed. Maybe that's what I wanted all along, someone to say that they'd miss me. I rang Aggie, a woman in London whom I had known when I'd lived there, and asked her if she would put me up until I got a place. I don't think she was too pleased. I hadn't spoken to her for about seven years. I told myself that I would stay for only a few days.

I sold the car for £400, and had £200 from work. Putting my trust in God, at forty-two years of age, and with six years' sobriety, I left Ireland once more.

Chapter Thirty-seven

I arrived at Heathrow, got the Underground into the centre of the city and made my way to Cavendish Road. Aggie's house was full of people; they seemed to be having a party in the middle of the day. The first thing they did was ask me what I wanted to drink. When I told them that I didn't drink, it seemed to put a right dampener on things.

'You always drank,' Aggie said, pressing a glass of God knows what into my hand.

'I don't any more, but I don't mind anyone else drinking. More power to them,' I said a little too cheerfully.

Aggie led me to a room that was full to bursting point with everything imaginable. Over in one corner was a bed.

'That's yours,' she told me.

'Thanks a million,' I said. 'It won't be for long.' I was reassuring both her and myself.

'The chipper is just around the corner,' she said, and returned to her guests. I went to get some fish and chips and then I walked around to familiarise myself with what was close by. I saw a job agency and went in. They told me to come back in the morning and they would have something for me. I told them that I would do cleaning or childminding. I bought myself a couple of magazines and went back to Aggie's. I got into bed and tried to read. I didn't want to start thinking of home or feeling afraid, so I got out of the bed, went down on my knees and asked God to be with me. Then I read until I eventually fell asleep.

The next morning, I was up at six. There were bodies all over the place and the smell of drink made me feel sick. I left the house without as much as a cup of tea. All I could find in the papers was pub work. Well, that's what I would have to do for the moment. I rang the Goose and Firkin at the Elephant and Castle and got an interview for the next day. I was there before they opened. They asked me if I would work that day and they would see how I got on. So I started immediately. It was hard until I figured out where everything was; then it was second nature to me. I got the job and it was live-in, so I went back to Aggie and thanked her for helping me out. She said to come back if I was ever stuck again.

The landlady and landlord were from the North of England and friendly. It was a young people's pub. The money was good — £129 a week — and I had no rent to pay. There was one big problem: because I was working days and evenings, I was not going to any AA meetings.

I rang Katie, who had exciting news. She and Jackie were both pregnant again, but it meant that she would not be coming to Birmingham as soon as she had expected to. I was overcome with homesickness. I was not going to be there for my daughters. She said that the minute the baby was born, they would be over. They were both four months' pregnant.

When I had been in the job a month, I asked for a weekend off to go home and see my family. I had presents for everyone and flew from Stansted to Waterford Airport. Jackie's husband, Tony, met me there. When Shauna and Amber saw me, they ran and threw themselves at me.

I stayed at Katie's and visited Jackie. They both looked healthy and were looking forward to their new babies. Ellen came to see me and said she was moving to London with her boyfriend, that he had some family over there with whom they would stay. She said she would bring her boyfriend to visit before I went back. I was happy to see her so full of life, and at ease with me. Philip arrived later in the evening and told me that he and his father were going to America for a few years, to work, because locally jobs were scarce. I was surprised but pleased for them. I thought it would be an education for Philip and he would get to see some of the world. Philip was a good carpenter and Michael a builder. J.J. said that he and half a dozen more of the young people around the village would go after a while if it worked out for his brother and Michael.

'I must go and see my father,' I said to Katie. 'Do you want to come with me?'

'You'd better go yourself,' she said. I had bought him a bottle of his favourite Courvoisier brandy. As I walked up the avenue, I could see that he had no light on — only the flicker of his television. Dear God, don't let me be hurt, no matter what he says to me, I said to myself. I climbed the stairs slowly, in no hurry to get there. I knocked on his door.

'Come in.' His voice sent a shiver through me as I gently opened the door.

'Hello,' I said cautiously. He was sitting on his chair. I stood at the end of the bed with the brandy on show to soften him. He turned off the television. With not a glimmer of emotion, he looked at me with cold blue eyes. 'You can leave that and go.'

I placed the brandy carefully at the end of his bed and left. When I got near the gate, I stood and looked back at his window. The television was back on.

I took my granddaughters to Sunday Mass the following morning. I had bought a new coat for going home — grey; I had paid £100 for it. I had never spent so much on one item of clothing in my life. As I went in through the church door, I heard a whisper: 'I wonder how long she was lying on her back for the money to buy that.' I clung to the warm hands of the little girls.

In the afternoon, we had a visitor I didn't want to see — Michael. He rambled up the path, not a bother on him, as if he owned the place.

'Calm down,' Katie said, noticing the red creeping into my face.

'Did you hear that we're going to America?' he asked me, the minute he walked in.

'Philip told me,' I said, trying to sound as normal as he was. I thought: Is there something radically wrong with me that I can't forget what took place the last time we were face to face? Does he not remember the way he drove to Dublin and took Ellen from me and let her leave college?

His voice broke into my thoughts. 'Maybe you'd come over to us after a while; bring Ellen with you. You would love it over there. They have a great lifestyle.' He was talking as if we were an ordinary couple discussing an everyday event. Frantically I searched my mind for that elusive right answer. Katie was behind his back making signs and signals with her arms and mouth. I had no idea what she was trying to tell me.

'Who knows what will happen?' I said. Katie sank into a chair in what seemed like relief. I must have said the right thing! Michael looked pleased with himself, which made me feel more uneasy.

'Thank God you said that,' Katie told me when Michael had left.

'Why?'

'Because he wouldn't go if he didn't think there was a chance you would go over after him.'

'Oh no! I can't let him think that, for God's sake.'

'Well, who knows, you might go.'

'Katie, would you like me to go back to your father after all that has happened between us?' I asked her in amazement. 'That would be the worst thing that could happen to either of us.'

'Yes. Well, I would love it to happen,' she said, tears in her eyes. 'I'm no different from anyone else. Every child would love their parents to be together.'

'Katie, please listen. I don't know what made me say that to your father, but I know in my heart that I could never again live with him. I'm not saying it's his fault, but I have to stop this vicious cycle of me coming back only to have to leave again when things get impossible. It's not fair on anyone. I'm always the baddie and I'm tired of it.'

I knew my children thought that I was the one who always spoiled everything. This offer from Michael changed the atmosphere between Katie and myself, and all the closeness I had experienced earlier suddenly evaporated. All I wanted to do now was to get away.

When I arrived back in London, physically I was there, but mentally I was still in Katie's kitchen, trying to explain myself. At work, I never stopped, so that at night I would fall into bed and just pass out with tiredness. It was over six months since I had been to an AA meeting. So, I added the guilt I felt about that to all the other guilt I was carrying, and struggled on.

One Saturday night, I had a phone call from Katie's husband to tell me that she had had a baby boy, James, my first grandson. He was two months premature, but doing well. I had the joy of his arrival, and the sadness that I wasn't there to see him. A couple of days later, Ellen and her boyfriend, Shane, arrived from Ireland, which gave me something else to think about. He was a lovely young man. We met at the Goose and Firkin a couple of evenings later. I was full of excitement, telling anyone who would listen that my youngest daughter was coming to visit me. She looked great when she walked through the door and I was so proud of her. We sat and laughed and talked. They were staying with Shane's sister, and having a great time seeing the sights before they started working. Ellen had found a job with the NatWest Bank. They told me that Katie and her family were looking forward to coming over to Birmingham in a couple of weeks. Michael and Philip were off to America around the same time.

Katie was over at last and I couldn't wait to see them. They were staying with her in-laws in Birmingham. I took a weekend off and went up to see my first grandson. In my eyes, the baby was the image of J.J.: he had the same hair colour and the same smile. Katie was anxious to get their own place since it was hard living with her in-laws. Amber was delighted to see me. She told me all the news of her cousins and her new granny and grandad. I had a lovely weekend. Katie said that I looked tired and should take it easy. She didn't understand that I was not able to do that. I had to keep going to be able to sleep at night.

Chapter Thirty-eight

There was something wrong with me. The headaches were unbearable, and in the pub I kept dropping glasses. I promised myself that I would take it easy the next week, but the next week never came. Then one morning, when I tried to get out of bed, I couldn't move. What was wrong with me? I was terrified. When I didn't surface for work, one of the staff knocked on my bedroom door.

'It's time for work,' she shouted.

'Come in,' I said as loudly as I could, the words coming out through the corner of my mouth. Thank God the door was not locked. When she saw how I was, she ran and got the landlady. An ambulance came.

'What's the matter with me?' I slurred.

'Don't worry. We'll have you in hospital in no time.'

They took me to Saint Thomas's hospital. I was falling in and out of consciousness. My eyelids and my limbs felt as heavy as lead. Sleep would be merciful, but between lights shining in my eyes, and pins being stuck in my legs, there was no hope. A doctor said, 'You've had a stroke, caused by a clot of blood on the right side of your brain, which is affecting the left side of your body.'

'I'll be all right, won't I?' I asked in terror.

'It all depends on the next twenty-four hours. You could have another. We'll put you in a ward, keep you under close observation and see how you are in the morning.'

The left side of my face felt numb, as if I'd been to the dentist. A nurse came and asked me if I'd like to contact anyone. I gave her Ellen's number. She came back and told me that Ellen was on her way. Ellen and Shane arrived with a big bunch of roses.

I was extremely lucky, and didn't have another stroke. My face would improve with time, they told me. After the twenty-four hours I started on some gentle physiotherapy for my arm and leg. I wanted to be fit again but I couldn't motivate myself to exercise. All I wanted to do was cry. Some of the people from work came to see me, and I wished they wouldn't. No one else from my family came to see me, only Ellen. The depression was the most crippling part of my stroke.

After a week in hospital, the time came for me to leave. I had no home, no job, and only about £300 to my name. The Social Services put me into a hostel in Petherton Road, in north London. It was nice, clean and well supervised. I was told that I would get a flat when I was well enough to look after myself. My physiotherapy continued and took up a lot of my time, but I gradually got well. I started going to AA again.

On my way to and from meetings, I would struggle up to the top of the bus and say, 'Dear God, you must have one little corner in this big city just for me, please.'

After three months, I got a one-bedroom flat in Islington. The minute I saw it, I loved it. It was in a small block of eight flats, in a quiet cul-de-sac. Right outside my sitting-room window was a most wonderful God-given ash tree.

I had been getting sick benefit for the previous five months and had saved most of it. I turned the place into a home, bit by bit. Within six months, I had it warm, cosy and comfortable. Photographs of my children and grandchildren hung proudly on the walls. I loved my home, my pink bedroom, my white-and-red kitchen, and white-and-green bathroom. Outside, I had ivy growing on the walls, and flowers on the windowsills. I felt safe and secure.

In April 1988, Jackie had her baby, Mia. I wanted to go straight away to see my new granddaughter.

When she was about a month old, I made the journey. I arrived laden down with presents. A bottle of whiskey for Tony, another bottle of brandy for my father, toys for Shauna and a little dress for baby Mia. I gave Jackie money to buy something for herself. Jackie not being a demonstrative person, I never felt that she was pleased to see me. Tony, on the other hand, always said to me, 'You're very welcome' and gave me a warm, firm handshake. Shauna, who was now four, was delighted to see me. The new baby had huge brown eyes and brown hair — the opposite of her big sister, who was blonde with blue eyes.

After our supper, Jackie, who was always great for the food — the best of everything — said, 'It's strange you should think of coming home this weekend. The tickets from Daddy arrived in the post yesterday, for you and Ellen to go to America.'

I was shocked. 'What do you mean?'

'The tickets for the two of ye to go to Boston. Sure, you must have said to him that you were going to go over.'

'Oh God.' I felt sick. Just then, in walked J.J. Straight away Jackie told him what was going on.

'If you go over to him, I will never speak to you again and that's final,' J.J. said to me.

'I don't want to go over there at all.'

'Give me that ticket,' he said. 'I'll go over myself. I hear they're doing well, building condominiums.'

'That's fine with me.'

'Well, one of ye better ring my father and tell him,' Jackie said. 'Because I'm not going to be the one.'

'I'll do it now,' I said. My heart was in my mouth as I waited for him to answer the phone.

'Well, girl,' he said, all friendly. 'Are ye ready to come over? You'll love it here, the two of ye.' He meant Ellen and me.

'I'm not coming.' There was a deadly silence.

'Well, don't send that young one over here to me,' he said. 'I couldn't mind her on my own. You would have to be here with her.'

'You know how disappointed she'll be if you don't let her go.'

'Whose fault is that then? Put Jackie on to me.'

'Your father wants to talk to you,' I said.

'No. I'm staying out of it,' she said. I told him what Jackie had said.

'You're some bitch,' he said, and then continued to call me all sorts of names.

Feeling sick to my guts, I went up to the bathroom to compose myself. I was full of guilt. J.J. had gone by the time I came down. Who could blame him?

Later on that evening, I went up to see my father, and brought him his brandy. Shauna came with me for company.

'Back again,' he said.

'I came home to see Jackie's new baby, and yourself.'

'Will you ever learn?' he said. I went bright red. His face was twisted with bitterness; he seemed to be searching for the ultimate humiliation.

'I've come to see my grandchildren,' I repeated. Shauna tugged at my hand and said, 'I want to go now, Nanny.'

'It wasn't worth your while coming up. Off with ye now,' he said.

When Shauna was going to bed that night, she insisted that I tuck her in. There was a great love between us and I felt blessed by it. When I looked at her long blonde hair strewn out over the pillow, a smile spread across my face.

I went down to the sitting room. Jackie had the fire lit; Tony had gone for a pint. She told me that my sister Mary wanted to come and see how I was after the stroke. Maybe my illness was a blessing in disguise. Perhaps Mary and I could be friends. To be able to call in and see my sister and to get to know her children again — I would love all that. Now that Michael had left the village, things could get easier for me.

Mary and Geraldine called the following morning. At first, it was awkward. I couldn't stop myself from talking.

'It's great to see ye. Thanks for coming in,' I said. 'Both of you look marvellous.' They were making a fuss over the baby and didn't seem to hear me. After about ten minutes, Mary said, 'Did you bring home any nice style?'

'I'll show you.' I was up to the bedroom like a flash. Down I came, struggling with my suitcase.

'That's a nice skirt,' she said rummaging away.

'If you like it, you can have it,' I said, without hesitation. She folded it and left it to one side.

'I bought it to go with the jumper,' I said as Mary held up a new jumper I had just bought. 'You might as well have that too.' I felt that if I gave her the new clothes, it would mean that we could get on better as friends. Getting a little braver, I began to feel I had the right to say a few things, to be myself.

'You're very quiet,' I said to Geraldine.

'Oh, I'm all right,' she said, with a quick glance at Mary.

'Aren't any of ye going to ask me how I am after the stroke?' My daughter was included in this. She had never inquired about my health since I'd come home.

'Well, I can see your left eye is wonky,' Mary said. 'But sure, only the good die young. We'll have to be off now,' she said, making for the door, with Geraldine close on her heels.

'Why did you give her all those lovely things?' Jackie asked. 'I would have loved them.' I just shrugged. I couldn't bring myself to tell her that I would give the last stitch I had on my back, if only my sisters would like me and be glad to see me.

The next morning, Geraldine called again. She came in the back door.

'I just want to have a word with your mother before she goes,' she said to Jackie.

'Right, come in.'

'I'm sorry about yesterday. I can't seem to talk in front of Mary,' she said to me. 'You know what she's like.' She was talking as if her life depended on it. 'How are you after your stroke? It's terrible that none of us asked you about it.' She stopped to take a breath and I jumped in.

'I'm getting stronger all the time. It was only a slight one, thank God.' I wanted to put my arms around my youngest sister and hug her.

'Good,' she said. 'Sorry again for yesterday.' I knew that she was sorry. I could see it in her face.

'I thought Alison might call to see me,' I said.

'She has her own problems but I'm sure she'll work them out in the end.' Geraldine looked uncomfortable, so I let the subject drop.

As we were leaving for the airport that evening, Mary was going in to Geraldine's house.

'I'm off again. See you soon, I hope,' I said. She barely acknowledged me. I could not believe it.

When I got back to London, I spent days going over the different things that had happened. I would never understand Mary. What had I done to her? She had everything: the nicest house in the village, a good husband, four lovely children and enough money to be comfortable. I felt that all those things paled into insignificance for her when I was around. It was unbearably sad.

Two months after my trip to Ireland, J.J. was on his way to America. He came to me first because he hadn't got a passport and he thought that all he had to do was go into an office and get it. Because he'd been born in London, he had to have a British one. I was delighted but anxious about his arrival. I hoped that he would approve of and like my little home.

Everything had to be as perfect as possible for him. At times, I thought he quite liked me. Other times, I felt that he couldn't bear even to look at or speak to me. It was with those undercurrents that I waited for him to arrive.

At four in the afternoon, there was a knock on the door. With my heart thumping, I opened it. My son stood there. I feasted my eyes on him. Then I reached up on my tiptoes and kissed him on the cheek as casually as I could.

'How ya?' he said.

'I'm grand. How was your journey?' I asked him as he went into the sitting room and put down his bag. 'Are you hungry?'

'Not really. I had a session last night with the lads and I've a hangover.'

'You have to eat something.' I went into the kitchen to put on a fry. I was picking things up and putting them down again. Please God, help me to think of things to talk about.

'Stop fussing in there,' J.J. said. I'm getting on his nerves, I thought. I stayed in the kitchen until I was finished cooking. Then I had a cup of tea with him. Anything else, I wouldn't have been able to swallow. After he'd eaten, he lay on the settee and fell asleep. I looked at him and wished I could be natural and normal instead of having to think about everything I said and did.

J.J. slept in the bedroom and I on a bed settee in the sitting room. The next day, he went up the Holloway Road and met some lads from home. They all went to the pub and it was the early hours of the morning when he came back, a big bag of fish and chips in his hand. He sat on the sofa, throwing a bag of chips into the bed to me.

'Where were you all day?' I asked.

'Having the craic.'

'Good,' I said. I loved my children to enjoy their life, have fun, be carefree, do all the things my sisters and I had never done. As he made a move to go to bed, I said in a coaxing voice, 'J.J., will you leave your cigarettes and matches here on the table? I'm terrified of a fire.'

He grinned at me, picked them up and went into bed. When I heard him snoring, I tiptoed into the room. There he was, arms above his head, his mouth open, just like when he was a little boy. I ached to reach out and pull the covers up on him, to stroke his head of curls, and kiss him on the cheek. Instead, I tiptoed away.

J.J. got a job bricklaying with one of the blokes he had met in the pub. 'I'm time enough going to America,' he said. That was J.J.: he would do things in his own time — no rush, no panic. Every evening, after work, he went to the pub and came home at all hours of the morning, with our takeaway. I gave him a key to the door, but it was no use; I couldn't sleep until he came in. We would sit there together and have pretend arguments about the time of night he was coming in at, and about his cigarettes and matches. He would grin at me. There was not one cross word between the two of us, and I loved him so much, it hurt.

'My son is staying with me,' I would say to people at my meetings. It made me feel like I was a real mother, a good mother. Still, it seemed that I could never get back to where I had been when I had left my children for those five dreadful years.

J.J. stayed with me for two months, but the time came when he was ready to leave for Boston. I didn't know how I was going to handle it. I was aware of how sad I felt, but I also experienced a great sense of relief: relief that nothing terrible had happened between us which would cause either of us any more pain. We had succeeded in our clumsy efforts to be almost natural with each other. I had not had the courage to talk to J.J. the way I really wanted to, but I did make one brave and rewarding move before he left. He was standing at one end of the room, ready to go, and I was at the other end, looking over at him. Walking towards him, I said, 'Give me a hug before you go.' My head came to his chest and I rested it there. My arms crept around him and, after a couple of seconds, I felt his tighten around me. I had not held my son for eighteen years, not since he was ten years old. I told him that I loved him and he said, 'I know you do.' We went to the airport together and were at ease in each other's company. I hugged him again when he left and then I went into the toilet and thanked God for the gift of this time with my son. I'm grateful that I didn't know then that I would not talk to or see J.J. for four years.

Philip rang the next day to tell me that J.J. had arrived safely. J.J. was not one for writing or talking on the phone. I kept in touch with him by sending him birthday and Christmas cards, always making sure to say that I loved him.

Philip would ring me every couple of weeks. He told me that they had an apartment each in the same house, that Michael had met a young woman and was living with her. I hoped they would be happy together. This could be a good time to ask him for a divorce and be free of him. I went to a solicitor as soon as I could and gave him Michael's address to send him the relevant forms.

The solicitor rang me when the forms were returned unsigned. We made another appointment, and he told me that I would automatically get my divorce after seven years, even though Michael hadn't signed the papers. I told him to go ahead, that I was in no hurry. I would wait, and so I did.

Ellen would come and visit me now and then, often when she'd had a problem of one sort or another. We had some great chats. She had no difficulty talking to me about anything, especially about the time I had left home. In fact, she was very like me in that respect. She would open a bottle of wine and we would analyse and scrutinise everyone and everything. Ellen had great insight, accompanied by a wicked sense of humour, and a self-awareness way beyond her seventeen years.

She decided that she wanted to see more of the world and was going to go to Boston, and that herself and Shane needed a break from each other. When I told Katie what Ellen was doing, she assured me, 'Ellen is quite capable of looking after herself.'

I'd just started doing a few cleaning jobs when Jackie rang

and asked me if she and the two children could come over for a week. I couldn't believe that what I'd dreamed of was happening. On a beautiful July day, they arrived at Liverpool Street station by train. I was so proud of my daughter and my granddaughters. It seems that Shauna had been upset leaving her father behind, because they had never been away without him before. Jackie told me that Tony had said, 'When Shauna sees your mother, she'll be fine.' I was delighted to hear that.

Jackie loved my flat and I was thrilled. I took them to see the sights of London: Buckingham Palace, Trafalgar Square and Tower Bridge.

We visited Katie in Birmingham. Katie, who had her own place now, met us at the coach station. She had Amber, and my one and only grandson, James, with her. We had two lovely days and a night there.

Back in my flat, Jackie and the little girls were sleeping in the bedroom while I slept in the sitting room. On their last night, Jackie wanted to get the girls to sleep early because they had the journey home the following day. She got a bottle of wine for herself for a treat as it was the last night of her holiday. When she was on her second glass of wine, I said to her, 'Would you like to talk to me about how you felt when I left home when you were little?'

'There's not much to say about it really, is there?' she said, without looking at me.

'I want to give you the opportunity to say anything you want to me, or ask me anything and I will answer you as honestly as I can. The last week has been very special to me. I feel close to you. I want us to stay that way.'

'When you left, I thought I would die,' she said. 'I told Aunt Mary to ask you to come back to me, and I really believed you would come if you knew how I felt.'

I felt as if I was going to choke on the ball of hurt that was in my throat. 'There are no words strong enough to describe how sorry I am for leaving,' I said. 'Do you believe that I never intentionally left ye, my children? It was your father I ran away from.'

'I thought it was me you left,' she said flatly. 'I don't think it matters now why you left. The harm's done.'

'There is not a day that goes by that I don't think of what I did and regret it with all my heart.'

'I know, I know.'

'I can't change the past. No one can — not even God,' I said. 'I'm so sorry for the pain and hurt I caused you all.' I was getting tearful now and I knew that Jackie did not like displays of emotion, so I thought it was time to stop the conversation.

'Thanks for talking to me,' I said. 'It means a lot.' We sat quietly for a while. I was thinking how much I would love Jackie to say that she forgave me, and loved me, but what right did I have to expect that?

'I think I'll go to bed now,' Jackie said.

'I hope I didn't upset you by talking.'

'No. We have a long journey tomorrow though,' she said, quickly leaving the room. There was never a sense of ease or solace after these short and brittle exchanges with any of my family. Had I any right to unburden myself on them in the vague hope of their forgiveness? I sat for a long time, mulling this over in my head, never coming to any satisfactory conclusion, and being left with a sadness that seeped into my very soul.

The next day, I said goodbye at the airport. Shauna was clinging and crying. My heart was heavy as I made my way back to Islington. I was beginning to think that I should try to let go of what had happened in the past, and make my amends to my children by showing my love and devotion to my grand-children. They rang me that night to say that they had got home safely and to thank me for a lovely time.

Chapter Thirty-nine

The following October, Jackie rang to tell me that my father was seriously ill, and that he wanted me to come home right away. It gave me a terrible shock. For some reason, I never thought about my father dying. He was in his early seventies and that did not seem old to me. I got a flight to Dublin the following morning, and then the train to Kilkenny, where Jackie picked me up. During the journey home, I had thought a lot about my father. I loved him so much and, though it seemed at times he just loved to hurt me, I could smile at some of the things he had said and done. I did not want to lose him. He gave me a strange kind of security and I could not imagine him gone.

'How is he really?' I asked Jackie.

'Well, he's not good. His kidneys are in a bad way.'

'Is he going to die? What did the doctor say?'

'The doctor won't commit himself.'

'I'm frightened of seeing him and am trying to prepare myself.'

'He looks the same as ever, so don't worry. They're all up there with him,' Jackie said, meaning my three sisters. How were they going to be with me? Were they going to talk or not?

It was five in the evening when Jackie drove me to the door of the nursing home and said she would see me later. I told her not to wait up. I took a couple of minutes to gather myself. I had an empty feeling as I walked slowly up the stairs. When I got to his door, I stood outside and made the sign of the cross. Then I knocked and Mary opened it. She never spoke, but I didn't expect her to. I focused on my father, who was resting against a heap of pillows. He looked very yellow. I went and sat on the side of his bed.

'How are you, Daddy?'

'Not good, girl,' he said. I took his hand in mine and held it gently.

'I'm here now,' I said soothingly. A faint smile reached his eyes. It reminded me of when I was a child, and I would reassure him with a smile or a look. This was a familiar role for me and it felt good.

'I'm staying with my father tonight,' I said. I felt that it was what my father wanted and I knew that it was what I had come home for. 'It doesn't matter to me who else stays. I can stay on my own.'

A silence fell on the room. It was as if I had broken some sacred rule or spoken out loud in church.

'I'll stay,' Mary said quickly. I looked at her properly for the first time in years. When she was young, she was very pretty; she was taller than me and slimmer. She used to have a great sense of humour, but now she never seemed to smile. It was so sad. Was she angry towards me because she felt that I was the one who had got away. Who knows?

The decision was made at last. Mary was staying with me. Alison and Geraldine remained with my father while Mary and I went to get some supper. Before I left, I told my father that I would be back in a couple of hours. He nodded in acknowledgment.

I went down to Jackie's to get something to eat, not that I was hungry.

Having eaten, I lay down with Shauna and dozed for a while. When I woke up, I felt terrible, as if I had just lived through a nightmare. I pulled myself together and set out for the nursing home. The village was quiet. The houses in the area were multiplying. There were lights scattered here and there in the countryside which I had never seen before. I felt a stab of sadness as I thought of all the times I had stood on the top step, watching to see if my father had got home safely.

Mary was there before me, and my two other sisters had gone home. She was sitting with her back against the wall. I went over to my father and asked him if he wanted anything. He said, 'No', and closed his eyes. I went to sit on a chair at the far side of the bed.

'Why don't you sit over here?' Mary said suddenly, patting the chair beside her. I went and sat next to her.

'He'll pretend to be asleep now so that he'll be able to hear what we're saying about him,' she said earnestly.

'Will he?' I said.

'I have to sit over here where he can't see me or he'll go berserk. If you don't believe me, ask Alison or Geraldine. They'll tell you,' she said, her face glowing.

'I do believe you,' I whispered. And I did because I knew that my father could be cruel.

Then my father moved in the bed. 'She's right,' he said.

'Didn't I tell you, he's not asleep at all,' she said gleefully.

'Well, stop talking about him if he can hear you,' I said. We sat in silence.

It was a very long night.

Morning arrived at last, and with it Alison and Geraldine. As Mary and I were about to leave, the nun in charge of the nursing home came to see how my father was.

'I'm Sister Imelda,' she said, shaking hands with me. 'Help yourself to tea or coffee from the kitchen when you're here.' She was pleasant and friendly, and I thanked her. Then I left for Jackie's to try to get some sleep.

I tossed and turned. I remembered how when my father had a few drinks taken, he would say that I was like him and that Mary was like our mother. I took it to mean that I liked a drink like himself, and that although this was a bad thing, he was more comfortable with it than with Mary, who seldom touched the stuff, like Mammy, who could not bear his drinking and constantly left him because of it. Maybe he transferred his feelings towards my mother onto Mary and being the kind of man who always wanted to be seen as the perfect father and husband, he resented the fact that Mary thought he was neither, hence the tension between them. Perhaps Mary thought that the only way to survive Daddy was to be like him. No one will ever truly know why they felt about each other the way they did.

Eventually I fell into a restless sleep, and didn't wake up until two in the afternoon. After a shower and a change of clothes, I had something to eat and left once again for the nursing home.

Geraldine was sitting with my father when I got there, and he appeared to be asleep. She looked worn out.

'Are you okay?' I asked her.

'I'm grand,' she said, a bit too quickly for my liking. I was sure that he'd been giving her a hard time, as usual.

'Do you want a break?' I asked.

'Could we go downstairs together for a cup of tea?'

'I suppose we can,' I said.

'We won't be long,' she whispered, catching me by the hand and pulling me through the doorway. 'God,' she said, clutching her stomach. 'Will this ever end?'

'Is it that bad?' I asked.

'Bad is not a strong enough word to describe it.'

'Tell me,' I said, dreading what I was going to hear.

'First, you'd better pray that he never turns on you, or you will never forget it as long as you live.'

'What do you mean?'

'One after another, he has called us evil and twisted. It's no use saying that he doesn't know what he's talking about, because he does. How can he say things like that to his own daughters?'

'I really don't know how he even thinks of the things to say; it beats me,' I said as I put my arms around her. We stood there, away from his door, clinging to each other, until we felt uncomfortable.

'We'll be dead before him, that's what will happen,' Geraldine said. We both doubled over in silent, hysterical titters.

'Are we terrible for laughing?'

'No, it relieves the tension,' I said. We never got to the kitchen for the tea, afraid that we had left our father on his own for too long. We rushed through the bedroom door to make sure he was all right.

'What are you two up to?' he asked.

'Nothing,' we said in unison, afraid to look at each other in case we might burst out laughing and he would go mad. We went and sat on two chairs like a couple of small children who had just been told off.

Alison came into his bedroom on the third afternoon, brisk and efficient, like a mother superior.

'How is he?' she asked, as she smoothed his covers and tugged at his pillows.

'Why don't you ask me? I can still talk and I'm not deaf either,' my father said to her.

'Well, how are you then?'

'Well enough to know that you're talking about me every chance ye get.'

'You sound fine to me,' she said in the same tone of voice that he used with her. I was amazed that she could speak to him with such courage, almost arrogance, and even more surprised when he seemed to draw in his horns.

'You go and have a rest and something to eat,' Alison said to me. 'No doubt I'll be here when you get back.' Giving my father a quick peck on the cheek, I almost ran out of the room.

I took a couple of deep breaths of fresh air as I walked down the avenue. It was a bitterly cold day. When I reached Jackie's, the house was empty. I slept for a couple of hours. Around nine, I went back to the nursing home. When I arrived, my three sisters were already in state. No matter how early I was, they would always be there before me.

A nun I hadn't met was making my father comfortable for the night.

'Aren't you the lucky man to have all your daughters here looking after you?' she said.

'I am, I suppose,' he said ungraciously. 'This one is home from London,' he said pointing to me.

'You must be Kay. Sure God love you, you poor thing,' she said, taking my two hands in hers. She looked hard into my eyes. Then she stood there, patting my hand and muttering prayers half under her breath. 'May the Lord look after you.' A surge of anger coursed through me. How dare she patronise me?

I pulled my hands from her. She took a step back and made the sign of the cross.

'Thanks for everything, Sister,' Mary said.

'Don't mention it, child. God bless ye all.' She sidled out the door, without looking at me.

'I think Geraldine should stay tonight. Anyone have a problem with that?' Mary asked. We shook our heads. 'I'll be here first thing in the morning.'

I hovered between irritation and anger — that nun treating me like a lost soul, and my three sisters acting as if I should feel privileged that they even spoke to me.

'I don't see why you can't make up your own mind if you want to be with me or not. I am your sister too,' I said. I especially wanted to be close to Geraldine; she was like one of my own children.

'I'd like to sit up for a while,' Daddy said. Geraldine and I heaved him up on the pillows. 'Thank God them two are gone.'

'Why? Are we your favourites?' I asked, trying to lighten the mood.

'I have no favourites. I treated you all the same. No one can say any different about me. Put that television on,' he said. 'I haven't heard the news for days.' We did as we were told.

Hardly had we put the TV on then he grumbled, 'Turn it off, for God's sake. I can't stand that yoke that's reading it. I'll have a cup of tea instead.'

'I'll get it,' I said.

'No, let herself do that,' he said. Geraldine jumped to attention and off she went.

We sat in silence until Geraldine appeared with the tea. When we had finished drinking it, he said he would have a sleep. It was nearly one in the morning and we were all tired. Geraldine and I sat like statues, afraid to move, until we heard a low snore and felt sure that he was really asleep. Then we crept outside his door to stretch ourselves and have a chat.

'Please, God, let him sleep for the rest of the night,' Geraldine said. 'Do you hate it when we give out about him?'

'I wish we were a close family and that we supported each other, instead of all this sniping,' I said.

Geraldine was rooting around in a big shoulder bag she had.

'Would you like a drop of brandy?' she asked me.

'No, thanks.'

She put the bottle to her lips and took a big gulp. The wondrous smell of it reached me and I imagined that feeling of power rushing through her mind and body, and I wanted it too.

'I'll be back in a minute,' I said, dashing to the toilet. I put my hands together and looked up at the ceiling and said, 'Dear God, don't let me drink or even want to, please.' I stood there until I felt calm and composed. Then I went back out to my sister.

'Are you all right?' she asked me calmly. 'How many years is it since you had a drink?'

'About eight.'

She stood there thinking, then blurted out. 'You know, you're his favourite, always have been,' she said.

I stood there, pawing the carpet with my foot. Was this the reason for all the tension between myself and my sisters? I had never in my life felt like a favoured daughter. But that was Daddy's way, to pit us all against each other.

'We'd better go in and see if he's all right,' I said.

My father was asleep. We sat down quietly, my mind racing with it all.

Mary arrived around eight in the morning.

'How did the night go?' she asked.

'Fine. Daddy slept most of the time,' I said.

'We've had some terrible nights here, haven't we, Geraldine?' Mary said.

'We have,' Geraldine confirmed.

'I have a splitting headache,' I said. 'I'm going to have something to eat and then get some sleep.'

I gave my father a kiss on the cheek and left them to it.

A soothing and refreshing veil of fine drizzle covered the village that morning. Instead of going down the avenue, I went out the side gates of the nursing home, which brought me on to the old school lane. As I started to walk up the steep hill towards the school, I recalled the morning Alison and I had coaxed J.J. to the top, and when we let go of his hands, he ran to the bottom of the lane in a flash. A smile flitted across my face at the memory. How I wished I could have those days back! I would do things differently; I don't know how, but differently.

The lane was tarmacked now, not like when I was at school; then it had stones the size of our heads sticking out of the ground. We had permanently cut knees. Taking the clear, intoxicating air into my lungs, I held it for as long as was possible, then let it out slowly. I wanted to inhale this beautiful place and make it a part of me, so that I would be able to enjoy it at any time and at will. Then tears began to roll down my face.

Tears for my young self, for my loss and my longings. I loved this place, and yet I had had to leave it. It had driven me crazy. The constant battle when I was among my family to hold on to my identity and not conform to their ways sapped me of all my energy.

I turned back, and bumped into a local woman called Ruth. She was a few years older than myself, and had been good to me when I was having my babies, years before. She was also a constant and true friend to Mary. As I passed, she was in the garden.

'I thought it was you,' she said. 'How is your father this morning?'

'He had a good night, thanks,' I said, trying to hide the tears in my eyes.

'It's a hard time for all of ye. Has Mary made her peace with him yet?'

'I'm afraid not.'

'Well, she's going to have to before it's too late,' she said, pulling a few stray weeds. 'I'm going up to see your father later, and then I'm going to have a chat with Mary.'

'That would be great. It would make it easier all round if they were civil with each other.' We said our goodbyes and I left for Jackie's. What was the point in forcing Mary to make her peace? My head was throbbing by now. When I got to Jackie's I took two tablets, hoping the headache would shift.

After a couple of hours' sleep, I woke up with a migraine. Recently, every time I was stressed, I got one. I didn't usually take the painkillers when I was up and about, but I was going to make an exception this time and take one when I got to the nursing home. As I walked up there, the angelus bell rang out, bringing back memories of childhood. I was surprised to find my father on his own.

'Where's everyone?' I asked.

'That Mary one only comes here to torment me,' he said. He was up high on the pillows and looked like his usual self, all polished and spotless.

'You look great,' I said enthusiastically.

'Thanks. The nuns have given me a wash down, but I'm tired after it. I think I'll have a snooze.'

'I might have one myself here on this nice comfortable chair,' I said. We both lay back and closed our eyes. Then I thought: I must take a tablet and maybe I'll sleep. Once more, I closed my eyes.

After an hour or so, I felt better, but I hadn't slept. I wasn't sure if my father was asleep or not, but he was resting and it was peaceful. There were so many things I would have loved to talk to him about, but the fear of upsetting him prevented me. A few hours later, I could feel the headache returning, so I took another tablet. Just then, there was a knock on the door. It was Sister Imelda, with my father's lunch.

'Ah, you have company. Aren't you the lucky one?' she said to him.

'It's hard to say,' he said. 'This one is taking pills all the time.' I couldn't believe what he'd said.

'I have a migraine,' I said.

'You thought I couldn't see you, but I can. Every couple of hours, you take some of your drugs.'

'They're not drugs.'

'You won't fool me,' my father said. 'I've known for years that any of ye that give up the drink start on the drugs.'

'I have a migraine,' I said, slowly and deliberately.

'Whatever you say,' he said, his voice full of sarcasm.

'Would you like a bit of lunch?' Sister Imelda asked me. 'Come with me and I'll get you some.'

We went to the kitchen.

'Sit yourself down. You're shaking all over,' she said. 'Don't take any notice of your father. Sure, he has his own ideas about things.' She placed a bowl of piping hot stew in front of me. 'Eat that up now and have a night off for yourself. You need a good sleep.'

When I'd finished eating, I made my way back to my father. I felt stronger after the food and was careful to speak calmly.

'Did you enjoy your meal?' I asked him.

'It was all right,' he said. 'Do you see that mirror on the wall at the foot of the bed? I can see everything that goes on in the room in that.' I hadn't taken any notice of the mirror before. I stood up to have a closer look, and, yes, he could see into every corner of the room.

'I have a headache myself now,' he said. 'Give me one of your tablets.'

'No, I can't. They're prescribed especially for me.'

'That proves my case,' he said with satisfaction. He kept it up all afternoon, saying that he had a pain in his head and wanting to know why I would not give him one of my tablets. He wouldn't let me get him something from Sister Imelda. I felt that if I gave him a tablet, he would say I was trying to poison him. Maybe I was going mad, but that's how I felt.

Alison arrived at six that evening and I left immediately for Jackie's.

The children were there and all excited to see me, but I was in no humour to play with them. Mia was starting to walk and I couldn't look at her falling all over the place; my nerves were gone. I was dying to talk to someone about Daddy and my sisters, but I got the feeling that Jackie would prefer not to know any of it. She had to live in the village with my sisters and my father.

I left Jackie's about half-past nine for my five-minute walk to the nursing home. Anxiously, I wondered how my father would be with me in front of the others. As I was going through the door of the nursing home, Ruth, the woman to whom I had been talking in the school lane that morning, was coming out.

'Just the person I wanted to see,' she said, grabbing my arm and manoeuvring me back out the door. 'I've had a few words with Mary and she's upset. I told her that herself and her father are the same — that's why they can't get on — but she will have to make her peace with him, for her own sake, before he goes.'

'Oh my God, she'll be very upset,' I said.

'It's for the best,' she said and off with her down the avenue.

I went into the hall and could hear this weeping and wailing noise coming from the laundry room. There she was, Mary, her head buried in a damp mop.

'Pull yourself together,' I said, but she got worse. She caught the mop and, with a high-pitched screech, threw it the length of the room. I put my arms around her and held her tight.

'Is what Ruth said true? Am I like him?' she asked me.

'Sure, we're all a bit like each other,' I said. 'We're related. I think you should try to forgive him for whatever it is that makes you feel this way about him, or it will haunt you for the rest of your life.'

'I can't bring myself to do it.'

'There's no such thing as can't, only won't. We'll all help you,' I said, stroking her hair. She pulled away from me and went up the stairs two at a time. Geraldine and Alison were there. Mary said, 'I want ye all to leave the room.'

'Come on,' I said.

'What's going on?' Alison wanted to know.

'She's going to make her peace with her father,' I whispered.

We stood outside the bedroom door. We heard Mary sobbing and my father telling her it was all right. It went quiet for a couple of minutes, and then Geraldine said, 'I can't stand this. We'd better go in.'

'No,' I said. 'Leave them alone.'

'At least let me have a peep to see if she's okay.' She opened the door gently and we could see that they were both quiet and composed. We closed the door quietly.

Geraldine and Alison looked as if they were in shock. Half an hour later, Mary came out. She was beaming. Holding her right hand up to her mouth, she blew on her nails, then rubbed her nails on the shoulder of her jumper and said, 'I'm the favourite now.' The three of us laughed. I was happy for her, but there was a feeling of fear in me as we went in to my father.

'I don't want her staying with me tonight. She's on drugs,' he said, pointing at me. 'Don't let her near me.'

I stood there, feeling like a powerless child again. If he said I was a drug addict, then I was. My belief in myself was shattered. I left the room. Geraldine came out after me.

'What was all that about?' she asked. I told her the story and she said, 'He just can't be friends with the four of us at the same time. He has to fight with one of us.'

'I'm going to go down to Jackie's and ring Katie,' I told her.

'Stop worrying,' Katie said. 'I'm coming home tomorrow to see him.' She had always been my father's favourite grandchild. 'I'll see you soon.'

I stayed away from the nursing home that night. When I went to bed, I cried with humiliation. After a restless sleep, I dreaded going up to my father, but I had to do it. The nuns were washing him when I got there.

'I don't want her near, do you hear me?' he thundered to them. 'You made a holy show of me yesterday, taking drugs,' he said pointing. I went and sat on a chair, ignoring him.

Katie arrived soon after. My father was in great form when he saw her, cracking jokes and looking like a young lad. Then he said, 'I know your mother's here. Look at her; she's gone all red. Be a good girl, Katie, and take her away from me, once and for all.'

'Come on, Mam,' Katie said, taking me by the arm and practically lifting me from the chair. She took me outside. 'You're distorted with pain. Please will you go back to London and look after yourself.'

'I have to talk to Sister Imelda first, to see if she can give me some answers. Why is he doing this to me?'

We found the nun working in the kitchen.

'When people are dying, they say and do strange things,' she said. 'Try not to let your father get you down.'

'Sometimes it's hard for me to rise above the things he says,'

I said. 'Now Katie thinks I should go back to London as soon as possible, but I want to make my peace with him first.'

'Wait until after Mass in the morning and you and I will try and talk to him,' she said, patting me on the back.

'Thanks, Sister,' I said, giving her a quick hug, a slight ray of hope blossoming.

The next day was Sunday. I went down to nine o'clock Mass and met Sister Imelda there.

'Please don't leave me on my own with him,' I said to her.

'We'll play it by ear,' she said with a cheery smile.

'Good morning,' she said to my father when we went in with a basin of warm water to wash him. I too wished him good morning.

'Good morning,' he said. I helped the nun remove his pyjamas and we started to wash him.

'I'll give ye some time on your own now,' she said when we were finished. I wanted to shout out: 'Don't leave me.' But I didn't. I looked at my father's forbidding face and didn't know what to do or say. He never moved a muscle to ease the situation.

'I'm going back to London today,' I said, so faintly I barely heard it myself.

'That's all you're good for is leaving.'

'I do love you, Daddy,' I said, my voice shaking. I stood at the end of his bed, willing him to say he loved me too.

'I know that,' he said bitterly. I held my breath and waited for more, but nothing came.

How I wished that we would talk and laugh about the things we had done together. If only he had been able to confirm for me that we had had good times — that would have been a priceless gift. I left the nursing home feeling lost. I'm glad that I didn't know then that I would never have the opportunity to speak to my father again. I think I might have thrown myself on the bed and begged him to say something that I could treasure for ever.

I went back to London and rang Jackie every second night to see how my father was doing, always remembering to ask her if he had said anything about me. I desperately wanted him to ask me to come home again, to say that he wanted to see me.

He died six weeks after my return to London.

Chapter Forty

'He's gone,' Mary said when she rang me at three in the morning. 'Are you coming home for the funeral?'

'I don't know,' I said. 'What's the point now?' That was the extent of our conversation. She hung up and I sat there holding the phone and looking at it as if I had no idea what it was. Now he would never be able to say whether he loved me or not; it was so final. My tears were dropping on to the humming phone. How could he be gone forever?

I had to talk to someone. It was too early to ring Katie in Birmingham. Then I thought of Philip in Boston. I couldn't remember if we were five hours ahead or behind in time. I dialled his number.

'I don't know if I should go home or not,' I said to Philip.

'You'll be sorry if you don't. Anyway, why won't you go?'

'Because he's gone and he won't ever be able to take back the humiliating things he said about me.'

'Mary said he was terrible to her too.'

'He was.'

'Well, Mother, you'll have to toughen up a bit.' We talked on the phone for ages. One thing I didn't tell Philip was that I didn't have the money to go back to Ireland. I had a friend in AA from whom I could borrow it, though, and that's what I did in the end. I borrowed £200 and home I went.

The journey was trance-like. I didn't feel sure of my memories any more and now that I didn't have anyone to verify them, they seemed the most important thing in my life. Now it was all too late. There was no leaving it until another day when he might be in a better humour or not so drunk.

My father had been brought out to the chapel of rest at the nursing home, from the hospital in Kilkenny, where he had died. He would be buried after eleven o'clock Mass the next morning. It was all so quick.

Jackie and I went up to the nursing home to see Sister Imelda and thank her for everything.

'You should see your father,' she said to me. 'It will help you to accept that he has gone.'

'I don't want to,' I said, sounding like a child.

She insisted.

'Please stay with me,' I implored her.

Jackie and I followed her to the coffin. When she opened it, I shut my eyes tight. When I did look, he was the same as always: not a hair out of place and his face clean-shaven. I reached out to touch him, but pulled back, thinking for a second that he was going to shout. Feeling the nun's reassuring hand on my arm, I touched him on the cheek and said, 'This is our last goodbye, Daddy.' My heart jumped in my chest as if I had been given an electric shock. Tears slid down my burning face.

At seven that evening, his four daughters sat in the front seat of the chapel, with Sister Imelda, to say the rosary for the repose of his soul. The nun started the first of the five decades, then Alison said the second, Geraldine the third, and then it was my turn. When the rosary was finished, the coffin was wheeled out and put in the hearse for my father's last trip down the avenue. The four of us walked behind the hearse to the village church.

It was a big turnout, and I wondered if he would have a small funeral the next day. My father would hate it if that happened. I met quite a few people who I had not seen for thirty years, not since I'd left Thomastown. It was a nice service and Jackie did one of the readings. When I looked up at her on the altar, I thought how pretty she looked. She had on a black suit and a red blouse. There was a red carpet on the steps to the altar and whatever way it reflected on her, it brought a flood of tears to my eyes. I felt such a rush of pride and love for my daughter.

After we left the church, a group of family and friends went to the pub. Afraid of my own misery, I started to walk. I felt lost, alone, a forty-three-year-old abandoned child. It was a dry, bitterly cold November night. I set off up the road where I'd spent most of my married life. Rambling by the old pump, I thought of all the buckets of water I had drawn from it. Quickly I passed by the nursing home, not wanting to indulge in that loss just yet. At Mrs Cuddihy's, I made the sign of the cross in memory of that good woman. Then I was at Michael's, the house where my children had laughed and played, and where I had abandoned them. Since Michael had left for America, it had been vandalised. Most of the windows were broken; net curtains flapped through them like sails on a ship. Standing under the copper beech once again, I listened to the wind whistle through the bare branches.

I could see for miles around. The lights were on in the old schoolhouse up on the hill, and I could almost imagine hearing my children's voices in the playground and down in the woods. I suppose I had a love-hate relationship with the whole area: it was where I had hurt and been hurt, and learned the most about myself. Eventually I began to walk back towards the village. Everywhere was so quiet. I wondered if my father could see me now, and if he might be having any regrets. My idea of hell would be to be up there somewhere and be able to see my family suffering and not be able to do anything about it.

The next morning, as we made our way to the church for the funeral Mass, it was so cold that we could see our breath as it left our mouths. It was as cold inside the church as it was outside. Three of my father's remaining sisters were there. One of them was too old to come, and two were dead. It must have been dreadful to bury their only brother and the youngest member of their family. When we came out of the church, it was about a quarter of an hour's drive to the graveyard. We would have to pass my father's house on the way. I wondered would they stop. They did, for the customary length of time. We moved on again slowly. Quite a few people walked behind the hearse. When we got to the graveyard, the north wind nearly took our breath away. My father was being buried in the same plot as his parents. It was great to see my Aunt Katy and my Uncle Tom and a few of my cousins there, all from my mother's side. A few people from AA came to pay their respects and to make sure that I was okay.

After the burial, my father's family went back to Mary's house.

She had a great spread of food for everyone, from a cooked meal to sandwiches and drinks. I had not been in my sister's house for about fifteen years. It was absolutely lovely. She had everything anyone could possibly want and yet it was not enough to get over the strain in our relationship. Would I ever be able to understand it?

I have little or no recollection of the journey back.

A couple of minutes after I returned to London, with my cup of tea in my hand, I huddled into my chair. My mind wandered, looking for a place to rest. I hungered for a family to close in and protect me.

A week after the funeral, I got a letter from Geraldine. She wanted me to write to her, in secret. We communicated like this for years.

I told myself that there was a sense of freedom in my father not being there any more. That there was no need to dread having to tell him something, and I didn't have to worry about him being constantly angry with me. But I missed him so much. I couldn't believe that he wasn't there for me any more. Because no matter how traumatic our relationship had been, I knew that my father loved me, in his own, eccentric way.

Just before Christmas, I was out doing some shopping when a Christmas card in a shop seemed to jump out at me. It read, 'To my dearest Dad'. I cried for hours.

Chapter Forty-one

The following year, in early spring, Philip came home to Jackie's for a few weeks' holiday. Of course, the minute I heard, I knew that I would go to Ireland to see him. He had been so good to me when my father died, talking to me for hours from Boston. I wanted to hear how J.J. was doing. Philip was great to have a chat with; he would never say anything bad about anyone, but at the same time, he would gab away. He acknowledged me and allowed me to be a mother, and how I valued that.

A couple of days before I left to go home, Ellen rang. Apparently she had been living in Cork for a couple of months. She rang Katie a lot, and Katie would tell me little bits about her sister's life, but if I started to probe, I would be cut off, so I was delighted that she'd contacted me. Ellen sounded cheery on the phone.

'I hear you're coming home to see Philip. Well, I have some news to tell you.'

'What?'

'I'm pregnant,' she said quickly.

I gauged every word I said, knowing it would be studied carefully. 'Are you pleased?'

'I suppose I am.'

'Well, I'm going home tomorrow. Why don't you come to Jackie's and we can talk properly.'

'I know you're coming. That's why I rang to tell you. I'm living in a caravan parked outside Daddy's and I'm working in the pub.'

'Okay. I'll see you there.'

My God, I thought, Ellen was as free as the wind in the trees; how would she settle down with a baby? She had come back from Boston after six months, and had gone to live in Dublin with a lad she had met in America. He was nice and he adored her; he supported her while she went back to college. Then it suddenly ended between them for some reason — no one knew why — and she moved to Cork. Maybe this baby was going to be good for her; it might encourage her to settle down.

I got to Jackie's about six in the evening. Philip arrived back from seeing friends. We gave each other a hug.

'Did you see Ellen yet?' he asked me.

'No, I'm only after getting here.'

'She's working in the pub. Come on down with me and see her.'

Ellen was serving one of the locals and having a good laugh. 'Well, Mother,' she said, a big grin all over her face.

'You're looking good,' I said.

'Thanks. You're looking tired,' she said back. She seemed not one bit worried about being pregnant and single. It made me think of the panic I'd felt when I was in the same situation. She was cool, calm and, from what I could see, proud of herself. It was so much easier these days, I thought. I wondered what it would have been like had I been sixteen now, and not in the 1960s. Would I have made all the mistakes I had, would I have married the baby's father if I'd had the choice? These thoughts ran through my mind as I looked at my youngest daughter.

'I'm getting big,' she said, patting her stomach. I dared not ask her if she was eating properly, or having morning sickness, or who the baby's father was, all the kinds of things a mother should ask.

Philip and Ellen told me one yarn after another about their time in America and all the mad things they'd done: many twenty-four-hour drinking sessions and tricky situations too familiar to need repeating. I would have preferred not to hear them. This was a problem with me and my children. We had blurred boundaries. I realise it is one of the reasons I always feel so anxious around them. But I had to ask Philip if J.J. was drinking much.

'Don't be worrying about us. I drink as much as he does,' he said, as if that was going to reassure me.

We stayed there until closing time, then we walked up to the caravan with Ellen. There was no light on or sign of a boyfriend. We didn't go in with her. I said I would be up to her first thing in the morning. When we got to Jackie's, they were in bed; we didn't see anyone. I was jaded tired.

In the morning, about half-past ten, I went to the little shop on the corner to get some fresh milk and bread to take up to Ellen's. It was a chilly morning. *God, help me to say the right things to Ellen*, I prayed. When I saw the caravan, with my daughter asleep inside, it was like a bad dream. I had to knock on the door several times before she opened it. Gas fumes nearly knocked me over.

'You shouldn't leave the gas heater on all night. It could kill you,' I said. I knew mornings were not her best time. 'I brought some milk and bread.'

'This caravan is freezing; that's why the gas is on,' she said and crawled back into bed. After three or four minutes of an uneasy silence, I perched myself on the edge of a seat, and said, 'I don't think you wanted me up so early.'

'That bastard never came home last night,' she said. I presumed she meant her boyfriend.

'What are you going to do?' I ventured calmly.

'How do I know!' she said.

Once more she hauled herself out of the bed. 'I'll make you a cup of tea. I feel too sick to eat or drink anything myself,' she muttered, going out the door with the kettle in her hand. 'This morning sickness.' I didn't know what to say to her, but I longed to comfort her.

'Daddy told Philip to open up the house to let me get water, so that I wouldn't have to drag it up from the pump,' she said, coming back in the door. It's a pity he didn't feel the same way about your mother dragging water from the pump, I thought to myself.

'That was good of your father,' I said.

'He should let me move into the house and that would be better for him,' she said. 'Why do the two boys get everything? Philip is getting this house and Granny is leaving hers to J.J. Why is that?'

'I have no say in any of this,' I told her in a resigned voice. 'It has always been like this in Ireland.'

'Well, it's wrong — totally wrong,' she said furiously. 'Look at what happened to your house below.'

'I know.' I wondered if she was aware that we had so much in common as women and as daughters.

'Have you any plans or are you going to stay here?' I said.

'Well, I'll tell you something now: I'm not going to be like all the other unmarried mothers around here,' she said.

'What are you going to do?'

'When they have a baby here, they hide away, never to be seen again. It's like they've died. I'm going to carry on working. I'll bring the child with me and God help anyone who says anything.'

'I hope it works out like that for you, I really do.'

'I'll tell you another thing. I don't need a man to help me either. I'm better off on my own,' she said.

'Will we go down to Jackie's?' I asked her, having listened to her set Ireland and all its men to rights.

'God knows what kind of humour she'll be in.'

'Why is she in such a bad mood?'

'No idea. I don't take much notice of her,' Ellen replied. With all the chatting, it was lunchtime when we got to Jackie's. I made a fresh pot of tea and there was bread and ham, tomatoes — anything anyone could want in Jackie's spotless kitchen. Just as we were about to sit down, Jackie came in from work at the post office for her lunch. I knew immediately that she was not happy to see us. She would not eat with us. With all the fuss and bad feelings, I was no longer hungry. I could feel a migraine coming on. Since my father had made such an issue over me taking tablets, I was so self-conscious about it that I felt I had to say something.

'I'm going to take a tablet for this migraine before it gets in on me,' I said. Neither of them spoke but the way they looked at me, you would think I'd said that I was going to shoot up heroin. My father's words lived on after him. Jackie went back to work and I picked at some food. Then it was time for Ellen to go to work in the pub again.

I went to the school to pick up Shauna. Her face lit up when she saw me, 'Nanny! Nanny!' she called, running into my arms. I picked her up and swung her around.

'This is my Nanny,' she told her friends. Then we picked up Mia from the babysitter, and went into the corner shop for sweets. I loved to look at their eyes dancing with excitement. With one of them each side of me, I held their hands. It reminded me of Ellen and Philip, and the years I'd missed when I could have been doing this with them. Then I thanked God for having given me this second chance with my grandchildren. Shauna was chatting away, telling me who was living here and there, the people she thought were nice and the ones who weren't. When we got to the house, we made sandwiches and had a party with the things that we had bought.

We sang songs, danced, had a fashion show with the Barbie dolls. We had first, second, and third prize for the best dressed, and we even had to have a fourth prize so that they could have two prizes each. This Barbie fashion show became a regular thing, every time I went home. We had some great laughs. Then they would do their Irish dancing and play their recorders for me.

'I don't want Nanny to go away any more. Why can't she stay here?' I overheard Shauna whisper to Jackie.

'I don't know,' Jackie said irritably.

When the children were in bed and she and I were washing up, I asked her how she felt about what Shauna had said about me not being around.

'Oh, for God's sake. It's just that I was tired and only half-listening to her,' she answered with a sigh. 'Why do you have to make a mountain out of everything?'

'I'm sorry, I really am,' I said.

Later that night, Jackie and I went down to the pub. I wanted to say my goodbyes to Ellen and Philip because I was going back to London early the next morning. Ellen said she would write to me, and Philip said he would ring me. Just before closing time, Jackie and I left. There was a heavy, uncomfortable lull between us as we walked back to her house. I searched inside myself for something that would span the years of pain, something memorable to connect and bind us together.

'Is there anything you'd like to talk to me about before I go?' I asked her. 'Have I done something to hurt you again?'

'It's just everything,' she said crossly.

'Perhaps I shouldn't come home again until you invite me?'

She agreed, too quickly, that that would be the best thing all round. I didn't let her see my hurt, and carried on as normally as was possible.

Chapter Forty-two

Philip rang me one Sunday afternoon. He asked me if I would
like to come to Boston for a holiday. I was full of excitement at
the thought of going to America. I took on a couple of extra
cleaning jobs, and saved like mad. I couldn't eat or sleep with
anticipation, and wanted to go as soon as I could possibly afford
it. This was typical of me: I had to go straight away in case
something happened to stop me.

About a month later, Philip rang again. I told him I was
telling anyone who would listen that I was going over to him.

'Well, I rang to tell you that Daddy wants to know would you
leave it until he can afford to go home when you're here?' Philip
said.

'I don't understand.'

'He wants to go to Ireland when you're here,' Philip said. 'He
said it would upset him too much and would you leave it for
now.'

'Are you seriously telling me that your father can't stay in
Boston if I'm there?'

Philip sighed.

'Do you want me to leave it?' I asked.

'I suppose it would be better if you did, just in case he starts drinking again.'

'Does he live near you?' I asked.

'No. About an hour-and-a-half away.'

'How can he see me then? Isn't he living with someone else?'

'Look, Mother, I'm only telling you what he said.'

'I'm sorry. It's not your fault that this has happened. The last thing in the world I want is for you and me to have bad feelings between us.' If Philip was not nice to me, I would cry, so I wanted to get off the phone quick.

Considering how I felt, I thought that I had handled the situation well. I wanted to scream with pain and rage. *Why don't you tell your father that I have a right to go wherever I want without his permission?* That's what I would have loved to say. But I was not going to put my children in the middle. The threat of Michael drinking hung constantly over our children. No one ever gave a thought to the fact that I might drink. I tried to take it as a compliment.

Ellen's baby was due. No one had heard from her for a couple of months, and then out of the blue she rang me.

'I'm living in Galway,' she said. 'I love it here. The scenery is beautiful, and the people are real friendly.'

'Are you with the baby's father? Joe, is it?'

'He works away from home most of the time. It doesn't bother me,' she added hastily. 'I have a good friend called Penny; we have a laugh together.' I had to act as if I thought all this was perfect or she would not ring me again.

'When you go into hospital, I'd love to be with you,' I told her. She said she would love it also, and would let me know when to come.

A few days later, she rang to say that she was going into hospital to be induced, and that the baby was overdue. She was to be there at nine the following morning. I reminded her of my offer — to come and be with her, but she told me she was fine;

she had Joe and Penny. After I had told her that I loved her and would be praying for her, we hung up.

The next day I was preoccupied. I must have given birth ten times, for Ellen, in my head. I found it strange that she didn't want me there. I couldn't imagine anything nicer than to have my mother with me at a time like that. Maybe that's what I was doing wrong — trying to give my daughters what I had wanted myself, and maybe they didn't want it from me. I rang the hospital, my heart pounding.

She was in labour, and I was told that I could talk to her later.

'Now you can stop worrying,' Katie said when I rang her.

At six that evening, I got to speak to Ellen.

'Hello,' I said, all excited. 'It's me. What did you have — a boy or a girl?'

'I had a boy a couple of hours ago.'

'Congratulations. I was worried about you.'

'Well, don't worry. I don't want you worrying about me. I'm fine, the baby's grand, end of story,' she roared. I was near to tears, so I thought I'd better finish the conversation before it got any worse.

'I'm delighted that you and the baby are well. You must be tired. Will I call you tomorrow?'

'Do. I'm going to lie down now. Bye.'

I rang Katie.

'I have to go over to see Ellen. I think there's something going on.' I started to sob. 'I want to see where she's living, but I'm afraid that I'll make things worse between us.'

'Give her a couple of days, then ask her again, and see what she says,' Katie advised.

When I did phone, Ellen was in a more receptive mood.

'I'm being discharged,' she said quietly. 'Would you like to come home and be with me for a couple of days?'

I was ecstatic. God was good. The money that I'd saved for my journey to Boston would now fund my trip to see my second grandson.

I cancelled work and flew to Dublin the next day and then drove for five hours non-stop to Clifden, in Co. Galway. Eventually I found where she was living. It was about three miles outside Clifden. As I pulled in off the road, there was a woman in the yard.

'I'm Ellen's mother,' I said. After we shook hands, the woman said, 'She must be gone to Clifden with her friend Penny.' I looked around me at Ellen's new abode. There was a fine big house and a small one joined on to the side of it.

'Where exactly does she live?' I asked.

'Ellen lives in the small place and I live in the big one,' the woman said. 'I let the little house to people in the summer for their holidays. Knowing that Ellen was desperate, I made an exception for her. It's lonely for a young one out here,' she said.

'That's good of you and I appreciate it,' I said. She asked me in for a cup of tea.

'You must think we're a strange family. Her down here on her own with a newborn baby as if she has no one belonging to her?' I said, feeling that I owed this kind woman an explanation.

'Not at all,' she said, as she bustled around, heating the teapot.

'We would do anything for Ellen but she won't let us. She won't even tell us where she's living at times,' I said.

'Young people today are like that,' she said, giving me a cup of tea and a big slice of fruit cake.

We talked about the weather, about how long I had been living in London and so on. Then I realised that I had been in the woman's house for over an hour.

'I'd better let you get on with what you were doing,' I said. 'Once again, thanks for everything.'

I drove in to Clifden and looked for Ellen everywhere. It was not a big town, so it took me an hour at the most. When there was no sign of her, I decided to go back out to the house and see if she had returned. I sat waiting in the car for over three hours. It was so quiet, I wondered how she lived there. Another hour went by, and not a person to be seen; the odd car passed, but that was it. I walked around the house. I looked in the windows. It seemed to have two bedrooms, a kitchen, bathroom and toilet. There wasn't much else to see. By now I was getting angry. I had been waiting for five hours.

I knocked on the landlady's door and asked her if she would give Ellen a note. I was glad that my ticket was only until the next evening.

Where could she be? I decided to go back through Clifden and see again if there was any sign of her. After a couple of miles, I saw a car coming towards me and just knew it was Ellen. I blew the horn frantically. When they stopped, I got out of my rented car and ran back.

Ellen was in the back with the baby on her lap. 'This is Penny,' she said, pointing to a woman about ten years older than herself.

'Hello,' I said. 'Ellen, I have been out at your place for the last five hours.'

'Penny came out to see me, and I had a few things to get, so I went with her when I had the chance,' she said, looking at me defiantly. 'Well, what are you going to do now?' she asked. 'Are you going to look at your grandson after coming all this way?'

'I've been looking at him while we were talking,' I said lamely. 'Can I hold him?' I asked.

'You'd better come back to the house. He needs changing.'

'I'll follow you,' I said.

I don't know how I felt as I walked back to the car. Had I got it all wrong again? Did she want me there at all? I hoped that Penny would leave and let us have a chat. When we got back, I asked Ellen if I could hold the baby.

'You can change him and all,' she said, putting him in my arms. He had blue eyes, and a little wisp of blond hair. He looked really healthy. I changed him and then cradled him in my arms.

'Are you going to stay tonight, Penny?' Ellen asked.

'Is your mother staying?' she asked.

'Are you, Mother?'

'Well, I was hoping to,' I said, adding quickly, 'I'll be going back tomorrow.'

'You might as well stay then,' Ellen said.

'I don't mind Penny staying if she wants to.' Ellen needed all the friends she could get.

'I'll go,' Penny said to Ellen. 'I'll see you later in the week.' And with that, she stood up.

'Nice to meet you,' I said to her.

When Ellen came back in, she seemed calmer.

'Will you hold him?' she said, handing me baby Robert. 'I'll make a pot of tea. You must be starving.'

'That would be great,' I said, with relief. Ellen made ham sandwiches with lovely fresh bread and a big pot of tea. After she had put the baby into her bed, she came and sat down.

We were eating away, not a sound coming from anywhere. I couldn't bear it. 'Do you like the quiet?' I asked.

'Sometimes. It all depends on the mood I'm in,' she murmured, thoughtful. I knew that my youngest daughter was not happy.

The baby made a noise, so she went and picked him up. 'You'd think he would try and come at least one night a week,' she said, referring to her boyfriend.

'I don't know what to say to you, Ellen.'

There was so much I wanted to know, out of concern for her. She had no transport, the shops were five miles away, and, as far as I could see, she had no one to talk to.

I took some photographs of the baby to help pass the time. Around ten o'clock, we decided to go to bed. My mind was racing. Should I ask her if she would like to come back to London with me? Having spent half the night awake, I got up around seven and brought Ellen a cup of tea. She was breast-feeding the baby.

'I didn't hear a sound out of the little one all night,' I said.

'He's good.'

'Ellen, is there anything I can do for you? I don't like leaving you here on your own with a small baby,' I said, trying not to sound too pleading.

'I'm fine,' she said, with a don't-push-it face. We sat there together, looking at the baby as he stretched and yawned.

'God love him,' I said.

'What do you mean, God love him?'

'I hope you never feel as helpless around him as I do with you this minute,' I said in a flash of anger. 'I'm going to have a wash,' I said. I went into the bathroom and tried not to let the tears flow, but my heart was breaking, for her and for me. When I had composed myself, I came into the kitchen. Ellen was there, talking to the baby.

'I have a long journey.'

'Right,' she said, standing up quickly. I was at the front door before I knew it. Kissing the baby on his little head, I nervously handed her £30. I wasn't sure if she would take it or be offended, but she took it.

'Thanks,' she said. I stood there, wondering if she would like a hug or not. In the end, I just left. She waved as I drove away. When I looked in the car mirror, I could see them standing in that lonely place, like lost souls. My emotions were all over the place as I drove back to Dublin. I was angry with myself for being so scared of Ellen, and angry with her for not letting me help her, like any daughter would let her mother with her first baby. More than anything, I wanted her to be happy, and she wasn't. No one knew more about that than me.

Chapter Forty-three

A week later, when I rang Ellen, she was moving again, this time to Cahir in County Tipperary. Her boyfriend had got them a place there. I was greatly relieved to hear that Joe was going to be living with her and the baby and that they seemed to have patched things up.

Three months after that, I went home for Robert's christening. By this time, Ellen had moved yet again, to a house on the grounds of a big estate near Clonmel. I arrived the day before the big event. Katie and her family had come from Birmingham and were staying at Jackie's. Katie picked me up at the station in Kilkenny and took me to Clonmel. The house was full of Ellen's friends; they were from all over: Dublin, Clifden, Cork. So I stayed in a B&B in Clonmel.

By the time I got to Ellen's, I was oozing tension. Nothing could have prepared me for the shock of seeing her. My beautiful daughter was haggard and worn; her lustrous golden hair was limp and wispy. It occurred to me that this must have been how my father felt when he saw me after J.J. was born. She threw her arms around me. 'It's lovely to see you, Mam,' she said.

'It's lovely to see you, too, and where's my grandson?' He was gorgeous. He came to me straight away, with a big smile. Katie had Jackie's two children, and her own two, with her. They were fighting over whose turn it was to hold Robert. I decided to take my five grandchildren to the village for treats, but discovered that there was no shop or village nearby. But there was a pub on the grounds, which sold sweets and crisps. We got a feast and went for a walk along the bank of the river that ran through the grounds of this truly lovely place. I had not felt so happy in a long time. We sang and danced, we took photographs, and I played the game my grandfather used to play with me. 'There's a leprechaun,' he would say, and I would rush to see it, only for him to say, 'Ah, you missed it again.' They were not as easily fooled as I had been.

When got back from our walk, I had a few words with Joe, Ellen's boyfriend. I said to Katie. 'He seems nice.'

'He is,' she said. About eight that night, Katie drove me to my B&B. Then they left for Jackie's and I went to bed. The thought of meeting Jackie in the morning was on my mind. I hadn't spoken to her since we had found out that Ellen was pregnant, ten months before. I will never be able to understand how Ellen and Jackie could meet me one time and be nice and pleasant, only to meet me the next time and treat me with total disregard; it absolutely unnerved me. Maybe they wanted me to stay away altogether, like my father had said. It would be far kinder if they came out and said that to me, if that was the case, rather than letting me in and treating me like the enemy.

In the morning, after a fitful sleep, I set out for the church. Katie, Jackie and the children were already there. It was a glorious day. They were all dressed in their best clothes. My heart was pounding loudly as I went to join them. How could I feel so alone? Here I was in the middle of my family.

'Hello,' I said.

The one I was concentrating on was Jackie. Her hello had been vague. My grandchildren were the ones who were thrilled to see me. They all wanted to sit beside me in the church, so I put Mia on my lap, and Amber and Shauna on each side of me. James was with his dad; he was not as possessive of me as the girls were.

There were two other babies being christened. I thought ours was the most beautiful. After it was over, we all went back to Ellen's. The pub was also a hotel, and Ellen had arranged for a meal for us. I thought it was a great idea and told her so. We were easy with each other, and this warmed my heart.

We went into the dining room where there was a great spread of good food. During the meal or afterwards, no opportunity presented itself to talk to Jackie and I didn't see any point in going out of my way to do so. If she really wanted to say anything to me, she could have, easily. At around three o'clock, I had to leave for Dublin, to get my flight. Ellen hugged me goodbye, and so did my grandchildren. Jackie gave me a feeble kiss on the cheek. Katie drove me to the railway station. I felt happy enough leaving, just a bit anxious about Ellen not looking after herself, but there was nothing I could do about it. I had lots to think about on the journey. It's a strange thing for a mother to say, but the sense of relief I experienced when it was over, and none of them had said anything to hurt me, was immense.

One of my greatest wishes was to be around my children and not to feel the full force of their dislike.

In 1995, after nearly five years in Boston, J.J. came back to Ireland to live. He was staying at the home of his grandmother, Mrs Kelly, who idolised him. I did think that it was ironic that my son should be her favourite grandchild. Maybe somewhere in the back of my mind it was my way of saying to her: 'I can't be all bad if you love my son.'

I would have to go home to see him. It took every ounce of courage I had to ring Jackie and ask her how he was. She sounded pleasant enough. 'He's put on a lot of weight,' she said.

Then she asked me if I would like to come home and see him. I said I would and thanked her for asking me. It had been over a year since I'd been to her home.

The following week, I went to Ireland

Jackie, Shauna and Mia picked me up at the station in Kilkenny. We went to a book shop. Shauna was collecting the Babysitter books and Mia got some for colouring. After we had supper, and a sing-song, the children went to bed. Jackie's husband, Tony, went down the village for a pint, and she and I went into the sitting room for a chat. I asked her how J.J. really was, and if he knew I was home.

'I told him you were coming, but whether he remembers it or not is another thing.'

'Is he that bad on the drink?'

'He's bad enough.'

'I wonder is there anything I can do?'

'You'd know the answer to that better than anyone,' she said.

When Tony came up from the pub, he said, 'J.J.'s down there and he's pretty full. He had blood tests done last week. It seems that his legs gave way under him and he couldn't stand up.'

'My God, that's terrible.' I was shocked, and determined to see him the next day.

When I slipped in between my two sleeping grandchildren, I felt my body relax as they instinctively moved closer to me, but my head was full of J.J. After I had exhausted all avenues of thought, I fell into a restless sleep.

We were up about nine on Saturday morning to go shopping in Waterford. As we were driving through the village, J.J. was going into the pub. Jackie stopped and I shouted, 'Hello'. I think I could have passed him without knowing it was J.J, he looked so different. He was only thirty-three but he looked ten years older. He had put on about four stone.

'Well,' he said. I knew that he didn't want me looking at him the way he was. His poor eyes were all bloodshot. Those same delicate green eyes that I used to wash open with cold tea, when he was little. He was gruff and offhand with me, but I understood how he was feeling. The conversation lasted only seconds. He said he would come up to Jackie's to see me, before I went back, three days later.

'He'll be all right.' Jackie's voice broke into my thoughts. I reluctantly let it drop.

The good was gone out of the day. That night, I looked after Shauna and Mia when Jackie and Tony went out. Then we went for a drive on Sunday. There was still no sign of J.J.

When I woke on Monday morning, my throat was sore and I felt sick and feverish.

'I'll go over to the doctor and get something for this,' I said.

I walked through the village and never met a soul. Passing by Mary's house, I did not raise my eyes to look at it.

'Hello there, Kay,' the doctor said.

'Sorry to bother you, doctor, but when I woke this morning, my throat was sore, and I don't feel great.'

'Let me have a look at it,' he said as he went and got his torch. 'Yes, you have a bad throat all right,' he said, writing me a prescription.

'When is that fella coming over for the results of his blood tests?'

'You mean J.J.?' I said.

'Who else?' he said, looking grim.

'Can you tell me what the results are?' I asked him.

'No. Tell him to come over here now.'

I left the surgery in a blind panic and ran to Jackie's.

'Will you go down to Granny's and get J.J. The doctor wants to see him straight away,' I said.

Jackie came back on her own.

'Did you drive him over?' I asked her.

'I did, but first I had to get him out of the bed.'

'Thanks, Jackie.'

I couldn't sit still, I was in and out to the front door. He could quite easily go into the pub when he was passing it and not come up at all.

I was resting against the worktop with a cup of tea when J.J. sauntered in.

'How are you?' I asked.

He shrugged but didn't say anything. He sat down, his elbows on his knees and his head in his hands. There was total silence. It was as if we were afraid to breathe. Then I saw a tear drop on to the floor.

'What's the matter, J.J.?' I asked, my voice shaking.

'I have cirrhosis of the liver,' he said quietly.

The floor felt like liquid under my feet.

'That never entered my mind,' I said, in a daze. I wanted to go to him, but felt paralysed. Why could I not think of something useful to say? As if out of nowhere, I said, 'Would you like a cup of tea?'

He nodded.

'I'll make it,' Jackie said, speaking for the first time.

With that, J.J. stood up and said, 'Don't bother with the tea.' He was leaving. Just as he got to the front door, he said to me, 'Will you walk as far as the gate with me?'

'I will,' I said. When we got to the gate, he rested his back against it. We looked each other straight in the eye.

'No matter what was going on, I always loved you,' J.J. said. 'I have to keep drinking. It's the only way I can forget the way I treated you when you were drinking.' Tears were flowing freely and unashamedly now for both of us.

'I never blamed you for that,' I said. 'You were driven to it — looking at your mother always drunk around the house.' Then I gave him the one thing I craved most in the world, forgiveness. 'Please, don't keep on drinking because of that. I forgive you and I love you.'

We stood there, crying, in each other's arms. I thought my

heart would burst with love and tenderness. I wanted never to let him go.

'I'm not going to ask you to promise me that you won't ever drink again, but that is my dearest wish for both of us,' I said. 'No matter what happens, you will always be my son and I will always love you.'

For weeks afterwards, I kept having conversations with J.J. in my head. Things that I wished I'd said when I'd had the chance. I spent one whole weekend writing and rewriting a letter to him. It wasn't so much a heart to heart as a soul to soul. Then I put it in the post with a prayer for both of us.

Chapter Forty-four

Would J.J. stop drinking now? A cold shiver ran through my body at the thought that he might not.

Later on that week, at ten at night, Ellen rang me. Straight away I knew by her voice that she was drunk.

'You are a mother now, Ellen,' I chastised her.

'I don't think we should go down that road, Mother, do you?' she said bitterly.

'I never took any of you to the pub when you were small.'

'Oh no, you just walked out and left us. That was much better.'

'I'm not going to have this conversation with you now.'

'Why — because I'm drunk? That's something you would know all about, isn't it?' she roared. I hung up.

Within seconds, she rang back. 'I'm not finished with you yet,' she shrieked.

Shaking, I took the phone off the hook. How dare she ring me up like that and abuse me? If she wanted to talk about how she felt, I was more than willing to listen, but not when she was like this.

The next morning, I rang Katie. She had some news herself.

Ellen had rung her, after she had spoken to me. It seemed that Ellen's lease was up and she was having a problem finding another home.

I struggled through my work, but I couldn't get the phone call out of my head and was worried about where Ellen would go now. That night, about ten, the phone rang again. 'Hello,' I said, tentatively.

'Hello, it's me,' Ellen said.

'Why are you ringing me? Is it to say sorry for last night?'

'Sorry to you?' she said. 'Never, not as long as I live.'

'Well, I have nothing to say to you, until you do,' I said and hung up. We had that same conversation over and over again until I left the phone off the hook at one in the morning.

It was not easy for me to bring this attack to an end, because a huge part of me needed and felt that I deserved to be hurt by Ellen, by all of my children. But I was beginning to realise that, by allowing my children to continue punishing me, they were doing indescribable damage to themselves.

Soon Ellen and her problems took second place for me to J.J.'s. Jackie rang to say that J.J. had left his grandmother's and had gone up to live in Michael's house. The last time I had seen that house, all the windows had been broken, and there was no electricity. I couldn't bear to think of him being there on his own.

I mulled this over in my head for the next couple of hours, and then I rang Katie with my master plan. Would she go home and ask J.J. to come and live with one of us? I said that I would pay her fare, and she could hire a car. She agreed. Katie and J.J. were close; he would listen to her. I would have gone myself, but I had just been diagnosed with high blood pressure and felt scared; I had to get it under control. However, there was another, more important, reason why I didn't want to go. Something might happen to ruin the fragile peace that now existed between J.J. and me. I wanted to hold on to that for ever if I could.

Every penny I earned cleaning, which was about £150 a

week, seemed to go on trips to do with my children. But I was delighted to be able to do it.

Katie was staying at Jackie's. She had two days to talk to J.J. and find out what he wanted to do. He was nowhere to be seen when she arrived home, but the next day she found him in the village pub. She rang and told me that she had gone in and sat up on a high stool beside him. She was treading on dangerous ground. He could make it impossible for her to talk to him. Katie related their conversation to me:

'What are you doing, sitting in here on your own?' she asked her brother.

'What are you doing here?'

'I came home to see you,' she said.

'Well, here I am,' he said, with a big smile. There is nothing in the world as nice as one of J.J.'s smiles; they're so rare.

'We're all worried about you. Will you come back with me, or go to Mammy and see if you can stop drinking,' she said, with a smile to equal his.

He didn't answer.

'We know that you're not living at Granny's any more, that you're staying at Daddy's. There's nothing there — no windows, no furniture, nothing.' She observed him closely, knowing that he could have stood up at any minute and walked away from her. He focused on his half-empty pint. Katie knew that he was on the turn.

'Can I buy you a drink?' she asked him.

He looked her in the eye. There was no smile now. She knew he was well aware of what she was trying to do, keeping him sweet with another pint.

'Well,' she said irritably. They sat looking at each other, waiting to see who would give in. It was a deadlock.

'I'm going to the toilet,' J.J. said. It took a great effort for him to get up off the stool casually, but he gave only a slight stagger. The barmaid, a local girl who had gone to school with J.J. and

Katie, came over and said to her, 'I won't come near you until you call me, in case I interrupt something.'

'Thanks. You know what he's like. I'm trying to get him to come back to England with me, to see if we can stop him drinking.'

'Best of luck,' the girl said.

'Give him another pint to see if I can talk some sense into him.'

J.J. came out of the toilet. 'Talking about me, are ye? I'm not going to make my mind up now.'

'Well, you don't have long to make it up. I'm going back tomorrow. I have a ticket here for you,' Katie said.

'Ye have it all planned, haven't ye?' Picking up the remainder of his pint, he drained the glass, pushed it away and pulled the full pint in near to him with a contented shrug. Katie left him there. She said to me later that she could not sit there and watch him slobber over another pint.

There was no sign of him for the rest of the day, but Jackie said that he had a load of washing in the machine at his grand-mother's. We took that to mean that he was coming back with Katie.

The next morning, they had to be at Dublin Airport at ten for their flight to Birmingham. Katie got up at six to be there on time. She had over two hours' drive in front of her. She went up the road to her father's house. J.J. was fast asleep.

'J.J., are you going to get up or what?'

'I'm dying,' he said.

'Where are your clothes?'

'I think they're in Granny's washing machine. I met someone last night and forgot all about them.'

'Get up and do whatever it is you have to do,' Katie said. 'I'll go down to Granny's and get your clothes.'

'No, wait. I'll come with you,' he said. With that, he crawled out of his makeshift bed and straightened himself. Katie said that he was purple in the face, and his lips milk white. She was afraid that he would not make the journey. They went out, J.J. grabbing two bottles of beer on the way. He got into the back of the car and curled up in a ball with two bottles cradled close to his chest.

Katie stopped at her grandmother's. She had parked away from the house so that Mrs Kelly could not see that J.J. was in the car.

'Where are you going at this hour of the morning?' Mrs Kelly asked.

'I'm collecting J.J.'s clothes,' she answered, making for the machine to get them out as quickly as she could. She stuffed the wet clothes into a plastic hold-all that Jackie had given her. As she was doing this, her grandmother was saying over and over again, 'Are ye taking him away from me? Where have ye got him?'

'Granny, it's the best thing for him,' Katie said. 'He'll be back to you soon, wait and see.'

J.J. slept for most of the journey to Dublin. Katie was terrified that they would not let him fly, he looked so bad. It was obvious to anyone that he was not himself. She put him sitting where he could be seen from the check-in and went up and checked both of them on the flight.

When they got back to Birmingham, an exhausted Katie rang me. J.J. had gone to the pub for a cure. She was adamant that he would toe the line the next day. I wanted to go up straight away and have a chat with him, but she said to leave it for a week or so.

Nevertheless, things went from bad to worse over the next couple of weeks. J.J. would not stop drinking. He would stay in bed for a couple of days to try, and then go on a ferocious batter. He started a couple of jobs but they would last only a few days and he would be too hung over to go.

In the end, I insisted on going up to see him. He had been at Katie's a month by this time. I went up by coach on a Friday evening. It was the cheapest way to get there. I had about £100 in my pocket. I wanted to take Amber and James shopping and give Katie some money for looking after J.J. The three of them met me at the coach station. Amber was now ten and James seven; they were beautiful. We didn't talk about J.J. in front of the children; we waited until they had gone to bed. Katie's husband, Martin, went out for a drink to let us have our chat. He was a nice chap and put up with a lot from us all. It's not every man who would allow his brother in-law to come and stay, especially in the state of health that J.J. was in. I thanked him for it. There wasn't much for Katie to tell me because we had spoken on the phone every day.

We were hoping that J.J. would come in soon; he'd been out all day, drinking. I got tired around midnight. I'd done a day's cleaning before leaving for Birmingham, so I went to bed. I was sleeping with Amber.

'Why aren't you asleep, love?' I asked Amber.

'I wanted to talk to you.'

'Is it about going shopping tomorrow?'

'No. It's about me not being able to sleep, because I'm afraid that J.J. and Daddy will have a fight,' she said.

I was wide awake now.

'Don't worry. I'm here now and I won't let J.J. fight with anyone.' I wished that I felt as positive as I sounded. She fell asleep before me and I was glad of that. I snuggled into her. She was a special little girl. When her teacher told the class that whoever believed in Jesus Christ would live for ever, the first thing she did was ring me and ask me if I believed in Jesus Christ. When I said I did, she said, 'Nanny, we will live for ever.' I fell asleep, thinking of this, and never heard J.J. coming in.

The next morning, Katie went to work early. She had been running a restaurant in town for a couple of years. The two children and I got up and had some breakfast, and then we went into the front room to look at a video of *The Lion King*. Their father was upstairs having a lie-in. Just then, I noticed J.J.

sneaking out the front door. I didn't do or say anything, but let him go with a heavy heart. I noticed it was nearly eleven — opening time. About ten minutes later, Katie rang to tell me that J.J. had phoned her. He wanted Amber to go over to the pub with some money for him.

'She's doing no such thing. I'm going over to him myself, this minute,' I told her.

Five minutes later, I walked into the dingy pub. J.J. was the only customer. If he was surprised to see me, he didn't show it. He carried on casually throwing darts at a board.

'Can I have a Coke, please?' I asked the woman behind the counter.

'You can pay for this while you're at it,' J.J. said, pointing to a half-empty glass of Guinness in front of him.

'Take the money for that and can I have another pint, please?' I asked. I wanted to make sure that we were not going to be disturbed.

'Put those darts away and come over here,' I said to him as if he were a five-year-old. I went into a dark corner as far away from the counter as possible.

'J.J., do you know what you are doing to yourself and us?' I began. 'We have to look on as you go out day after day killing yourself. We all feel so helpless.' He was so hunched over his body, his head was nearly on the floor. I knew that he was in despair. 'What are you going to do about yourself?'

He took a big gulp out of his drink.

'I suppose you don't care what happens to you. That's how I used to feel, but could you try and do something about it for me?'

I couldn't see his face. I searched frantically to find one thing to say that would reach him and ignite some hope. 'J.J., I love you with all my heart and I know people say you have to stop drinking for yourself or it's no good, but trust me, no matter who or what you stop for, it's better than this. Could you stop for me? I did it for ye.'

'I don't know,' he said quietly. He still had his head down. I was terrified that he would start crying or get angry with me. I wasn't sure which would be the worst.

I said the first thing that came into my head. 'Surely anything would be better than being in this stinking place, on your own, first thing in the morning?'

'I know you're right, but I'm not ready. I don't want to stop yet.'

'I'll leave you alone so,' I said, putting my hand on his shoulder and stroking him. There was no more to be said; I knew that. He had no money, and I knew what I was about to do was textbook wrong. But I wanted to see the relief and perhaps a smile on his face before I left him. I took £40 out of my pocket and put it on the table in front of my son. He finally looked at me, and an uneasy smile crossed his face.

'If I could do it for you, I would,' I said, kissing the top of his curly head. Then I stood up and left.

Chapter Forty-five

All along, I'd thought that when my children got older, they would have more understanding of life and marriage. I hoped that as they formed relationships, they would think, What if I had married the first boy or girl that came along, like my mother did? I believed that they would develop the wisdom that usually comes with living life, and with age, and the ability to look at situations with an open mind; to see things from both sides, mine and their father's, and to care about both of us.

How long more would I have to wait? As I write, J.J. is forty-six, Katie forty-five, Jackie forty-three, Philip thirty-eight and Ellen thirty-six. I had waited so long for them to forgive me, love me, let me back into their lives, but by the end of the century it was beginning to dawn on me that it was never going to happen. Nearly thirty years before, I had put myself on the outside in an act of survival, when I didn't even know what that was, and I had never been let back in.

When I got Ellen's phone call, I was astonished. She was inviting me back to see her and the boys. Her tone was warm and friendly: 'You can stay with me. I'm still in the same place and

I'd be delighted to have you.' Was this the same girl who had been roaring down the phone at me a couple of weeks previously?

I got a cheap flight with Ryanair. Once again, Jackie picked me up from the train station in Kilkenny; she had Shauna and Mia with her. They were dressed up in their Christmas clothes. I gushed and admired their pretty dresses and boots, knowing that they had put them on especially for me to see. They said that they had so many toys to show me when we got to their house. We were going to have a busy night ahead of us.

Jackie knew that I was to stay at Ellen's for a couple of nights. Philip, who had been home about two weeks, wanted to know if I would wait until he was going up to Ellen's, and we could travel together. That was okay with me. I decided that I would take Shauna and Mia with me, to give Jackie a break. They were delighted and looking forward to seeing their cousin Robert, who by now was over a year old and walking. I hadn't seen much of this grandchild but Shauna told me that he knew me from a photograph. After a lovely evening at Jackie's, we went to bed tired and excited.

The next day, Philip came to collect us around one and we set off for Ellen's. It would take us about an hour to get to Clonmel and another half an hour to get to the estate where she was still living. Philip and I chatted effortlessly as we sped along.

Ellen was waiting for us. 'How are ye?' she said, standing at the front door with Robert.

'Fine,' I said, remembering an AA saying: FINE *means fed up, insecure, neurotic and emotional.* I smiled to myself.

'How are you?' she asked Philip.

'Fine,' he said too.

'I thought you'd be up to see me long ago. You're home over two weeks,' she said, taking a deep pull out of her cigarette.

Shauna and Mia asked if I would take them to see the film *Santa Claus.* I said I would.

I was delighted to have the opportunity to take my grandchildren to the pictures. We got popcorn and drinks, and then went to our seats and settled down. I sat in the middle, and when we were not eating or drinking, we held hands. Now and then, I would sneak a look at my beautiful grandchildren and feel proud to be part of their lives.

The film had been two hours long. Philip, Ellen and the baby were waiting for us when we came out of the cinema. A sense of doom came over me when I saw them.

I opened the door with a false bravado saying, 'Here we are.' I gushed about the film, then stopped as Ellen put her finger to her mouth. She pointed to Robert asleep in her arms.

'Sorry,' I said.

'He's awake now,' she said.

'Sorry,' I said again, looking at Philip for support. He moved his gaze to Mia, asking her if she'd enjoyed the film.

'Yes,' Mia said feebly and put her hand into mine. I promised myself that no matter what was said, I was not going to upset those two children. It was obvious to me that there had been a drastic change in Philip and Ellen's mood since we had left them.

When we got back to Ellen's, she asked me. 'Did you enjoy the film?'

'Yes, thanks.'

'You don't seem too sure.'

'I am sure.'

'I heard that you're not happy about J.J. being at Katie's,' she said, eyes blazing mad for an argument.

'Who told you that?' I asked her, looking at Philip.

'Yes, Mother, I told her that you were talking to Amber about J.J.,' he said.

'You'd want to get your facts right, Philip, before you say things like that,' I said, my eyes blazing now. 'I didn't want the child worrying about her father and J.J. having a fight when J.J. arrives back from the pub at night.'

'What do you mean?' they both asked.

'I don't want to talk about it in case I get upset and the children notice,' I said through clenched teeth.

'They're all right,' Philip said.

'How can you say I didn't want J.J. over there? I was the one who paid for him to go over,' I said. They looked at each other. 'I paid for Katie to come home and get him, and I paid his fare also. And another thing: I told Katie to tell him he could come to me if that was what he wanted.'

I stopped to catch my breath, and Ellen jumped in. 'Don't you ever come into my life again until you're invited,' she said.

'What are you talking about now?' I asked.

'Clifden!' she said. 'J.J. is drinking himself to death because he hates you so much.' I stood up to go into the bathroom and compose myself before the girls noticed the tears in my eyes. Ellen caught me by the hand as I passed her.

I pulled my hand free and said, 'Don't follow me,' as I walked away from her.

She followed me in. I was shocked when I saw her behind me. I turned around to face her. Then she said, 'When I look at my baby, I wonder to myself how you could leave me when I was two years of age. When I'm in bed at night, I think about you. I would love to have you in front of me and tell you exactly what I thought of you.' She was very angry and upset.

I stayed calm, and said, 'I know that it was a terrible thing that I did.' No matter what I said, it would sound feeble in comparison to her rage and pain. Telling her that I loved her with all my heart and had never stopped thinking of her, of all of them, made her even more angry.

'I hope you never forget what you did,' she hissed.

'Please, go away and leave me alone,' I pleaded.

'Nanny, are you coming out?' It was Mia outside the door.

'In a minute, love.' Ellen stood as if in a trance.

'Are you all right?' I asked her.

'Fuck off,' she said and flounced out.

Dear God, get me through this evening, I begged as I tried to make myself look normal. How was I going to stay the night at Ellen's? Mia put her hand in mine once more. If only that child knew how much it meant to me at that moment. I gave it a squeeze; she looked up at me and smiled. It gave me strength.

Ellen was now sitting in a corner of the room with the baby on her lap. She spoke only to the baby for over an hour. This is the girl who could not wait to see me and have a nice chat, I thought. Mia was sitting on my lap, and Shauna was wandering around, looking bored. It was a wild night. The rain and wind lashed against the house. Then we started playing a game of Jenga. This was putting wooden blocks on top of each other to see how high we could go. I was glad when Philip started playing the game with us; it kept our minds occupied. When the blocks fell, we would all shout, which was a natural reaction, but Ellen was furious because we were making a noise. Then out of the blue she said, 'I'm going to bed.'

It was after eleven when I said to the girls, 'Will we go to bed?'

The three of us climbed into bed. The children were asleep in no time, but I had so much going around in my head, it was ready to take off. Ellen and Philip must have had a right old mother-battering when we were at the cinema. The hatred and anger in Ellen was getting worse every time I met her. And I couldn't get over how much Philip had changed. He seemed to have his mind made up that I was against J.J., no matter what I said.

The last thing I heard that night was Ellen and her boyfriend talking in bed, in the next room. In the morning, I sent the children down first, to break the ice.

Philip was up. He'd slept in the sitting room. I asked him if he would drive us to Jackie's.

He said that he was going back himself anyway.

Then I rang Jackie and asked her if that was okay with her. She didn't sound too pleased.

'I'm sorry about this,' I said. 'I'll look after the children if you want to do something yourself.'

'Right,' she said.

Philip was asking Ellen to get up, telling her that we were leaving.

He made a fry for himself. The children and I had cereal. Then Ellen made her entrance, 'Did ye sleep all right?' she asked.

'Grand,' I said, daring her to look at me. She gave a fleeting glance in my direction.

'I'm going to go back to Jackie's today,' I told her bravely.

'Whatever you want,' she said, cool as a breeze. That was the end of that conversation. I needn't have worried that she might try to persuade me to stay. She waved us off with a look of relief. Philip had given her £60 and I gave her £30.

'I don't want to know why you came back early,' Jackie said when we got to her house. Philip had dropped us off, and then gone on somewhere. He and I never mentioned the previous night.

On Sunday, Jackie took the children and me for a drive after we had had an early dinner. It was pleasant; we didn't talk about anything heavy. As we drove along, memories of different things that had happened in my life came flooding back. I longed to share those experiences with my daughter and granddaughters. They were simple things like me riding along with my grandmother, Ma, in a donkey and cart, and her buying me a polka-dot dress in Power's in Callan, or the many journeys I had made on the bar of my father's bike. But I knew that Jackie could not bear to listen to me going on about such things.

The next morning, I left for London. I had come up with something new to think about. Was it the biggest mistake in my life to believe that my children now wanted me and my love? They didn't want anything from me. Was my constant insistence on being in their lives a bad thing for all of us?

Philip rang to say he was going back to Boston. It was a strained conversation. It's my nature to want to get everything out in the open and fix it, but I was too cowardly to ask him why he was so sure that I was against J.J., in case I made matters worse. It was the same with Katie. I wanted to sort things out with her, and ask why she hadn't told Philip that it was I who had paid for her and J.J.'s flights over and back. But my fear of losing Katie, in particular, was too great. I tried to remain positive, but what I really did was to start acting. I stopped being myself, and became instead a superficial woman who talked about the weather, clothes, and what was on television. I wanted Katie to notice and ask me, 'What's happened to you?'

'Daddy is coming back home to Ireland to live,' she said excitedly when I rang. 'He's going to do up the house and live there with Norah.' Norah, apparently, was American, and the woman in Michael's life. 'They're going to stay at Iris's until the house is ready to move into.' Iris was Michael's sister.

Katie was full of news and I was full of resentment. The thing that made it worse was the excitement in her voice.

Chapter Forty-six

I didn't have long to wait for the solicitor's letter. Even though I was expecting it, when I saw the brown envelope with the Irish stamp, I didn't want to touch it. My heart pounding, I read it and decided there and then that I was going to sign it straight away.

My decision came at the end of three months of wrangling with my children since Katie had rung me to tell me that Michael wanted me to sign my share of the house over to him. I had been devastated, not by Michael's behaviour, but by the willingness of my children to go along with him and to try to persuade me to sign. It seemed that my children wanted me out of their lives.

Wearily, I went down to the solicitor on the Caledonian Road who had handled my divorce and asked her to witness it for me. She said that I would have to get it done in Ireland.

'Are you sure about that?' Katie asked when I rang to tell her.

'I'm sure,' I said. I hadn't wanted to upset Katie, as she was in the throes of a divorce. A couple of hours later, Philip rang me to say that his father would pay my fare home.

'No, thanks,' I said. 'I don't want anything from him. I will go when I can afford it and not before.' I knew that Michael wanted it done immediately in case I changed my mind. This was my way of punishing him. He would have to wait until I was ready.

In the meantime, Ellen rang me to tell me that she was six months' pregnant. She was pleasant and it was as if she and I had a great mother-daughter relationship. I went along with it as usual — I didn't dare mention our last encounter. She seemed pleased about the pregnancy, and I was glad about that.

It was three months later when I went home. When Katie told Michael that I was on my way, he went through his usual routine of going away for the weekend, in case he ran into me.

When I went to the solicitor, in Kilkenny, she asked me, 'Are sure you want to do this?'

'Yes,' I said.

'You are a foolish woman.'

'I know,' I said. I signed it and posted it to Michael.

Jackie said that Shauna and Mia would love to see me when I was home. I went there and she said that she hadn't been up to see Ellen for ages and that we should go and see her together the next day. I hesitated but she said, 'The baby is due any day now.'

'Right,' I said. 'Let's go.' I was not sure about it, but I didn't want to make a fuss.

'Maybe we'll stay the night,' Jackie said. 'You haven't seen the place she's living in now. It's still close to Clonmel.'

'How many times has she moved since Robert was born?' We counted: five different homes in two years.

'It's true what she said when she was little — that when she grew up, she wanted to be a tourist,' I said to Jackie and we laughed. Ellen had been a chubby, smiling, always-ready-for-fun child. How had she grown into this hostile young woman?

We went up the next day. The house she was now living in was quaint and homely. After a lovely meal, Ellen and Jackie went to the pub next door to get a bottle of wine. When they came back, they were in fits of laughter. Apparently there had been a really drunk man in the pub, who was seeing double, and when they went in, he had said, 'What are ye four havin ta drink? Come on, come on, have a drink with me.' It's not easy to make Jackie laugh, but she enjoyed this. To hear Ellen imitating the man was a scream; she could be so funny. We had a great night and all went to bed around midnight. Neither of my daughters had mentioned Michael or the house.

About four in the morning I heard Ellen calling, 'Mammy, I think the baby's coming.'

I jumped out of the bed and said, 'Don't worry. We'll get you to the hospital straight away.' She was doubled up with pain. Everyone was now awake. We got the three children dressed and into Jackie's car. It was half an hour's drive to the hospital in Clonmel.

We were there in no time, and got Ellen settled in. I asked the nurse how long she thought it would take.

'A couple of hours,' she said. We were in and out to the car with Robert, trying to keep him occupied. Then we had just gone to the hospital canteen to get a cup of tea when I heard my name being called over the intercom. When I got to Ellen, she was in the last stages of labour.

'How could I forget what this pain is like?' she said. The nurses were telling her to push.

'You'll forget again,' I said. 'Come on and push, good girl.' This went on for about half an hour, and then I saw my grandson being born.

Ellen, Jackie, the girls and I were all trying to hold the baby at the same time. Then Ellen's boyfriend came, and we took Robert out with us, to let Ellen and Joe be with the new baby together. Maybe things would be easier between Ellen and me now, I thought. Maybe she would realise that I wanted to know what was going on in her life, because I cared about her.

Joe came out after about ten minutes and took Robert. Then we left. We went back to Jackie's. Her husband, Tony, was there; the children told him all about the new baby. Then Shauna shouted down from her bedroom, 'Can I go up to Michael and Norah?' No one answered her, so she repeated it.

Tony said, 'What's she on about? Since when did she start going up there?'

'Shut up, Shauna,' her mother shouted. 'They've gone away.'

That was that, but I had noticed that the last couple of times I'd been around Shauna, she had scarcely spoken to me. My God, I thought. Is this poison going to run through another generation?

Someone suggested going for a walk. I thought it was a great idea; it was a beautiful warm evening.

'Will we go up to see Michael and Norah's house?' Shauna said. 'It's gorgeous, and Mammy has the key.'

I stood still for a second or two, and then said, 'Why not?' I was curious to see what had been done to it.

We walked up, the two children and Jackie and myself. On the outside, it was painted a brilliant white, with brown window frames and doors. It looked very impressive against the big copper beech, with its full plumage of dark red leaves. We went in the front door. The hall was painted cream. Shauna led me into the main bedroom, now twice the size. There was the most wonderful wooden floor, a huge double bed, and a dressing table with gold jewellery carelessly tossed on its polished surface. It was so grand. We then went into the sitting room which had also doubled in size. The furniture and carpet were very American, but again it left me speechless. Then into the kitchen, cosy and cheerful; a little stove made it so warm and wonderful.

'Daddy has cut off the three new rooms he built on, just for the time being,' Jackie said. 'Later he's going to make it into a separate apartment for any of us who want to stay.'

'That's a good idea. When Katie or Philip come home on holidays, they can stay there. It's great,' I said, throwing my hands in the air. 'He's done a great job; he should be proud.'

This is what I said, and I meant it, but my heart was aching at the same time.

If Michael had done a fraction of this, or shown some interest in the children and me, maybe we would have been there together on that day, celebrating the birth of our sixth grandchild. I was keeping up a good front for Jackie, for the girls, and for myself, but I could have screamed with loss, and a deep longing for the fulfilment of my dream of a happy family.

Mrs Kelly died shortly after this and left her house to J.J. I was delighted for him, and wrote and told him so. I said I was sorry his grandmother had passed away and that I knew she had been more than a grandmother to him because of the circumstances of his life, and that he was bound to miss her, but that he had been with her at the end and that was what she would have wanted.

Chapter Forty-seven

When I got back to my flat in Islington, I thought about Shauna. I know that she was only thirteen, but it hurt me that she didn't seem to see me as her Nanny any more. Perhaps she had begun to pick up on Jackie's attitude and to think she had to treat me in the same way.

Katie and I talked a lot about her split from her husband. 'How are the children taking it?' I asked.

'Not too bad. That's one of the reasons I rang — to know if you'd take them for another week.'

'Of course I will. Isn't it great that you can make a decision about your life and marriage and not lose your children?' I wanted her to imagine what it was like to go through the loss of a marriage and to lose your children as well.

'I know.' She sounded disinterested.

Katie brought them down to me and we had a good time together, as usual. Amber, now thirteen, talked a lot about her father. She was worried that he would be lonely not living with them. I did my best to reassure her. James was ten and going around with one fist tightly closed. He refused to open it. When he was asleep, I opened it gently and I got a shock. He had DAD written in large print on the palm of his little hand. He woke up and knew that I had seen it. He cried for a long time that night. I told him he could write Dad any place he wanted to, and talk about him as much as he liked. He said he was afraid of upsetting his mother if he kept talking about his father. We had a long chat about it all, and after that they felt easier in themselves.

My sister Alison came to London to visit her eldest daughter, Rebecca. Rebecca was a lovely girl of nineteen, and had come to visit me a couple of times. She said that her mother would like to see me. This meant so much to me. I hadn't seen or heard from Alison since my father's funeral. We were to meet in Hammersmith, where Rebecca was living.

It was a beautiful summer's day. Alison's two youngest sons were with her, big lads in their early teens, nice young fellows. When we met, I knew that Alison, too, was anxious.

'How ya?' we said to each other from opposite ends of the room.

'Grand,' we said nearly together. We shook hands and glanced nervously at each other. She looked well. I was glad to see that she was trim and slim; you would never think that she had six teenage children. I told her this and a big smile swept across her pretty face.

A little time afterwards, her daughter said, 'Off out with the two of you and enjoy yourselves.'

I dreaded the first few minutes on our own, the uncertainty, not knowing what to say. Alison said she wanted to get something nice for Rebecca's flat. This gave us something to focus on. We went into one shop after another.

'Haven't they lovely things now? Not like when we were setting up house,' I said. We seemed to be drawn to the same books and ornaments. Alison bought me a Susan Howatch novel, *The Wheel of Fortune*. The excitement of my sister buying me a present was childlike. Our shopping finished, we went and had something to eat. Alison talked about her children all the time. I talked about mine also, Alison didn't respond to any of it, as if I didn't have the right to speak about mine. I'm not sure if it was intentional or not, but it was painful to me.

When I was leaving, she walked to the station with me. We stood on the platform and she thanked me for meeting her. I told her that I'd enjoyed the day and thanked her for meeting me. I wished so much that the train would come before something went wrong. At last, there it was. I wanted to run towards it! Alison was saying, 'The next time I'm over, we'll meet again. I hope you enjoy the book.' She leaned towards me and I towards her, and we hugged for a second or two. I jumped on to the train, willing it to move away.

'Do you want to go?' I asked my sister.

'No,' she said. 'I'll wait and see you off.'

With that, the engine started and I breathed a sigh of relief. Alison stood on the platform, waving, and I waved back at her as the doors closed. Then she was out of sight and I was alone again. I hoped she hadn't noticed how uneasy I had been before leaving her. I didn't want her thinking that was I tired of her company. There was so much love in my heart for her, if only I could have told her. I rang her before she went back to Ireland and she told me that she had had a lovely time and she would see me again, next year, please God.

Ellen rang one evening. Immediately I was on my guard. Would she be insulting, cross, even pleasant? I never knew. I hadn't spoken to her since the birth of her baby, two months before. She asked me if I was coming home for the christening.

'I'd love to! When is it?'

'Tomorrow.'

'Really? This is the first I've heard about it,' I said, trying to keep my voice from quivering.

'Is it? I thought Katie would have mentioned it?'

'No, she didn't. She has a lot on her mind with the break-up and so on.' I could hear myself making excuses for both of them, but in my gut I knew it was all rubbish. When an incident such as this happened, it seemed obvious to me that there had been discussion between Katie and Ellen about whether they should tell me about my grandchild's christening. I was making myself ill wondering what conversations were going on amongst my children about me, their mother. I began to feel that I was suffering from paranoia. But the denial in me concerning my family was stronger than the denial about my alcoholism.

'Daddy and Norah are coming,' I vaguely heard Ellen say.

'Oh, well, there'll be plenty of ye there without me. How is the little chap?'

'He's great.'

'Well, at least I saw him being born,' I said, to reassure her and myself that the christening was not as important as his being born.

'You did. That's right,' she said.

'Have a great day and take plenty of photos,' I said with false cheerfulness. With that, she was gone.

One phone call from one of my children and I was in the depths of despair.

I said nothing to Katie about the fact that she had never mentioned the christening. What was the point? By now, I did know, though, that my not mentioning things that bothered me, and carrying on as if everything were okay, was not solving anything. It was building up inside me. I was exhausted from it all.

Things started to change yet again. Philip decided he wanted to leave Boston. I was relieved that he was going to be nearer to his family. And Katie had a new man in her life, Leo. The children seemed to get on well with him. Then Philip decided he was going to live in Birmingham. He moved in with Katie, her man, and the children, until he got a place of his own.

When he had been there for a couple of weeks, Katie and Leo came down to London for me to meet him. Philip was looking after the children. Leo was a big man, over six feet and about sixteen stone. He made himself at home quickly, was very chatty, and they stayed the night.

After a couple of weeks, Philip got his own place, but he had no job and no money. Since he had come back from America, he had spent a small fortune. He asked me for a loan of £300 which was about as much as I had. I gave it to him, and he promised to give it back to me when he was working. I was glad that I had the money to give him. He did get a job. He was a great carpenter, so he got the first one that he applied for. After a couple of months of work, he bought a car and met a nice girl. He seemed settled.

I was pleasantly surprised when Ellen began ringing me regularly, and I dared to hope that things were improving between us. She was getting older and learning a lot about life. I was longing to see her and the children, but didn't want to go and stay with them. If she came to me, maybe things would be different. I decided the best thing to do was to bring her and the children over to London. She said she would be terrified of flying on her own with the children; apparently she had developed this fear since the children had been born. I got some reasonable flights for me to fly over and come back with her. Then Katie would fly back with Ellen after her visit.

This trip for Ellen was costing me every penny I had, but I'd promised and I couldn't disappoint her. I flew to Dublin to meet her, praying that we would not fall out or hurt each other. I was at the airport an hour before I was to meet her. As I wandered around, doing nothing in particular, I heard a man's voice saying, 'My God, is it yourself?' It was P.J., the man I had finished with ten years before. I was delighted to see him. He had put on a bit of weight, but he had the same twinkling eyes and big smile.

'Are you coming or going?' he asked me.

'A bit of both.' I told him that I'd come over for Ellen.

'Will you ever get sense?'

'God knows,' I said with a smile.

'Are you living with anyone or anything?' he asked.

'I was with someone in London for a while but he went back to live in Ireland and there's been no one since.'

'Here's my phone number. Give us a ring sometime,' he said, grinning all over his handsome face.

'Here's mine. You give me a ring after this week's over.'

I went to meet Ellen and my two grandsons. Three-year-old Robert was all excited about going on a plane. He was with me and had his own seat by the window, while one-year-old Dylan sat with Ellen. They were the kind of children you could not help but notice: slightly tanned from always being out in the open air; blond, with eyes that shocked with their blueness. No matter what happened for the next week, it was worth it just to see the amazement on Robert's face.

Ellen was thoughtful.

'They're good children,' I said to her.

'They are,' she said.

We got to the flat after hours of travelling, and had something to eat. Then we brought the children to the park and the swings across the road. I took Dylan from Ellen, and he came to me with a big smile. He had a roguish grin that made you want to laugh. After that, he wanted to be with me all the time. Of course, I was thrilled, and there was no jealousy between my precious grandsons.

Ellen was distant. I was delighted she was with me but disappointed to see her so unhappy. I didn't want to probe by asking her if there was something wrong. She would tell me in her own time, if she wanted to, I thought to myself.

When we got back to the flat, Dylan wanted to sit on my lap when I was eating.

'No,' Ellen said to him.

'I don't mind. Honestly I don't,' I said.

'Don't undermine me in front of my children,' she replied.

'Sorry,' I said. 'It's just that it's been a long day for them and everything is strange,' I said lamely.

Ellen didn't reply. She stood up and put the baby on her hip, then she caught Robert by the hand. They went into the bedroom. That was the last I saw of her that night.

The children were awake at seven. I could hear them laughing in the bedroom. I went into the room and asked Ellen if she wanted a cup of tea.

'I'll get up for it,' she said, busying herself. She didn't seem to be in any better humour. We were both talking to the children but there was nothing being said between us. Then the phone rang and it was Katie. I spoke to her for a couple of minutes then I gave Ellen the phone. I took the boys into the bedroom.

Ten minutes later, Ellen came in. 'Katie's coming down for us tonight. We're going up to her for the rest of the week.'

A coil of pain tightened in my stomach and I heard myself say, 'If that's what you want.'

I had to go to work for a couple of hours and on the way I rang Katie from a phone box.

'What reason did Ellen give for going to Birmingham after spending only one night with me?'

'She didn't give me a reason,' Katie said. 'She just asked me would I come down and get her, and I said I would.'

'I see,' I said, even though I didn't see at all. 'What time will you be down?'

'Myself and Leo will be down around nine. I have to get a babysitter for Amber and James. They're looking forward to seeing the boys.'

'I'll see you then.' I felt raw.

When I got back to the flat, Ellen and the children seemed to be happy. I asked them what they would like to do.

'Go to the park,' Robert said.

Off to the park the four of us went. Then back to wait for

Katie and Leo. I wished Ellen would say something to me, anything about why she was leaving.

One evening, I decided I would ring P.J. I had kept putting it off because I was scared of getting hurt. However, I rang and he was delighted. We started to ring each other often and it became something else for me to think about, other than my children. Of course, I would talk to him about them, and he had met three of them over the course of the years. It was nice to talk to someone who cared about me and my feelings in this whole sorry tale. He came over on holiday and eventually we ended up living together. We are still happy to this day.

Chapter Forty-eight

Once again, I was thrown into confusion when Katie invited P.J. and me to Birmingham for Christmas 1999. P.J.'s ten-year-old son, Eoin, was over with us and he was welcome too. Philip was going to be there and Leo's parents. When we got to Katie's, I noticed that a lot had changed. Leo would not let me have five minutes on my own with her. At dinner, he would tap the table beside him with his finger to tell her she was to sit there. I felt sick to my stomach watching this. Katie had always been her own person. I used to love to see her independence shine. We came back to London on St Stephen's Day. I couldn't stay any longer. James and Amber came with Eoin and us.

On New Year's Eve, we went to Alexandra Palace to celebrate the beginning of the new century. From there, we could see all over London. Fireworks lit up the sky and the Thames, and we could see the Dome in the distance. The children had tall hats with the year 2000 written on them. People with picnic baskets were handing around glasses of champagne. I was careful. I knew how easy it would be to get carried away on a tide of emotion. P.J. stood with his hands on Eoin's shoulders and I was beside him, with my arms around my grandchildren; it was a wondrous night. When they rang in the New Year, I had tears of happiness in my eyes. Back in the car, we sang along to an Abba tape, until we reached home. I'd bought two bed settees for the children to sleep on when they visited.

'Your mum will be down for you tomorrow,' I said as I tucked them in.

Katie and Leo arrived for the children the following evening. They didn't stay long; they were gone in half an hour.

The final humiliation for me with my children came with Mia's confirmation. I'd never missed any of my grandchildren's Communions or Confirmations. When Amber was making her Confirmation, she had asked me to be her sponsor. I had said it would be a privilege, and I felt so proud going up to the altar by her side.

I desperately wanted to be there for Mia's big day. She used to write to me nearly every week and I would write back by return post. Once, she sent me a badge which said: *Loveliest person in the whole wide world.* I keep it on my mantelpiece all the time. Recently I'd noticed that her letters to me were getting fewer, but I put that down to the fact that she was getting older and I knew she was a busy and popular little person.

Now I patiently waited to see if Jackie would ring or write and put me out of my agony.

I started to think about my future. At fifty-six, dashing around from one house to another cleaning was getting too much for me. I decided to go to college and do a counselling course. It was a great challenge for me and something I had always wanted to do.

We had a lot of role-play in college. All mine was about my family. I could hear myself going on and on about them and I was getting sick of listening to myself. People looked at me with pity. I was so angry with my children and my sisters. I was finding it very difficult to speak to Katie, and she didn't ring me either. Two weeks went by without contact. I rang Katie, and started a stupid conversation with her about the weather and things — dialogue of the deaf, I call it.

'Are you going to go to Mia's Confirmation?' she asked. 'I know if it was me, I wouldn't bother going.'

'We are two very different people, you and I,' I said wistfully. 'You know that I won't go unless I'm asked. Why is this so important to you?'

'No reason,' she said.

A couple of days later, Jackie rang and left a message on the answering machine saying, 'Mia's Confirmation is on the eleventh of July. You can come if you want to.' Once again, I got ready to go home.

Philip rang me a couple of days before I left. 'I hear you're going to the Confirmation,' he said. 'Are you going to see Ellen?'

'Does she want to see me?'

'You can't go home and not go and see her.'

'I suppose you're right,' I said. That was as much as I could say to him.

I hired a car in Dublin and drove to Kilkenny. This was on a Friday and the Confirmation was on the Sunday. As I drove along, I prayed that everything would be all right this time. When I got to Kilkenny, I rang Ellen to get the most difficult thing out of the way first.

'Hello,' I said to her.

'I was expecting you to ring today,' she said. 'Where are you staying tonight?'

'In a B&B. But I would love to see Robert and Dylan.'

'Right,' she said. 'Do you want to come here?'

'That would be great.'

Then I asked her what I should get the children — would she like some clothes for them?

She said, 'There are two water pistols that they're mad for and I won't buy them, so you can.'

When I drove out to her house, Robert and Dylan were

playing in the front garden. Robert was delighted to see me and he knew I was his granny, but Dylan didn't remember me.

'Come in,' Ellen said. 'I'll make us a cup of tea.'

We sat down with our drinks and then she said, 'How do you think it's going to be with Daddy on Sunday?'

'I'm sure it will be fine; he wouldn't go otherwise, would he?'

We had a chat and I heard all about the children and Joe, and when I was leaving, Ellen said, 'Give me a ring tomorrow night, and I'll meet you in town for an hour.'

'I'd love that,' I said, and kissed her and the boys goodbye.

On Saturday morning, I was meeting Jackie and the children in Waterford to do some shopping. After hours of shopping, we went to have something to eat. Jackie didn't have much to say.

'How's your father?' I asked her.

'The same as usual,' she said.

'It's great that he doesn't mind me being there tomorrow.'

'Actually he's decided that he's not coming. Himself and Norah are going away for the day.' Her face was expressionless. I was just about to say, 'I'm sorry', when I thought, Why am I sorry? It's his decision.

'How do you feel about that?' I asked her.

'In future, I will ask you both to come to those things, and then ye can decide yourselves to come or not.' Shortly after that, we left. As we were going in the same direction, Mia came in my car and Shauna went with her mother. Mia roared with laughter at my flat voice as I insisted on singing 'Doe a deer'.

'Please, please stop singing Nanny or I will be sick,' she begged.

I was disappointed that Shauna didn't want to travel with me as we didn't get to see much of each other any more. She had definitely pulled away from me. When we got to Barnatastna, we had to go in different directions. I was going to Carrick-on-Suir. We said our goodbyes until the morning.

As I drove past the slate quarries, the sun flitted in and out through the lush green trees and hedges. The car felt empty and hollow after all the chatting and singing. When I reached Carrick, it was like a ghost town. I parked the car and sat in it to nourish the pain and inevitably experience the hurt. Why would I not stay away from this pain? It was like the way a sore tooth constantly draws your tongue to it.

Eventually I booked into a B&B and rang Ellen to see if she wanted to meet me.

'Hello,' I said cheerfully as I lay back on the pillows.

'Well.' I knew by her voice that she was in a bad mood.

'Don't worry. I just rang because I said I would,' I said lamely.

'Right,' she said, and then she was gone.

Dear God, please get me through this one more time, I prayed. I slept with these words on my lips and in my mind. When morning arrived, I wondered what this day would bring.

The weather was glorious as I drove along those familiar roads. They held a memory at every turn. I was early as usual as I came into the village. Why not go and see Jackie's new house before I went on to Michael's? Turning off the Carrick road, I drove down the hill on to a boreen. There it was; it was going to be a fine house. Parking the car in the drive, I could see that there was no one about. Having climbed up on a couple of planks, I got inside. I couldn't make out what rooms were what, except the kitchen and bathroom, but they were all a good size. Suddenly I was overcome by a feeling that I would never be in this house again. Happiness and good health were the blessing that I wished for them before I left.

It was getting near the time for church. I freewheeled down the hill to Michael's and stopped. All the memories came flooding back, good and bad alike. I got out of the car and went to the door and knocked. Shauna opened it. 'Nanny's here,' she shouted into the room.

Mia was eating her breakfast, dressed in her school uniform. 'You look lovely,' I told her.

'Thanks,' she said, giving me one of her big smiles. I stood there, looking around me.

'This used to be Mammy's room before she got married,' I said.

'Was it, Mammy?' Mia shouted up to her mother, wherever she was.

'It was,' she said. So she is here, I thought.

Just then, Tony, her husband, came in.

'Nice to see you,' I said, putting my hand out to shake his.

'Lovely day,' he said, barely touching it. He had never done this to me before. I could feel my smile fading and I was at a loss for words.

'I went to see the new house,' I said, a silly grin on my face.

'My place?'

'Yes, it's lovely,' I finished lamely.

He went out to do something or other and I breathed a sigh of relief, but 'my place' rang in my ears.

Jackie came down from the room at last.

'You look marvellous,' I told her, and she did, in a pale blue suit, tall, slim and blonde.

'Who owns the other car outside?' I asked her.

'It's J.J.'s,' she said.

I could feel my face light up.

'He's up the back, walking the dogs,' she said. 'He's breeding them now.'

'I must go out and see him,' I said, making for the door. I went out to the yard gate and called his name as loudly as I could. There was no answer. I stood there, looking at the school house and the surrounding woods. Then I looked down at Mrs Cuddihy's and felt as if I had been blotted out of my own life: I knew all that had gone on around there but no one seemed to know what had gone on with me.

Jackie and the children came out of the house. Then I saw J.J. coming towards me, followed by a couple of dogs. He seemed to be in no hurry to reach me. It was like an eternity passed before he did. The gate between us was locked. 'I thought I recognised that voice,' he said.

I took in his whole appearance, to reassure myself that he was in good health. Then I said, 'You look great.'

'Thanks,' he said.

'I'm delighted that I got to see you,' I said. I had so much more that I wanted to say but they were all sitting in the car, waiting.

'I have to go or we'll be late for the Confirmation,' I said. 'Give me a hug.' I didn't want to miss any opportunity to let him know how much I loved him.

'You'll get all dirty.'

'I don't care,' I said as I threw my two arms around his neck and kissed and hugged him. He was delighted, I knew, but he was not half as delighted as I was.

They were calling me from the car. Another precious moment with my son had come and gone. I knew that I could handle only snatches of this, in case something happened that would take it away from me forever. Of all my children, I felt he was the one who had forgiven me for my past mistakes.

My body got into the car but my mind was scattered all over the place.

'He looks great,' I said to anyone who was interested.

When we got to the chapel, the first person I saw was my sister Mary with her family.

The chapel looked great. The Bishop was there to confirm the children.

When the Confirmation was over, there was the usual congregation of people outside the church, taking photographs. I dreaded this part of it because I was afraid of being left standing on my own.

We left the chapel and went up to Michael's so that Mia could change out of her uniform.

'Ellen rang Daddy last night,' Jackie said. 'She was upset that he wasn't coming today.'

'I see,' I said. 'Will we take some photos outside, of Mia in her new clothes?' I asked.

'Ellen, Joe and the boys are sitting in her car waiting for us,' Shauna said.

'Tell her to come in,' Jackie said.

Shauna ran out to ask her in. 'She doesn't want to,' she said when she returned.

'Oh, all right,' Jackie said.

When the girl of the day was ready, we went outside to take the photos. I was doing my best to act naturally as Ellen glared at me from the car. Shauna reluctantly stood in but without as much as a trace of a smile. When we had finished, I thought that perhaps there was a chance of a photo of Ellen with the two boys dressed in their best. One quick glance told me not to bother asking. She had both her hands on the dashboard and she looked as if she were ready to lunge at me. I went into the house to pull myself together. I wanted to cry out, 'Why won't you forgive me? Instead, I said nothing.

We went to the Park Inn, in Carrick, for the meal. I was sitting beside Ellen with Jackie opposite me and beside her Mia's Confirmation sponsor, Zoë, Michael's niece, Iris's daughter. The men were at the end of the table. They put the children at a table on their own, with Mia looking after Ellen's boys. They would do anything she asked them to do. We ordered our meal. Ellen didn't speak one word to me; she spent most of the time talking to Joe who was sitting at the other side of her. Jackie and Zoë were talking to each other at the far side of the table. I tried to cover up that I was not being included in any conversation by talking to the children at the next table. It was all unreal. I couldn't even taste the food. I was like a trapped animal looking constantly for a way to escape. When the meal was finished, I got up to go to the toilet.

'Can I come with you, Nanny?' Mia asked.

'Of course,' I said, delighted. Then Mia wanted me to ask Ellen to go to Tramore with them because she would love Robert and Dylan to go. I said I would, but asked her why she did not ask Ellen herself.

'I don't want to,' Mia said.

I thought that asking Ellen to go might break the silence between her and me.

Zoë was in the toilet when we got there, washing her hands.

'Hello,' I said to her.

'Hi,' she said back.

Then Ellen came into the toilet.

I let my guard down and said, 'Mia wants to know will you and the boys go to Tramore with them?'

'You liar,' she said. 'She never said that.'

I took a step back and said, 'I beg your pardon. I'm not a liar.' For a minute, I thought she was going to hit me.

'It's a family day out; they don't want me around,' she said, looking at Zoë for support.

'We're all family here, Ellen, whether you like it or not. Zoë is your cousin, and I'm your mother.' I was shaking with temper.

'You're a liar,' she said, just to have the last word.

'Mia,' I said to the child in the toilet, 'did you ask me to ask Ellen to go or not?'

'No, I didn't,' she said.

With that, Zoë spoke up and said, 'Yes, Mia did.'

I turned on my heel and walked out of the toilet. I took my jacket off the back of my seat and started to put it on. I was leaving. Something terrible was going to happen if I didn't. I'd known in my heart that Ellen would start an argument with me before the day was out.

All of a sudden, everyone seemed to be in a hurry to leave. Out of the corner of my eye, I could see Zoë whispering to Jackie. I knew that she was telling her what had happened in the toilet. I thought I would never get outside.

When we were outside, Jackie said to me, 'Are you coming or not?'

'No, I'm not,' I said. 'Thanks for the meal; it was lovely.'

Mia came over to me, looking ashamed, and whispered in my ear, 'Nanny, I'm sorry for telling a lie.'

'Don't worry, sweetheart. Enjoy the rest of your day and remember I love you.'

'I love you too,' she said. I stood there looking at them drifting away. Ellen got into Jackie's car. So she was going after all. They left without a backward glance. I walked slowly over to my car, got in and slumped against the steering wheel like a drunk. When this thought came into my head, it was quickly followed by an even more destructive one: I could go into any pub here and have a couple of quick drinks to stop me from hurting. 'Dear God, get me out of this place,' I said aloud to the empty car.

Chapter Forty-nine

I'm finding it exceptionally hard to write this chapter. I started to write this book at a time in my life when I had to believe in myself, or go mad. I know I have my truth and others have theirs.

When my family left me on the day of the Confirmation, I was covered in a cold sweat. I ran my hands up and down my arms and could feel goosebumps standing out on them. This was the nearest I'd come to drinking in a long time. It felt so powerful that I was afraid to let it go; I didn't know what I would be left with. Loneliness washed over me. There were no tears, just a tight feeling in my throat that made me have to swallow the hurt.

Slowly I travelled back from Carrick-on-Suir and on to Dublin. P.J. was waiting for me there. He had been visiting his own family. We had a flight early the following morning, back to London.

Usually the first thing I would have done when I got back was to ring Katie. I would tell her every word that had been said, pouring out all my pain and anguish, but not this time.

'How did it all go?' she asked.

'More or less the same as always.'

'You're very quiet,' she said and waited. 'Well, anyway, I just rang to tell you that Ellen and the boys are coming over to me tomorrow, for a week.'

The rage that surfaced in me was like a volcano erupting. My heart was thumping in my chest and there was a film over my eyes.

'Are you there?' she asked. 'Why are you so angry with Ellen?' she asked in a restrained voice.

'Ask her. I wouldn't know where to start. She has my heart broken and I allow her to do it over and over again, but no more; this is the end.'

'That's a terrible outburst.'

'It's only a fraction of what's going on inside me. Ellen should take a good look at herself, instead of pointing the finger at me.' I don't remember any more of the conversation.

I felt that I was the one that Ellen should be coming to, but I knew that if she came, she would make my life a misery. Yet I still wanted her. Could I accept that I had no part to play in my children's lives? I could feel my eyes burning and dry for the want of tears. The luxury of crying I couldn't allow myself, because I was too frightened that I would end up running around the road screaming and be locked up in a mental home.

In the meantime, I had to live and work. This was July and college was finished until September, so I didn't have to think about that. Part of my counselling course meant that I had to be in therapy myself. I tried a couple of places before I met Maggie, my counsellor. She was a God-given gift. Just what I needed.

My first session with her coincided with Ellen being over at Katie's. It was on Monday mornings at half-past nine. At first, everything was coming out all over the place. Would it ever be all said? My biggest fear was of going insane. I told Maggie this. Neither Katie nor Ellen rang the whole week my youngest daughter was in Birmingham. I found this hard to bear.

A couple of weeks later, Philip rang. 'Pick up the phone,

Mother,' he said through the answering machine. I felt weak as I picked it up.

'Well,' I said.

'What's wrong with you now?'

'Why didn't Katie or Ellen ring me when she was over?'

'Why didn't you ring them?'

'Because Ellen treats me like she despises me.'

'Don't be so dramatic. You know what she's like.'

'Yes, I do, and I've decided I'm not going to take it from her any more.'

'It's like this, Mother. When you say one word against any one of us, we all get together against you.'

'That's news to me, Philip.'

'You always cause murder when you go home. You went over to Jackie's house without being asked or being told you could,' he said triumphantly.

'What harm was it to go and see her house?'

'You should have waited until she was with you.'

'Is she angry with me over that?'

'I'm only saying you had no right to do it.'

I couldn't believe what I was hearing.

'That's it in a nutshell,' I said. 'I have no right. I'm always in the wrong. If I didn't go over at all, I would be wrong, and if I bothered Jackie on the Confirmation day to take me over, it would be something else. If I didn't go to see it at all, ye would say I had no interest. I'm damned if I do and I'm damned if I don't. Where do I go from here?' I asked.

'You should think before you do things.'

'Think. I give my whole life thinking what's the best thing to do, and where does it get me?'

'Well, maybe you should stop thinking.'

'I rest my case, Philip.'

'Will you ring Katie?'

'No.'

'Okay,' he said, 'And I do love you.'

'I love you too,' I said. No wonder I felt as if I were going mad. Even as I said never again, I had allowed myself once more to be drawn in and abused, and then feel guilty. There was an almighty struggle going on in me. I was slowly realising that I had never been the mother that my children wanted. They just wanted to punish me. I was not going to allow them to do that any more. I was well able to torture myself without any help.

Months went by without any phone calls. I couldn't believe that they were prepared to let go of me, just like that. It was as if my whole family had been wiped out in one swoop.

Maggie told me that I was going through a grieving process. I had been deprived of my mother's love because of her illness. Then I had been denied my children's love by my mother-in-law and my husband. Now my grandchildren's love for me was being destroyed by my own children. And there was nothing I could do about any of it. Being alone was my reality now.

What was I going to do with the rest of my life? I never realised how much my children and grandchildren occupied my thoughts and actions until I tried to break the habits of a lifetime — such as planning trips to see them, and sending cards for every little and big occasion. I would wake up in the middle of the night terrified that letting them go was totally wrong. Other times, I just felt beaten. I knew I was not without blame, but I couldn't let this abuse continue. It was damaging for my children, for my grandchildren and for myself.

A week before Christmas, I was feeling that I would be able to get through it, even though I had only to hear a song, or a mother and daughter talking to each other and the tears would fall in big drops from my eyes.

I got Christmas cards from Mia and Shauna in Ireland.

This started me on another guilt trip. How awful I was to be distancing myself from my grandchildren. Immediately I posted Christmas cards to all my grandchildren, with money in each one.

Two days before Christmas, the phone rang and it was

Philip. 'Pick up the fucking phone, Mother. Do you hear me? P.J., are you there? If you are, pick it up.'

'Oh God; why did this have to happen when I was doing so well?' I asked P.J. He held me in his arms. I was sobbing hysterically.

'I'll ring him back or else I'll be living in fear of him ringing again,' I said.

I felt ashamed that P.J. was witnessing my humiliation. I rang Philip back.

'Hello,' I said tentatively.

'What's going on?' he asked.

'I don't know.'

'I want to talk to P.J. about you. He's a sound bloke, but he doesn't know you at all. Put him on the phone to me.'

I handed P.J. the phone and said, 'He wants to talk to you.'

'Well, Philip, what's bothering you?'

'You don't know my mother at all. She's a liar. My father never did anything to her, never, never.'

'I'm afraid you're the one who doesn't know your mother.'

I took the phone from P.J. and said, 'I never gave out about your father to any of ye.'

'Katie's in Ireland for Christmas,' he shouted over me. This was to end the conversation about his father.

'One time that would cut me to the bone, but not any more.'

'Everything is changed for ever, isn't it? I might ring you on Christmas Day.'

'That would be nice,' I said. With that, he was gone.

'You're crimson. Go and lie down,' P.J. said in despair.

I didn't want to lie down and start thinking. P.J. did all he could to keep me from pining. We sat and looked at videos, one after another, but I didn't have any idea what they were about.

Apparently we went to Southend one day but I have no recollection of it. When P.J. showed me the photos that we'd taken, I asked him, 'When did we go there?'

'After Christmas. You were a terrible mess that day.'

Philip didn't ring me on Christmas Day. His thirty-third birthday was in January. I did a lot of agonising about ringing to wish him happy birthday. In the end, I did.

'Thanks for ringing,' he said. We spent five minutes discussing the weather. It was torture.

J.J.'s birthday was also in January. I sent him his card; he was forty. I knew that it would not be acknowledged. At least he was consistent in never responding.

'How does it feel when the cards are not acknowledged?' Maggie asked.

'It's a rejection.'

'What would happen if you stopped sending them?'

'If I stop, everything will,' I told her, with tears in my eyes.

'How would that feel?'

'I'm not ready to find out yet,' I said.

'How long have you been trying to make everything right?'

'At least since I stopped drinking, over twenty years ago.'

'That's a long time. How long do you think it will take? How many more years will you give to knocking at the doors of their hearts to see if they will let you back in? You are still that two-year-old knocking on your grandmother's door. The only difference is that she gave you a loud and clear "No".'

'I've been punished enough. How dare they do this to me!' I said to her, eyes blazing.

'Which would be the hardest thing to do — keep knocking or let go of them?'

'One is just as hard as the other.'

'We all make our own choices in life. You make yours and your children make theirs. There are consequences to each choice.' She said that I had made a healthy choice for myself years before, when I had decided to leave and survive, as opposed to staying and destroying myself and all around me. I didn't leave my children. I left a hopeless situation.

'There are lots of different ways of leaving,' Maggie said gently. 'You could have stayed and died, or gone insane; that's also leaving. You could have continued to drink and committed a slow suicide and that would be leaving. There would have been many different consequences to all those choices.'

P.J. and I were going to Ireland for Easter to stay with some good friends of ours, Dessie and Carol, in Gorey. When I was at home, I wanted to go to all the places I had written about: to see my grandparents' houses, my parents' graves, Michael's house, and Jackie's new home. I wasn't sure how this would affect me, but I knew it was something I had to do. We took the car and crossed by ferry.

In my last session with Maggie before I left, I told her what I intended to do. She told me that I reminded her of the little boy in the story about the Emperor's New Clothes. My family all wanted me to shut up and go away, and I refused to do that. My sisters all found it easier to be friends with Michael than to go through the pain of talking about their past feelings. My children didn't want their father to be that kind of man and I can understand that. What about their mother, though?

The Tuesday after Easter, we set off from Wexford where we were staying, to go on my journey. It was a dismal day; thick clouds milled the dull sky. I felt anxious in case I was doing something that was going to set me back. I assured P.J. that if I didn't want to go any further, I would tell him.

We were quiet as we drove along the narrow roads from Rosslare. I looked at the mental home in Enniscorthy and thought of my fear of ending up in one. We drove on to New Ross and then took the old road to Mullinavat.

Through Ballyhale, Knocktopher, Newmarket and Aughvillar. Then we came to the Grand Gates. We stopped and took some photos there, before going up the narrow road to my grandmother's in Ballintee. The fresh spring well where we used to get the water was still there and the trees formed an arch under which we drove. It was so beautiful. We stopped and I got out to breathe some of the air. All the sounds were still the same, mostly the sound of silence. There was just one new house on the road, after fifty-eight years of my life.

Then we were there, outside the house where my mother had died, the house that was in so many of my memories. We stopped and I got out of the car. I looked at the same long path with the high hedges on either side. It sent a shiver through my body as I thought of the nights I had walked up that path to ask my grandmother if I could come in. I had tears in my eyes for that small child with the curly hair who had been turned away time and time again. The front of the house had a new red door and windows. I could see the window to the bedroom where my mother had been waked. My mind went back to that terrible day. I remembered being asked if I'd like to see my mother one last time. I'd hesitated but my grandmother had pushed me towards the room. After a couple of seconds spent adjusting my eyes to the dim light, I had looked and there was my beautiful mother. I remember thinking, I will never hear her big hearty laugh again.

I dragged my thoughts back to the present. P.J. was asking me if he should take photos.

'Yes,' I said in a faraway voice. Someone else was living there now. It was strange to think of other people being in there. Then I heard a car coming up the road behind us. I didn't turn around to look, but when it passed, I knew it was J.J. He drove past slowly, looking to see who was taking photos. I was speechless. I could see the back of his head as he faded away in the distance.

Oh my God, I thought. How could this happen? When P.J. came back to the car, I told him.

'Are you all right?'

'I am.' I felt anxious in myself, as if this were a bad omen or something. My grandmother had been a great woman for talking about the fairies and the banshee, and a sense of danger and mystery seemed at that minute to hang in the air around me.

When we left, we went to my mother's grave. It was well looked after and had fresh flowers on it and a new headstone. I didn't feel as close to her here as I had back where she'd died. The graveyard had changed a lot since my mother had been buried in 1960. Then it had been badly neglected.

As we were passing through Dunamaggin, there was J.J. up on a roof working.

'Do you want to stop?' P.J. asked.

'No. For God's sake, keep going.'

About a mile down the road, I said to him, 'I suppose you think I'm a terrible mother?'

'No, I don't,' he assured me.

Why didn't I stop? I asked myself. Then it came to me. It was for fear that it might spoil the goodness that I felt between me and my oldest child. This was a sign of maturity in me. Once I would have jumped out of the car without thinking of the consequences of my actions until it was too late. It was good to see J.J. working and looking well.

I didn't go to see my father's grave for some reason. We were coming into the village now, up past where his house used to be. It looked as though it was being well looked after. Up to Mrs Kelly's where J.J. now lived, on his own. He had changed the front of the house: it had a big bay window looking out on to the street. He obviously took great pride in it, and that did my heart good. On up past the Catholic and then the Protestant church. I looked at the nursing home where my father had died. Then Mrs Cuddihy's. A married niece of mine lived there now. Then there it was: Michael's house. I asked P.J. to slow down because I wanted to get a photo. It looked neglected and desolate. Red paint was running off the roof of the garage, down on to the white paint on the walls underneath. The curtains on the windows were yellow and not pulled properly.

The man himself just walked out the front door. It was less than three years since the evening I had walked up there with Jackie and the children. Then it had been like a show house. It made me feel sad for Michael. Then we turned off to see Jackie's. This was a fine house and I felt glad for her.

That was the village and I had survived it once more. We went from there to Thomastown. As we drove along, I said to P.J., 'Isn't it amazing the two people we saw — J.J. and Michael? Who would believe it?'

'It's strange all right,' he said, giving me a pat on the knee and a smile.

P.J. is a good man. I knew that he was as relieved as I was that the trip was over.

When we got to Thomastown, we went up to Ladywell to see where I had lived as a child. I couldn't believe how small it was; it was like a doll's house. TINTEÁN was written over the door, the Irish for 'hearth', the centre of a home. We went and took more photos at 18 Newtown Terrace, the other house in Thomastown where we had lived. We drove up by the Convent of Mercy where I'd been to school until my grandmother died. It was weird and wonderful to see all those places.

I thanked God for letting me see J.J. getting on with his life, and for giving me the sense to let him be.